Precisely how Eugen[e O'Neill]
achieved what he did in [... and]
just what aesthetic workings he laid
into his plays and why, has to date been
only marginally understood. This study,
however, focuses directly on O'Neill as
a craftsman. It both illuminates and
evaluates his attempts to restore to the
theater its ancient religious function
and to create a modern form of tragedy.

Apart from his apprentice works, the
only play of O'Neill's never produced
professionally was *Lazarus Laughed*,
which he completed in 1926. *Lazarus*,
with its elaborate mask scheme and almost operatic lyrical effects, was the
climax of his efforts to make the modern
theater "a Temple where the religion
of a poetical interpretation and symbolical celebration of life is communicated." Yet for Broadway it was far too
costly as well as difficult to perform, and
O'Neill was subsequently much more
realistic in his technique. At the same
time he never gave up his attachment
to *Lazarus*. And *The Iceman Cometh*,
written thirteen years later, was virtually
a transposition of the earlier play into

used the magic of ritual and pathos to
make the theater what it had been at
the time of its Dionysian beginnings—
a place of spiritual communion with life
itself. Along with a distinct interpretation of the plays, a provocative view
emerges of religious as against political
theater. And a strong argument is made
for the Nietzschean, or aesthetic, idea of
tragedy as against the widely held Aristotelian, or moral, idea.

literary magazine of the air.

RITUAL AND PATHOS

Photo by Francis Bruguière, courtesy of Hoblitzelle Theater Arts Library, University of Texas in Austin

Projected set design by Norman-Bel Geddes for *Lazarus Laughed*

RITUAL AND PATHOS—
the Theater of O'Neill

Leonard Chabrowe

Lewisburg
Bucknell University Press
London: Associated University Presses

© 1976 by Associated University Presses, Inc.

Associated University Presses, Inc.
Cranbury, New Jersey 08512

Associated University Presses
108 New Bond Street
London W1Y OQX, England

Library of Congress Cataloging in Publication Data

Chabrowe, Leonard
    Ritual and pathos.

    Bibliography: p.
    Includes Index.
    1. O'Neill, Eugene Gladstone, 1888-1953—Criticism
and interpretation.   I. Title.
PS3529.N5Z579   812'.5'2   74-4985
ISBN 0-8387-1575-3

To all those who have aided me,
especially in spirit

contents

Preface   ix
Acknowledgments   x
Synopsis   xi

DRAMATIS PERSONAE
    Dionysus   1
    Lazarus   34
    Hickey   73
    Oedipus   100
    Electra   140
    O'Neill Himself   169

Chronology of First Productions   199
Notes   202
Select Bibliography   215
Index   220

preface

Precisely how Eugene O'Neill achieved what he did in the
theater, just what aesthetic workings he laid into his plays
and why, has to date been only marginally understood,
perhaps because most scholars and critics cannot quite imagine the significance of craft. Yet to understand an artist
fully, even to understand him at all, is impossible without
grasping the intricacies of his art.

In this study of O'Neill's art I have tried to combine
scholarship with criticism, scholarship at its best being illuminating and criticism at its best discriminating. I have
also tried to write a book that could be read both as a
companion to the plays and independently of them.
O'Neill's pursuit of his craft constituted a drama in its own
right, a two-fold drama with plot and subplot, reversals,
recognitions and a climactic denouement. In sum, I have
tried to re-create that drama.

acknowledgments

I wish to express my gratitude to the publishers and others listed below for permission to quote as follows:

Cambridge University Press—from Jane Harrison, *Themis*

Dodd, Mead & Company—from Carl Gustav Jung, *Psychology of the Unconscious*, trans. Beatrice Hinkle

Estate of Eugene O'Neill—nondramatic writings of Eugene O'Neill

Estate of Kenneth Macgowan—from Kenneth Macgowan, *The Theater of Tomorrow*

Jonathan Cape Ltd.—from *The Plays of Eugene O'Neill* (for the British Commonwealth excluding Canada)

Random House, Inc.—from Friedrich Nietzsche, *The Birth of Tragedy*, trans. Clifton Fadiman, copyright 1927 and 1955 by The Modern Library, Inc.
—from *The Plays of Eugene O'Neill* (for the United States and Canada)

Viking Press, Inc.—from Friedrich Nietzsche, *Thus Spoke Zarathustra*, in *The Portable Nietzsche*, ed. and trans. Walter Kaufmann

Yale University Press—from Eugene O'Neill, *Long Day's Journey Into Night*, copyright © 1955 by Carlotta Monterey O'Neill

synopsis

There are only two kinds of theater just as there are only two kinds of art generally—religious theater and political theater, or religious art and political art. Art is religious when its primary intention is to evoke emotions, whether tragic or comic or in some combination. Art is political when its primary intention is to be instructive, usually in the ways of a higher morality. Art for art's sake on the one hand, art for the sake of social improvement on the other. Just plain commercial art, or more to the point just plain commercial theater, is only the religious corrupted by lack of faith. It flourishes when a culture grows cynical and begins to degenerate. The church is defiled and put to vulgar uses, the money lenders set up shop in the temple. Eugene O'Neill hardly chased the money lenders out of the temple, but he was a man of the religious theater uncorrupted. For him aesthetics took the place of formal religion, art made life livable.

Perhaps a better slogan for O'Neill than art for art's sake would be art for life's sake. He tried to convert the theater back into a church because he had a deep psychological need to do so. Only art could turn doubt into will and despair into acceptance. Only art could release his pain of spirit and allow him to transcend himself. O'Neill was driven by personal demons in all his work, demons that had to be exorcised over and over. The inward turn of his mind away from political or social preoccupations toward its own workings was the turn of his plays. The tension of his inner conflicts was his plays' tension. And this tension, this pain of spirit, could only be released if shared by an audience, by a body of fellow sufferers who in the sharing became father confessors. The exorcising could only take place through the performance of rituals that were communal in nature.

Yet O'Neill's plays amount to more than elaborate confessions or disguised autobiography. For his attempt to make of the theater a place where rituals were acted out had broad cultural significance. It was an attempt to restore to the theater the function it had possessed in ancient Athens and, in more sublimated form, in Elizabethan England—the function of life celebration. The attempt was shared in by others, some of whom considerably influenced O'Neill. In fact, the theater avant-garde in America was then dedicated to just this ideal. While the emotional wellspring of O'Neill's work was wholly personal, he was constantly reminded of the need to keep his plays objective enough to have a wide appeal. The shapes they assumed were even derived from the outer currents of other people's thoughts and the theater itself. So the secret of O'Neill's achievement lies as much outside the realm of his demons as inside. He manifested his genius not merely in dramatizing his conflicts but in making them into a religious experience. Indeed, to properly evaluate his work one must first understand his conception of a religious theater.[1]

This conception couldn't have been further removed from the American theater at the time he began writing. In America there had never been anything but a commercial theater, which existed between the poles of burlesque and melodrama. The culture may not have been degenerating, but the materialism out of which it was born had made it vulgar prematurely. And to make up for the vulgarity, it had bred an aristocracy of politeness rather than of honor or spirituality. Owing largely to this politeness, nobody had ever held the mirror up to nature in the New World. When O'Neill began to hold up what was a very introspective mirror, established dramatists like Augustus Thomas were looking the other way in the best manner and style of the Genteel Tradition.

Before World War I the only contemporary drama in which American audiences could see three-dimensional human beings was by Europeans, Ibsen and Shaw in particular. And even the European repertory was rarely to be found in the legitimate theaters. It was usually played in the converted residences and stables of the Little Theater movement, composed of such groups as the Neighborhood Playhouse, the Washington Square Players and the Provincetown Players. The European drama was in the mainstream of things, expressing the Western cultural upheaval and regeneration that had its roots in the last decades of the nineteenth century. But it didn't reflect the American scene, however three-dimensional the image may have been, and the American theater was without any vision of its own. If native drama had the excuse of being a cultural infant, it was an infant abandoned in a wicker basket and set adrift in the wrong current. The Provincetown group first put on an O'Neill play, the one-act *Bound East for Cardiff*, in the summer of 1916 in a fish house at the end of a wharf in Provincetown. As it happened, the tide was in and sprayed through the holes in the floor, supposedly enhancing the production with its rhythmic flow.[2] No doubt this was an expression of the mainstream of things and not the Broadway undertow.

Only from this time did the American stage begin to develop from a combination burlesque house and wax museum into what could be taken seriously as a theater. In 1891 William Dean Howells and others had called for the establishment on a cooperative basis of a theater free from commercial pressures, a "Stage whereon the Drama shall be considered a Work of Art, and produced as such—independent of cheap popularity, and where Americanism and modernity shall be the prime requisites." But twenty-five years went by before a stage of this kind was set up by the Provincetown Players and the other Little Theater groups. George Cram Cook, the vital force in back of the original Players, later said that their hope had been "to bring to birth in our commercial-minded country a theater whose motive was spiritual." This was when he was disbanding the group in the belief such a hope had withered. He explained that in the dry heart of the American community he had "vainly tried to create an oasis of living beauty."[3]

The purpose of the Players, at least in an aesthetic sense, was religious. And O'Neill's own purpose was equally, if not more, religious. Remaining faithful to his purpose for over thirty years as a playwright, he realized drama on a higher aesthetic level than most American playwrights even contemplated. Not surprisingly, the way to the aesthetic heights was through the psychological depths, and for that reason, along with his personal need, he explored the psyche and its motives without quarter. To dramatize what he uncovered meant shattering genteel morality and conventional dramaturgy. Consequently, there were legal and artistic struggles, but he managed to shatter the morality and dramaturgy both. Through his passion, imagination and daring the American theater finally became three-dimensional in the tradition of the European.

No one, of course, disputes the historic role O'Neill played in the American theater. He was the instrument of its coming of age. But historic value isn't the same as aesthetic value. It doesn't make an artist's work endure. It gives him a place in the textbook of his art but doesn't keep his work alive. Only aesthetic value keeps art alive, giving it a currency outside of history. So the question about O'Neill is whether his work has enough aesthetic value to command much response now that its novelty and intellectual fashion have died out. And in the answer to this question, in the clarification of just what the aesthetic value of O'Neill's work is and how he achieved it, lies his story as an artist.

In 1925 the playwright wrote a letter about his work to Arthur Hobson Quinn, an American drama historian of genteel sensibilities with an enthusiasm for O'Neill something like the love of an English dowager for Irish whiskey. In this letter he spoke of "the transfiguring nobility of tragedy, in as near the Greek sense as one can grasp it, in seemingly the most ignoble, debased lives" and of "trying to interpret Life in terms of lives, never just lives in terms of character." The Greek sense of tragedy might have had little place for what seemed debased and ignoble, but here O'Neill was feeling his own way. He went on to talk "of the Force behind—"

(Fate, God, our biological past creating our present, whatever one calls it—Mystery certainly)—and of the one eternal tragedy, of Man in his glorious, self-destructive struggle to make the Force express him instead of being, as an animal is, an infinitesimal incident in its expression. And my profound conviction is that this is the only subject worth writing about and that it is possible—or can be—to develop a tragic expression in terms of transfigured modern values and symbols in the theater which may to some degree bring home to members of a modern audience their ennobling identity with the tragic figures on the stage. Of course, this is very much of a dream, but where the theater is concerned, one must have a dream and the Greek dream in tragedy is the noblest ever![4]

For O'Neill, then, the theater meant writing plays in the spirit of the Greeks. And this meant restoring to the theater its original function as a place of ritual and religious experience. Accordingly, his aesthetic outlook or idea was twofold. It was both an idea of the theater as a temple of the god Dionysus and an idea of life as an inevitable tragedy. In fact, his plays are most easily understood as having one or the other emphasis. *The Great God Brown, Marco Millions, Lazarus Laughed* and *The Iceman Cometh*, for example, are attempts to celebrate life by embodying it in ritual forms. *Desire Under the Elms, Strange Interlude, Mourning Becomes Electra* and *Long Day's Journey Into Night*, on the other hand, are attempts to reveal man's struggle—with its paradox of triumph in failure—against the mysterious force that shapes his existence and limits him.

In other words, the emphasis is sometimes on the celebration of life in the abstract and sometimes on the life struggle of the individual. As these are two aspects of the same thing and there is an intermingling of naturalistic and expressionistic forms, the two areas of emphasis overlap. Yet this is very much to the point. O'Neill's ultimate purpose was to achieve an effect in the modern theater like that in the ancient Athenian. And such an effect meant not only finding equivalents for the Theater of Dionysus and Greek fatalism but reuniting them. It meant the celebration of life not in the abstract but in the flesh. The reunion came closest to being realized in his last two major plays. The ritual of *The Iceman Cometh* is a celebration of the individual life struggle, and the life struggle of *Long Day's Journey Into Night* is a ritual of celebration.

The idiom of these plays is something O'Neill was seeking in both areas of emphasis since the early Provincetown days. In his emphasis on ritual he was greatly influenced by Nietzsche. Presumably he read *The Birth of Tragedy* when he first began writing.[5] Nietzsche's book had helped give birth in Europe to the New Stagecraft of Adolphe Appia and Gordon Craig and to Max Reinhardt's Theater of the Five Thousand. These innovations, which started the movement toward a celebratory theater, were part of a full-scale rebellion on the Continent against photographic realism. And the more or less Dionysian spirit of this rebellion crossed the Atlantic shortly before O'Neill started his apprenticeship. The American avant-garde, including the Little Theater movement, was already picking up Nietzsche and becoming intoxicated with him.

Actually, the intoxication wasn't from Nietzsche so much as the cultural ferment in general. Shaw said in 1912 that "the movement voiced by Schopenhauer, Wagner, Ibsen, Nietzsche, and Strindberg, was a world movement, and would have found expression if every one of these writers had perished in his cradle."[6] At the same time Nietzsche's thought was what provoked the most excitement and was most at work in the plays of O'Neill. Cook, H. L. Mencken and George Jean Nathan, each of whom had a hand in O'Neill's early success, were all influenced in one way or another by the philosophy of Nietzsche. And O'Neill's later associates in Experimental Theater, Incorporated, the designer Robert Edmond Jones and the critic-producer Kenneth Macgowan, were disciples of Appia and Craig and of Reinhardt respectively.

In 1921, two years prior to the association, Macgowan published *The Theater of Tomorrow*, a virtual manifesto declaring that theater was an "instinctive expression of godhead" and Greek tragedy its prototype.[7] The same year O'Neill began writing *The Fountain*, a historical romance in which Ponce de Leon finds eternal youth in a revelation of Eternal Recurrence, that is, in the Dionysian metaphysics of Nietzsche. This was the first time O'Neill dramatized Nietzsche's vision of the Dionysian nature of things, though in his apprentice piece *Fog* he had intended the crying of a dead child as a similar kind of revelation. *The Fountain* had to wait for production until 1925 when Macgowan, Jones and O'Neill put it on at the Greenwich Village Theater. In the meantime O'Neill had written *The Great God Brown* and *Marco Millions*, leading up to *Lazarus Laughed*, which he completed in 1926. This climactic work he called "A Play For An Imaginative Theater," by which he meant

> the one true theatre, the age-old theatre, the theatre of the Greeks and Elizabethans, a theatre that could dare to boast—without committing a farcical sacrilege—that it is a legitimate descendant of the first theatre that sprang, by virtue of man's imaginative interpretation of life, out of his worship of Dionysus. I mean a theatre returned to its highest and sole significant function as a Temple where the religion of a poetical interpretation and symbolical celebration of life is communicated to human beings, starved in spirit by their soul-stifling daily struggle to exist as masks among the masks of living![8]

Lazarus Laughed was O'Neill's most obvious attempt to celebrate life by embodying it in ritual acts, in singing and dancing. The Imaginative Theater was laid on the foundations of the Theater of Tomorrow, and the play itself expressed the complete affirmation of life proclaimed by Nietzsche in *Thus Spoke Zarathustra*. As a ritual of celebration, however, it defeated its own purpose. The technical difficulties and expense of production kept it from the professional stage, which has been the case ever since. It was premiered in 1928 at the Pasadena Community Playhouse, an amateur repertory theater and workshop, where it received a full-scale treatment and enthusiastic reviews. But, ironically, what should have been the culmination of a movement in the mainstream remained in a backwater. The celebration was impracticable, which the worship of Dionysus never was. Yet in a special way O'Neill thought of the play as his best for many years after. And when there was little hope left of its being professionally produced, he transposed it into the wholly modern idiom of *The Iceman Cometh*.

At the time *The Iceman* was on Broadway and then later off-Broadway it gave rise to a certain amount of confusion. This wasn't O'Neill's fault since the action of the play is complete and understandable in itself. Nothing about *The Iceman* requires an explanation by outside reference, neither the action nor the aesthestic dynamics of the action. Just as the action is self-contained, the aesthetic dynamics are directly experienced in the theater. However, if one wants to understand as well as experience the aesthetic dynamics, reference to *Lazarus Laughed* and O'Neill's emphasis on ritual generally is essential. The experience of the dynamics doesn't require an understanding, and O'Neill thought it would be more genuine without one. But it doesn't preclude one either, which only goes to prove the validity of it.

Under the surface *The Iceman* is extraordinarily similar to the earlier play in almost every respect. In fact, in the light of a couple of letters written in 1944 *The Iceman* appears to be *Lazarus* thirteen years later. Clearly, it is a reworking of the same dramatic material, if not of the earlier play itself.

There is, of course, an obvious difference in outlook. While the laughter of Lazarus ecstatically affirms life, Hickey's evangelistic nihilism despairs of it. But while O'Neill's outlook changed, his conception of the theater didn't. The despair is as ritualistic as the ecstasy, the nihilism as religious as the affirmation. Where *Lazarus* failed, *The Iceman* succeeded. The theater was once more a temple for the celebration of life.

In his emphasis on tragedy O'Neill was greatly influenced by both Freud and Jung, and also to a lesser extent by Schopenhauer. He found the problem of tragic action very complex and made use of various explanations of human experience in solving it. Yet for the sake of evoking a greater pathos—the emotion of tragic suffering—he finally submerged the philosophical or psychological tragedy in what might be called the aesthetic tragedy.

When O'Neill first tried to write tragedy, he had only an intuition of what it was, an intuition inspired by Nietzsche and the Greeks. The Greek sense of it, of man struggling against something greater than himself, was expressed for him in the fatalism of *Oedipus Rex* and the *Oresteia*. More than anything else the inevitability of defeat was what made the struggle tragic. Although man possessed free will enough to struggle against his fate, he couldn't ultimately escape it. And as his fate was divinely imposed, it had a religious significance such that he was able to triumph over it spiritually. What O'Neill tried to do was find for this inevitability from above an equivalent which, as he later wrote in his notes for *Mourning Becomes Electra*, "an intelligent audience of today, possessed of no belief in gods or supernatural retribution, could accept and be moved by."

In *The World as Will and Idea* and possibly other works by Schopenhauer, which he had come to know sometime before he began writing, O'Neill saw a philosophical equivalent.[9] Man was controlled by an irrational force that was neither understood nor perceived, a universal will without purpose other than to perpetuate itself, a ceaselessly striving energy that beguiled the individual into doing its work with illusions of personal happiness, then destroyed him through frustration and waste. Life, in other words, was "one eternal tragedy, of Man in his glorious, self-destructive struggle to make the Force express him instead of being, as an animal is, an infinitesimal incident in its expression."

A philosophical equivalent, however, wasn't really suitable as a dramatic equivalent. For no matter how graphically O'Neill might show the workings of frustration and waste—in *Beyond the Horizon*, for example—the idea of the will as the ultimate source of man's destruction couldn't achieve the effect he wanted. As he was paraphrased as saying in 1924, "What I am after, is to get an audience to leave the theater with an exultant feeling, from seeing somebody on the stage facing life, fighting against the eternal odds, not conquering, but perhaps inevitably being conquered."[10] The trouble with Schopenhauer was that the audience was scarcely familiar enough with the idea of the will to accept and be moved by it in this way. The response O'Neill was after required no more than a belief in the Force as something mysterious, but even that was expecting too much.

Eventually he found the equivalent he was seeking in the Freudian and Jungian theories of psychoanalysis, especially in their deterministic aspects and their concepts of ambivalence. Psychoanalysis had revealed ambivalence to be the source of the life struggle and the deterministic factors in man's behavior to be the reason for his inevitable defeat. Further, the Jungian view provided man with the means of a spiritual triumph over his defeat. His fate was no longer divinely imposed, but it proceeded from the nature of his being with a significance that was equally religious. And the audience was becoming familiar enough, however superficially, with the idea of unconscious motivation to accept and be moved by it even to the point of exultance.

The Little Theater movement imbibed the psychoanalytical spirit along with the Dionysian, and O'Neill first came into contact with it through the Provincetown Players. The value it was to have in his work became visible as early as 1920. In *The Emperor Jones* he dramatized the alienation of man from himself and his environment in terms of a psychic regression to the primitive. While he had successfully dramatized the theme of alienation before, this was the first time he was able to suggest its inevitability. The suggestion of inevitability grew stronger in the plays that followed. But only in 1931 with *Mourning Becomes Electra* did he realize a fate proceeding unaided from within. The unconscious was made entirely determining of the conscious, and the destructive experiences of the past repeated themselves in the present. Man's struggle against something greater was a struggle against the inexorable force of his innermost self. The fatalism of the *Oresteia* and of *Oedipus Rex* had been translated into an equivalent that was dramatic. In addition, the inexorable force was overcome, if only in a symbolic or moral sense, and the paradox of triumph in failure was complete.

Yet as *Mourning Becomes Electra* was derived from the *Oresteia* in plot and structure, it had a considerable aesthetic distance from the audience. Its pathos was consequently muted, the tragic effect too removed. The fate equivalent could have its full impact only when cast in an intrinsically modern idiom. And not until *Long Day's Journey Into Night*, written a decade later, did O'Neill cast it in such an idiom. By then his philosophical outlook had turned despairing, a state of mind that worked against any spiritual triumph of the characters. But by purely aesthetic means he was able to bring about a greater release of tragic pathos than ever before. In the very defeat of man in the life struggle there was an exultation.

The fact is that O'Neill achieved nothing less than a renaissance of an art form long thought dead. Since funeral orations have been delivered many times over the petrified body of tragedy, a renaissance is just what his work amounts to. The orations have usually been delivered by scholars and critics with a strictly Aristotelian or moral perspective, but O'Neill's perspective was more from the Nietzschean or aesthetic side. Through the magic of ritual and pathos he evoked the tragic emotions in the theater as of old. In varying degrees, depending on the play, he made the audience feel what life was in its essence, not think about how to deal with it in its detail. To instruct or shake the opinions of an audience—the aim of political theater—is no mean feat. Still it is less difficult and in the long run even less relevant than to move an audience to catharsis.

In a 1943 letter to his first biographer, the critic Barrett Clark, O'Neill remarked that *The Iceman* and *Long Day's Journey* gave him greater satisfaction than any other plays he had done. Presumably this was because they both embodied his idea of the theater as a place of spiritual communion.

Photo by Nicholas Muray

O'Neill by the sea in 1924

O'Neill in New York in 1946

RITUAL AND PATHOS

DRAMATIS PERSONAE

Dionysus
Lazarus
Hickey
Oedipus
Electra
O'Neill Himself

dionysus

When the Provincetown Players opened shop in New York in the fall of 1916, their purpose was to set up an experimental stage for native playwrights. In the words of George Cram Cook they intended "to create a soul under the ribs of death in the American theater." The group felt it had a mission to help bring back to life a sacred institution, and in that sense its purpose and spirit were religious. In the dining room of his home in Provincetown Cook had a prophetic fresco of the history of the theater. The panels, according to his wife Susan Glaspell, were—"Theater born of Primitive Dance. Theater hardening into Church. Pure Dead Church. Church giving birth to Theater. Pure Dead Theater. Theater transforming itself into Living Church."[11] And O'Neill, in a 1928 letter to George Jean Nathan about *Dynamo*, implied that the purpose and spirit of the modern playwright should be religious in a further sense. In terms reminiscent of Nietzsche he confessed a

1

preoccupation with the search for meaning in a world apparently without meaning.

> [*Dynamo*] is really the first play of a trilogy that will dig at the roots of the sickness of today as I feel it—the death of the old God and the failure of science and materialism to give any satisfying new one for the surviving primitive religious instinct to find a meaning for life in, and to comfort its fears of death with. It seems to me that anyone trying to do big work nowadays must have this big subject behind all the little subjects of his plays or novels, or he is simply scribbling around the surface of things and has no more real status than a parlor entertainer.[12]

O'Neill's one-act play *Fog*, written early in 1914 and produced by the Players during the first New York season, was already in line with these ideas. The piece was crude in form, and O'Neill later repudiated it along with almost all his other apprentice works. But it still anticipated the revival of a religious theater. In the play a poet and a businessman are adrift in a lifeboat that also bears a peasant woman holding her dead child. As the two men give voice to the conflict of artist and Philistine in American life, the lifeboat, lost in a heavy fog, is carried up against an iceberg. At this point they hear a ship coming near. The businessman wants to call out, but the poet prevails on him not to for fear the ship might hit the iceberg in the fog. When all hope seems to be gone, however, the fog suddenly lifts and reveals a rescue party in one of the ship's lifeboats. After the peasant woman is discovered to be dead along with her child, the captain of the crew says they heard the child's cries and were following them through the fog. These were the birth cries of the Dionysian child—the saving spirit—in America.

The Dionysian spirit that moved O'Neill had appeared, or reappeared, in Europe as long ago as 1872 with the publication of *The Birth of Tragedy*. The complete title had we must also include in our picture of Apollo that delicate boundary, which the dream-picture must not overstep—lest it act pathologically (in which case appearance would impose upon us as pure reality). We must keep in mind that measured restraint, that freedom from the wilder emotions, that philosophic calm of the sculptor-god. His eye must be "sun-like," as befits his origin; even when his glance is angry and distempered, the sacredness of his beautiful appearance must still be there. And so, in one sense, we might apply to Apollo the words of Schopenhauer when he speaks of the man wrapped in the veil of Mâyâ [the Hindu personification of illusion]: *Welt als Wille und Vorstellung* [*World as Will and Idea*] . . . "Just as in a stormy sea, unbounded in every direction, rising and falling with howling mountainous waves, a sailor sits in a boat and trusts in his frail bark: so in the midst of a world of sorrows the individual sits quietly, supported by and trusting in his *principium individuationis* [principle of individuation]." In fact, we might say of Apollo, that in him the unshaken faith in this *principium* and the calm repose of the man wrapped therein receive their sublimest expression; and we might consider Apollo himself as the glorious divine image of the *principium individuationis*, whose gestures and expression tell us of all the joy and wisdom of "appearance," together with its beauty.[14]

Apollo, then, embodied life as it appeared to the consciousness of a civilized individual. He was the god who preserved the appearance of things. But if instead of the appearance of things it was the perceiving consciousness that was shattered, even in dreams and art all life's harmony and order were lost. The individual was drowned in the world of sorrows, in the formless reality of life itself. However, life itself redeemed him by allowing him to become one with it. And appearance, subjective in its individual forms, dissolved into the selfless, objective union of all things and beings. The perceiving consciousness was shattered by emotions, by emotions which had the effects of drunkenness and were most directly expressed in movement, in singing and dancing. The Apollonian gave way to the Dionysian.

It is either under the influence of the narcotic draught, which we hear of in the songs of all primitive men and peoples, or with the potent coming of spring penetrating all nature with joy, that these Dionysian emotions awake, which, as they intensify, cause the subjective to vanish into complete self-forgetfulness. So also in the German Middle Ages singing and dancing crowds, ever increasing in number, were whirled from place to place under this same Dionysian impulse. In these dancers of St. John and St. Vitus, we rediscover the Bacchic choruses of the Greeks, with their early history in Asia Minor . . .

Under the charm of the Dionysian not only is the union between man and man reaffirmed, but Nature which has become estranged, hostile, or subjugated, celebrates once more her reconciliation with her prodigal son, man . . . . Now the slave is free; now all the stubborn, hostile barriers, which necessity, caprice or "shameless fashion" have erected between man and man, are broken down. Now, with the gospel of universal harmony, each one feels himself not only united, reconciled, blended with his neighbor, but as one with him; he feels as if the veil of Mâyâ had been torn aside and were now merely fluttering in tatters before the mysterious Primordial Unity.

Dionysus, embodying the primitive, unconscious emotions that belied individuality, was opposed to Apollo. Yet one god couldn't exist for very long without the other—neither emotion without form nor form without emotion. The expression of each involved a distinct aesthetic impulse. At the same time one expression was dependent on the other for renewal. A work of art could be dreamlike, ecstatic, or dreamlike and ecstatic together. But it could only be dreamlike and ecstatic together when it revealed to the beholder in an Apollonian dream picture his oneness with the primordial universe.

Such a revelation was at the heart of Greek tragedy. The tragic chorus had originated in the singing and dancing crowds, the Dionysian throngs that appeared from time to time in the Mediterranean world. The first chorus in the theater was neither a representative group of common people in contrast to the aristocracy nor a collective ideal spectator commenting on the action. It was simply an imitation of a real Dionysian throng. And the spectators recognized the chorus as a satyrlike incarnation of themselves. Accepting their oneness with the chorus, they even felt they had been transformed into satyrs and that the tragic heroes on the stage were but an Apollonian image of their own being. Their being then reached to the very heart of things, to the most intense sensation of life itself. They had passed out of the suffering of their own existence into the joy of universal existence, dying in their individuality but being reborn in the eternal cycle of all life. The tragic image always reflected this suffering, death and rebirth. Behind the masks of all the individual heroes was the godhead of Dionysus.[15]

As Nietzsche pointed out, this idea of tragedy was different from Aristotle's, which was moral rather than aesthetic. The release of pity and terror Aristotle required was an effect proceeding from the action of the masked hero, but to Nietzsche the hero's action was only the image of an underlying pathos. "Everything was directed toward pathos, not action," he said, adding further on that "the deepest pathos can in reality be merely esthetic play." In other words, tragedy resided less in events or character of moral significance than in a movement of the psyche toward pathos, toward the emotion of tragic suffering. Not toward mere pity for suffering but—as the word *pathos* was understood in the original Greek—the feeling of suffering itself. The tragic myth on the stage revealed suffering as the underlying reality of existence, enabling the audience to experience and accept it as such. In a metaphysical sense suffering was justified as an aesthetic phenomenon. The function of tragic myth was "to convince us that even the ugly and unharmonious is an artistic game which the will [or life] plays with itself in the eternal fullness of its joy."

However, not all Greek tragedy was the same, and in Euripides' plays Nietzsche found an alien spirit, a spirit emanating from the mortal Socrates rather than the gods. This was the spirit of reason, logic and intelligibility, which substituted thought for Apollonian dream and passion for Dionysian ecstasy, bringing about a decline of the tragic in favor of the naturalistic. The decline could be seen in a lessened or more superficial use of the chorus and a more extensive use of the *deus ex machina*, which combined in appealing to the critical instead of the musical faculty. The plays still had a mythical content, but the Dionysian element had been lost and without it the Apollonian failed to remain compelling. The tragic stage was no longer an image of the inner world but an idea of the outer. Its spirit was no longer ritualistic and unifying but intellectual and individualizing. And this latter spirit was to be dominant in the West from Euripides on.

Nietzsche's understanding of tragedy derived from his interpretation of Dionysus. O'Neill's understanding of tragedy derived from Nietzsche's. But there was another basis for belief in the Dionysian origin and ritual nature of tragedy, and O'Neill was evidently familiar with that also. The findings of a group of scholars known as the Cambridge School of Classical Anthropologists had substantiated and elaborated on Nietzsche's idea. George Cram Cook and Kenneth Macgowan both approached the theater in terms of what these scholars had uncovered about the nature of drama as a Dionysian ceremony. In fact, early in his career Macgowan had interviewed the classical scholar Gilbert Murray, connected with the group, and covered a series of lectures by him on Greek tragedy. Moreover,

O'Neill himself came to be quite well-read in books dealing with primitive societies.

One of the Cambridge books soon taken up in interested circles was Jane Harrison's *Themis (A Study of the Social Origins of Greek Religion)*, first published in 1912. In it she gave an account of the social conditions out of which the Dionysian spirit arose. And in an "Excursus on the Ritual Forms Preserved in Greek Tragedy," included in the book, Gilbert Murray emphasized the religious nature of the dramatic form that spirit took in Athens. Later scholars have qualified the Cambridge view. Yet directly or indirectly O'Neill's understanding of tragedy was shaped by what Harrison and Murray had to say.[16]

On the basis of archaeological evidence Harrison argued that godhead was the projection of human emotions which were socially reinforced. Accordingly, in the early Mediterranean world the divine figures of Mother and Kouros (a youth about to enter into manhood) were projections of emotions reinforced in a matrilinear social group, the genealogical descent of which was through the woman. From a consideration of extant primitive societies Harrison concluded that the main characteristic of such a group was solidarity, the lack of differentiation between individuals as well as between the group and nature. The individual had but slight social or psychological awareness of himself. And when he acquired enough awareness to emerge from both the group and his surroundings, a new society with Olympian gods emerged with him.

The early Mediterranean or pre-Olympian gods, then, were characterized by solidarity. They had no personalities and were indistinct in their forms and functions. Harrison described them as potencies, as cyclic, seasonal, Eniautos or Year-daimons, which generally assumed plant or animal shape and shared the one and only purpose of giving yearly

food and increase to man. They were fertility-daimons that
lived and worked for the survival of the group. And they
also died for the group so they might be reborn and live
again the next year. This cycle of reincarnation was the
essence of the Year-daimon.

> Out of this cycle came all his manifold, yet monotonous life-
> history, his Births, his Re-births, his Appearances and Disap-
> pearances, his Processions and Recessions, his Epiphanies, his
> Deaths, his Burials, his Resurrections, his endless
> Changes...[17]

The more the Year-daimon changed, the more he remained the same. Yet as man developed more individual
consciousness the year itself changed. In fact, this change in
the year expresses the evolution from pre-Olympian to
Olympian godhead, which is to say from matrilinear to
patriarchal social conditions. There were three phases of
the evolution—the year being measured first by the earth,
then by the moon and finally by the sun—with the Year-
daimon taking on corresponding characteristics along the
way. At the same time the daimon retained his cyclic nature,
at least prior to becoming Olympian, and experienced an
annual birth, death and rebirth.

So in origin the Year-daimon was a fertility-daimon of
the earth, evolving only later into a figure of the moon and
then a sun god. Man, however, didn't distinguish himself
from nature. The fertility of the earth and the fertility of
man weren't just two related things giving rise to similar
human emotions. They were one and the same, giving rise
to but a single emotion. The fertility-daimon wasn't only a
projection of the change in season, from summer to winter
and back to summer again, from the old year to the new. He
was also a projection of the change in man's life from one
age to the next, from birth and childhood to puberty and

manhood, from manhood and marriage to parenthood and death.

The most important of these changes was the one that renewed the group, the change from childhood to manhood, at which time the male child was initiated into the community. This is why the projection of godhead most often took the form of a youth at the time of initiation, a ritual ceremony which celebrated the group's renewal through the fertility of the mother. And this initiation most often took place in the spring, the fertility of the mother being one with the fertility of the earth. The resurrection of life was embodied in the Mother and Kouros figures.

> There came then to Delphi, tradition tells us, two Kouroi, the greatest Kouroi the world has ever seen, Apollo and Dionysos. Were they, who seem so disparate, really the same? So far as they are Kouroi and Year-Gods, yes. But they are Kouroi and Year-Gods caught and in part crystallized at different stages of development. Apollo has more in him of the Sun and the day, of order and light and reason, Dionysos more of the Earth and the Moon, of the divinity of Night and Dreams. Moreover, Apollo is of man's life, separate from the rest of nature, a purely human accomplishment; Dionysos is of man's life as one with nature, a communion not a segregation.

Dionysus, the vegetation daimon, was the youth of a matrilinear society, or the son of his mother. Apollo, the youth of a later patriarchal society, was the son of his father. As social conditions changed from matrilinear and tribal to patriarchal and relatively democratic, the projected divinities underwent a metamorphosis. They surrendered their old group functions and came to embody individual principles. Instead of the life-and-death cycle of the year they were characterized by personal immortality. Harrison pointed out that though an individualized god might seem to be a higher thing than an impersonal daimon, he didn't move a people to ecstatic union. His appeal was emotional only to an educated few and no longer to the whole group, whose life he had left behind.

> We touch here on the very heart and secret of the difference between the Olympian and the mystery-god, between Apollo and Zeus on the one hand and Dionysos on the other: a difference, the real significance of which was long ago, with the instinct of genius, divined by Nietzsche. The Olympian has clear form, he is the *'principium individuationis'* incarnate; he can be thought . . . The mystery-god is the life of the whole of things, he can only be felt . . .

The Dionysian spirit intuited by Nietzsche in Greek tragedy corresponded to the emotions dominant in an earlier period of social development. Naturally, as this period became more remote such emotions became less accessible. But in the fifth century B.C. they were quite accessible. In the last play of the *Oresteia*, for example, Aeschylus dramatized the resolution of the recent conflict between the matriarchal and patriarchal orders, or between the emotions generated by these orders. Presumably the spectators of Athenian tragedy still felt matriarchal emotions. In matriarchal society the death and rebirth of the chief, usually the high priest as well, had been the death and rebirth of all life. With his death all the individual members had experienced the emotions of their own death, and with the crowning of a Kouros as the new chief the emotions of their own rebirth. Nietzsche's Primordial Unity was the aesthetic counterpart to this psychological unity.

As the mystery-god (in effect chief or king, high priest and Kouros all in one) was a projection of human emotions, those who projected him existed before he did. In worshiping him in a ritual act they both invoked and celebrated the renewal of their conditions of life. Godhead proceeded from this act of ritual, which Harrison defined as "the utterance of an emotion, a thing felt, in *action*."

Such action had obviously to be caused by the great events in life, especially its changes, for it was only about birth, initiation into manhood, marriage and death that the emotions felt were strong enough to require ritual expression. These changes in life were group changes just as the emotions felt were group emotions. And it was the psychological reinforcement given these emotions by the social conditions of the group that enabled them to be maintained. As Harrison wrote, "The individual in a savage tribe has but a thin and meagre personality. If he dances alone he will not dance long; but if his whole tribe dances together he will dance the live-long night and his emotion will mount to passion, to ecstasy." The ritual act in which these group emotions were uttered was a tribal dance, and in such a dance Greek tragedy, like Greek religion, had its origin. Murray, in his "Excursus on the Ritual Forms Preserved in Greek Tragedy," took this for granted.

> The following note presupposes certain general views about the origin and essential nature of Greek Tragedy. It assumes that Tragedy is in origin a Ritual Dance, a *Sacer Ludus* [Holy Playing], representing normally the Aition, or supposed historical Cause, of some current ritual practice . . . . Further, it assumes, in accord with the overwhelming weight of ancient tradition, that the Dance in question is originally or centrally that of Dionysus; and it regards Dionysus, in this connection, as the spirit of the Dithyramb or Spring *Drômenon* [initiation rite] . . .an "Eniautos-Daimon," who represents the cyclic death and rebirth of the world, including the rebirth of the tribe by the return of the heroes or dead ancestors.

Harrison also defined myth as an utterance of emotion, though an utterance in words rather than action. Myth was a direct expression in its own right, but the emotion that gave rise to it was the same as gave rise to ritual. So when the emotion of a ritual was forgotten, making the ritual meaningless, the corresponding myth was soon made meaningless as well. Harrison's distinctions between myth and ritual paralleled Nietzsche's distinctions between Apollonian and Dionysian art impulses. Once an emotion was dissipated to the point where its Dionysian ritual expression became meaningless, its Apollonian mythical expression soon became equally meaningless. And as tragedy had declined with the loss of the Dionysian spirit, its fall was really due to the subsiding of those emotions which were expressed in ritual, or rather with the change in the social conditions which had reinforced them.

So the problem O'Neill took on was more complicated than *The Birth of Tragedy* alone made it appear. He wanted to evoke the primitive religious emotions in the theater by aesthetic means. But such an evocation had to be of a psychological character since those emotions, not being socially reinforced, were far removed from the consciousness of a modern audience.

In the Athenian theater the primitive emotions had already been partly evoked and reinforced by the occasion of the Festival of Dionysus itself. Similarly, the Medieval town cycles in England and on the Continent had taken place on religious festival days, although the passion, miracle, mystery and morality plays performed were more didactic than ritualistic. By then, of course, secular ritual embodied the life of the community as much as religious ritual. As a result the very orthodoxy of the Medieval church plays worked against their achieving a communion in the Dionysian sense. But the Elizabethan theater, as Francis Fergusson has argued, achieved such a communion at times despite a lack of reinforcing religious occasion.

In Renaissance England the Church had been taken over in effect by the Tudor monarchy, and royal and civic pageantry was invested with a much greater significance than priestly ceremony. Consequently, the figure of the King in Shakespeare stood quite close to the figure of the King in Aeschylus or Sophocles. Both were priest as well as king and the unquestioned father of the community. Shakespeare's great tragedies didn't end with the death of the hero but with the assumption of the throne by his successor. Fortinbras in *Hamlet*, for example, renewed the communal life. And Malcolm performed the same function in *Macbeth*, as did Albany somewhat dubiously in *King Lear*. Furthermore, a great deal of the religious culture of the Middle Ages was still alive in Shakespeare's time. The Globe stage itself, covered by a painted canopy representing the heavens, symbolized the traditional cosmos inherited from the Middle Ages. The Medieval cosmos had even become a part of the psychology of the Renaissance man, and Shakespeare could anticipate that his audience would recognize itself in the common idea of a hierarchy of angels, man and beast. This anticipation was the Elizabethan equivalent of the anticipation by the Greek playwrights that their audience was ready to respond to a drama in the ritual forms inherited from an earlier society.[18]

O'Neill had no such anticipation of a traditional readiness on the part of his audience to respond in a religious way to any idea or form. On the one hand, the public appeared to share no deep-rooted belief of any spiritual significance. On the other, the theater commanded no more devotion in the community than any cocktail party around town. This lack in America of any association between religion and the theater, or of any attachment to particular dramatic conventions, was one of the reasons his plays were continuously experimental.

Yet he had become convinced, partly through his reading of Jung, that the civilized individual still retained the psychology of primitive man in his unconscious mind. "Our emotions are instinctive," O'Neill told an interviewer in 1922. "They are the result not only of our individual experience but of the experiences of the whole human race, back through the ages. They are the deep undercurrent, whereas our thoughts are often only the small individual surface reactions."[19] Accordingly, he used many ritual or rhythmic devices in his dramas for the purpose of reaching the emotional undercurrent. His aim as a dramatist was always to make his audience respond on some deeper level to the life on stage and so experience a Dionysian communion with life itself.

In the five years following the production of his apprentice piece *Fog* O'Neill saw all his remaining one-acters and six full-length plays performed. These full-length plays included *Beyond the Horizon, Anna Christie* and *The Emperor Jones*. Then in 1921, the year he began *The Fountain*, he wrote two others, *The First Man* and *The Hairy Ape*. The latter of these soon made its way to Broadway after opening in Greenwich Village in March of 1922. Paradoxically, just this success by the Players was what convinced Cook of their failure in the light of their original purpose. The values of an experimental stage appeared lost in playing each piece for an eventual Broadway success, and rather than continue working under a commercial influence he decided to leave the theater altogether.

The Hairy Ape dealt directly with man's struggle against his fate. In this sense it had more the emphasis of tragedy proper than of ritual. But it was the first time O'Neill made use of a unifying chorus on a large scale. Some of the one-act plays, particularly *The Moon of the Caribbees* in the "S.S. Glencairn" group, had been given dimension by a choral mood. And this same mood from out of a seamen's forecastle was the means by which he both built up the primitive identity of the men and then tore it down again. In the fourth scene, after the hero's feeling of belonging has been shattered, the isolation of the primitive from the civilized is heard in echoes of harsh, roaring laughter.

> YANK. (*resentfully*) Aw say, youse guys. Lemme alone. Can't youse see I'm tryin' to tink?
> ALL. (*repeating the word after him as one with cynical mockery*) Think! (*The word has a brazen, metallic quality as if their throats were phonograph horns. It is followed by a chorus of hard, barking laughter*).
> YANK. (*springing to his feet and glaring at them belligerently*) Yes, tink! Tink, dat's what I said! What about it? (*They are silent, puzzled by his sudden resentment at what used to be one of his jokes.* YANK *sits down again in the same attitude of "The Thinker"*).
> VOICES. Leave him alone.
> He's got a grouch on.
> Why wouldn't he?
> PADDY. (*with a wink at the others*) Sure I know what's the matther. 'Tis aisy to see. He's fallen in love, I'm telling you.
> ALL. (*repeating the word after him as one with cynical mockery*) Love! (*The word has a brazen, metallic quality as if their throats were phonograph horns. It is followed by a chorus of hard, barking laughter*).
> YANK. (*with a contemptuous snort*) Love, hell! Hate, dat's what. I've fallen in hate, get me? . . .
> LONG. . . .And what're we goin' ter do, I arsks yer? 'ave we got ter swaller 'er hinsults like dogs? It ain't in the ship's articles. I tell yer we got a case. We kin go to law—
> YANK. (*with abysmal contempt*) Hell! Law!
> ALL. (*repeating the word after him as one with cynical mockery*) Law! (*The word has a brazen metallic quality as if their throats were phonograph horns. It is followed by a chorus of hard, barking laughter*).
> LONG. (*feeling the ground slipping from under his feet—*

desperately) As voters and citizens we kin force the bloody governments—

YANK. (*with abysmal contempt*) Hell! Governments!

ALL. (*repeating the word after him as one with cynical mockery*) Governments! (*The word has a brazen metallic quality as if their throats were phonograph horns. It is followed by a chorus of hard, barking laughter*).

LONG. (*hysterically*) We're free and equal in the sight of God—

YANK. (*with abysmal contempt*) Hell! God!

ALL. (*repeating the word after him as one with cynical mockery*) God! (*The word has a brazen metallic quality as if their throats were phonograph horns. It is followed by a chorus of hard, barking laughter*).

As ironically subtitled, the play is "A Comedy of Ancient and Modern Life." It is a comedy with tragic overtones and has great power in its choral scenes, where the physical health of the ancient is opposed to the disease of soul in the modern.

The First Man, on the other hand, produced at the Neighborhood Playhouse five days before, was deservedly a failure. It had no chorus and was hardly more than a naturalistic family drama. In addition, it was forced and overdrawn. Yet again O'Neill was concerned with opposing the ancient to the modern. The wife of an anthropologist, preparing to go with him on an expedition to find the remains of the first primitive man, reveals that she is pregnant. This touches off a whole series of antagonistic reactions among the anthropologist, his socially outcast best friend, and various puritan members of his upper-class family, all of which results in the wife's death in childbirth and another series of antagonisms. But the anthropologist is finally moved to accept his newborn son, whom he had refused even to see, leaves him with the one member of the family he can trust and goes off to find the first man alone. The promise is of a future reconciliation of the modern with the primitive, the modern being meant to stand for conscious or surface life and the primitive for its unconscious source.* George Jean Nathan criticized this play along with *Welded* as an unsuccessful attempt to imitate Strindberg. However, the similarities he had in mind were those of sexual hostility and psychological intensity. And as O'Neill made clear later on, his debt to Strindberg wasn't so superficial.

About a year after the disbanding of the original Provincetown Players the group was reorganized under O'Neill, Robert Edmond Jones and Kenneth Macgowan as Experimental Theater, Incorporated.[20] Their policy was to produce European as well as American plays, and they were to use both the old theater and the Greenwich Village Theater. The old theater, which at O'Neill's suggestion had first been called the Playwrights' Theater, was now to be known as the Provincetown Playhouse. In *The Theater of Tomorrow* Macgowan had set forth the dramatic ideal for which they were to strive.

The problem, as Macgowan saw it, was to find a way for the religious spirit to make a reappearance on the stage. But orthodox faith in America, if not everywhere, was too weak to provide the means. Its dogma had been broken down by Darwinism and its spirit hadn't been Dionysian in the first place. An artist was needed to create a world of spiritual reality in the theater, a drama of the inner life to take the place of the old surface realism. Macgowan speculated that

*A related aspect of *The First Man* has been pointed up by Louis Sheaffer, *O'Neill, Son and Artist*, p. 47. This is the parallel between the Greek legend of Jason going off in search of the Golden Fleece, and O'Neill's story of Curtis Jayson, the anthropologist, going off in search of the first man—in each case the hero looking for fulfillment, a fulfillment beyond the means of ordinary men. The parallel extends to Curtis Jayson's conflicts involving his wife, Martha, equivalent to Medea. O'Neill was already attracted in his early plays to the larger-than-life themes to be found in Greek myths and the Bible.

this drama would probably have a greater multiplicity of
scenes, dialogue that was less natural than rhetorical, a
return to the soliloquy and the aside, and action in movement, music, design and color rather than in words alone.

It will attempt to transfer to dramatic art the illumination of
those deep and vigorous and eternal processes of the human
soul which the psychology of Freud and Jung has given us
through study of the unconscious, striking to the heart of
emotion and linking our commonest life today with emana-
tions of the primitive racial mind.[21]

On the surface this neo-primitivism was more reactionary than progressive, reviving as it did all the devices of
romantic melodrama. Yet the aim was a psychological truth
more far-reaching than in any drama since Shakespeare.
The Theater of Tomorrow was to be a modern equivalent
of what the theater had been in Elizabethan England and
Athens, though not until some profound change in our way
of life had restored to the theater the communal devotion
of those times.

Macgowan was very much impressed with the beginnings
of a movement toward a new kind of theater in Europe, a
movement led by Gordon Craig and Max Reinhardt. Craig
had taken off from what Appia had done and developed a
technique of production based on a highly imaginative use
of color and light. This was the New Stagecraft, from which
Reinhardt had drawn inspiration in his conception of the
Theater of the Five Thousand. In this theater all the effects
were to be directed toward monumentality. There were to
be austere lines and large spaces, which would bring the
spectator into closer contact with the actor. And the pauses
in the movement of the drama itself would be filled by
music, perhaps by the rhythmic chanting of a chorus.
Reinhardt's idea was eventually realized to a great extent in

the Grosse Schauspielhaus in Berlin, which before it was remodeled had been a permanent circus building. Even before this he had been using circus buildings for productions of plays like *Oedipus Rex, Orestes, Everyman, The Miracle* and Gerhart Hauptmann's *Festspiel*. Macgowan took this as an indication of things to come.

> The theatre of the circus opens up possibilities for the playwright that seem singularly broad and singularly pregnant with the spirit of the age. Such a theatre enables him to write in terms of movement as well as of words, to dramatize life upon varying levels of consciousness and of actuality, to reach ever closer to the life-giving vigor of vast audiences, to arouse in such mighty gatherings emotions which sweep in one gigantic swell to the players and are thrown back in still more majestic power to the audience again. In such a playhouse is born a sense of drama which transcends individual action.

One possibility in such a theater was a drama in which large groups or choruses would move in unison around individual figures given a universal quality or aspect by masks. O'Neill was to realize a variation of this idea in *Lazarus Laughed* just as in one way or another he was to realize most of the ideas Macgowan set forth. The heroes of this new drama wouldn't be the individual figures but the groups, which would represent the people. The Theater of Tomorrow was to be democratic in content as well as primitive or neo-primitive in form. And the other possibilities in such a theater were of a like kind. They were all forms of a ritualistic, communal drama of the inner world. With *The Theater of Tomorrow* as its credo Experimental Theater, Inc., attempted to bring Dionysus back to life by removing the technical barriers to his appearance on the American stage.

In 1923 Macgowan collaborated with the designer Herman Rosse on *Masks and Demons*. The year before he had written *Continental Stagecraft* with Robert Edmond Jones, exploring further the technical innovations being made in the European theater. *Masks and Demons* was a study of the mask as a religious symbol and tried to show that it had always been part of the ritual in theater as well as religion. In effect, the book suggested that the artist of the new theater would have to make the mask reappear on the stage as a symbol of godhead. If O'Neill didn't already feel the same way himself, he was greatly influenced by this suggestion. During the next few years he experimented with masks in *All God's Chillun Got Wings*, an adaptation of *The Ancient Mariner*, *The Great God Brown*, *Marco Millions* and *Lazarus Laughed*. Then in 1932 he published "Memoranda on Masks," in which he stated his findings. Although he wouldn't use masks for all plays, he would use them for the genuinely modern play that so far had only been foreshadowed in a few clumsy specimens.

For I hold more and more surely to the conviction that the use of masks will be discovered eventually to be the freest solution of the modern dramatist's problem as to how—with the greatest possible dramatic clarity and economy of means—he can express those profound hidden conflicts of the mind which the probings of psychology continue to disclose to us . . . .
For what, at bottom, is the new psychological insight into human cause and effect but a study in masks, an exercise in unmasking? . . . this insight has uncovered the mask, has impressed the idea of mask as a symbol of inner reality . . .
(3)
Dogma for the new masked drama.—One's outer life passes in a solitude haunted by the masks of others; one's inner life passes in a solitude hounded by the masks of oneself.
(4)
With masked mob new type of play may be written in which the Mob as King, Hero, Villain, or Fool will be the main character—The Great Democratic Play! . . .
(6)
Consider Goethe's "Faust," which, psychologically speaking,

should be the closest to us of all the Classics. In producing this play, I would have Mephistopheles wearing the Mephistophelian mask of the face of Faust. For is not the whole of Goethe's truth *for our time* just that Mephistopheles and Faust are one and the same—*are* Faust?[22]

The first production offered by Experimental Theater, Inc., was Strindberg's *The Spook Sonata*. This was the first performance of the play in America, and O'Neill joined in the decision to use masks in interpreting it. The theater program included some notes by the members of the triumvirate on various aspects of the new drama. O'Neill wrote about Strindberg, calling him the "precursor of all modernity in our present theater." He said that if one were to think of any other playwright's work as naturalism, Strindberg's had to be thought of as supernaturalism. And it was only through some form of supernaturalism that the conflicts of the spirit could be expressed. He added that *The Spook Sonata* was one of Strindberg's most difficult "behind-life" or supernatural plays but that to imaginatively cope with such difficulty was the reason an experimental stage was needed. For the truth, "in the theater as in life, is eternally difficult, just as the easy is the everlasting lie."

The reason for O'Neill's strong attachment to Strindberg was that Strindberg had been a forerunner of the Dionysian era in the theater. His devices had been the miraculous ones of the New Stagecraft and his conflicts of spirit the religious ones that obsessed Nietzsche. The German Expressionists, by contrast, influenced O'Neill only in his means, not his ends. Georg Kaiser's plays, for example, encouraged O'Neill to make the stage image more psychological or subjective.[23] O'Neill felt no real affinity, however, to Kaiser's ultimately political kind of theater, which partly explains his reluctance to acknowledge any influence at all.

When O'Neill was awarded the Nobel Prize in 1936, he decided against going to Sweden to accept the award personally. Instead he wrote a letter to be read at the ceremonies and in it acknowledged his debt to Strindberg. He attributed his first urge to write for the theater to the inspiration he felt in reading Strindberg's plays. And he said that Strindberg "remains, as Nietzsche remains, in his sphere, the master, still to this day more modern than any of us, still our leader."

The first production of an O'Neill play by the new management was in an uptown theater in March of the 1923-24 season. It turned out to be unsuccessful. Like *The First Man* the play was forced and overdrawn. It was a psychological love story called *Welded*, the title referring to the lovers' being held together by an unbreakable bond. The idea for the story came out of O'Neill's marriage to Agnes Boulton. But though the lovers in the play were husband and wife, the psychology of their bond was more mystical than marital. It was the psychology of the primordial union of life itself.

> ELEANOR. ...And then we fight!
> CAPE. Then let's be proud of our fight! It began with the splitting of a cell a hundred million years ago into you and me, leaving an eternal yearning to become one life again. ... You and I—year after year—together—forms of our bodies merging into one form; rhythm of our lives beating against each other, forming slowly the one rhythm—the life of Us—created by us!—beyond us, above us!

O'Neill realized the necessity of playing this expressionistically, although rehearsals were already under way by the time he did. His idea was to hide the realistic settings in drapes and isolate each of the characters at certain moments by spotlights that would be like halos or auras of egoism. The device didn't save the play, but it did contribute to the psychology of it. Out of egoism the lovers do fight. Only they both find themselves incapable of violating the bond, she with an old suitor and he with a prostitute. Then in the last act the preserved sanctity of the bond takes the symbolic form of the cross.

> CAPE. ...Listen! Often I wake up in the night—in a black world, alone in a hundred million years of darkness. I feel like crying out to God for mercy because life lives! Then instinctively I seek you—my hand touches you! You are there—beside me—alive—with you I become a whole, a truth! Life guides me back through the hundred million years to you. It reveals a beginning in unity that I may have faith in the unity of the end! . . .
> ELEANOR. (*with deep, passionate tenderness*) My lover!
> CAPE. My wife! (*His eyes fixed on her he ascends. As he does so her arms move back until they are stretched out straight to right and left, forming a cross. CAPE stops two steps below her—in a low, wondering tone*) Why do you stand like that?
> ELEANOR. (*her head thrown back, her eyes shut—slowly, dreamily*) Perhaps I'm praying. I don't know. I love.
> CAPE. (*deeply moved*) I love you.
> ELEANOR. (*as if from a great distance*) We love! (*He moves close to her and his hands reach out for hers. For a moment as their hands touch they form together one cross. Then their arms go about each other and their lips meet.*)

A few weeks after *Welded* a dramatization of *The Ancient Mariner* was put on at the Provincetown Playhouse. O'Neill arranged it without altering the words, and Jones staged it. Masks were used for all the characters except the Mariner, this scheme being the model for the one employed later in *Lazarus Laughed*. An arrangement of the Book of Revelation was also to be put on around this time, and O'Neill had gotten as far as figuring out the staging and sound effects. The Coleridge, however, had been given a bad reception and plans for the St. John were dropped as a result.

In *All God's Chillun Got Wings*, written the previous year

but presented a month after *The Ancient Mariner*, an African religious mask was an important part of the setting. In *The Fountain*, completed the year before *All God's Chillun*, a mask had represented the figure of Death. And in the production of *The Hairy Ape* masks had served in the Fifth Avenue scene, though the text hadn't called for them as such. But the dramatic effect of these devices was limited, and *The Ancient Mariner* constituted O'Neill's first real experiment in Macgowan's Theater of Tomorrow. The next ritual play he completed was *The Great God Brown*, in which the action was partly expressed in terms of masks alone.

Before the production of *The Great God Brown* there was another failure to be suffered. *The Fountain* lasted just two weeks. Again the failure was deserved. One reason for it was that Juan Ponce de Leon's search for the fountain of youth demanded a romantic style which American actors could no longer bring off. O'Neill had even made an attempt to give the prose dialogue the rhetorical qualities of blank verse. Yet the play as a whole was rhetorical. Despite its metaphysical intent it was romantic—or melodramatic—not only in style but action. Written in between *The First Man* and *Welded*, it suffered from the same fault of having more going on and being felt than was realistically motivated. In short, it was unconvincing.

O'Neill's trouble was that he was trying to intensify from outside what could only be intensified from inside. This was obvious here in the language among other things. Ponce de Leon's search for the fountain of youth turned out to be a search for eternal life and his discovery of it a spiritual revelation. The Nietzschean doctrine of Eternal Recurrence was personified in the figure of Beatriz. Juan, lying wounded and in a delirium of fever in the Florida jungle, sees the figure of Death in the waters of the imaginary fountain. Yet Death metamorphoses before his eyes into the eternally creating Beatriz. And the Dionysian life cycle, now revealed, redeems all the destructive pain and sorrow of his life by uniting them to its own creative force.

> JUAN. . . .Light comes! Light creeps into my soul! (*Then he sees the* FIGURE *walk slowly from its place and vanish in the fountain*) Death is no more! (*The* FIGURE *materializes again within the fountain but this time there is no mask, the face is that of* BEATRIZ, *her form grown tall, majestic, vibrant with power* . . . .) I see! Fountain Everlasting, time without end! Soaring flame of the spirit transfiguring Death! All is within! All things dissolve, flow on eternally! O aspiring fire of life, sweep the dark soul of man! Let us burn in thy unity! . . .O God, Fountain of Eternity, Thou art the All in One, the One in All—the Eternal Becoming which is Beauty!

He is released from the fear of death. And when death finally comes in the following scene, it is understood and justified as an aesthetic phenomenon, as "an artistic game which the will plays with itself in the eternal fullness of its joy."

> JUAN. . . .One must accept, absorb, give back, become one-self a symbol! . . . I begin to know eternal youth! I have found my Fountain! O Fountain of Eternity, take back this drop, my soul!

Years later O'Neill himself summed up these failures. In the "Memoranda on Masks" he thought about what he would change if he could live through the productions of his plays again. Some plays obviously had to be rewritten in part. But others, including *The First Man, Welded* and *The Fountain*, were "too painfully bungled in their present form to be worth producing at all." The one thing he wouldn't change in the early productions was the use of masks, which he regarded as having been wholly successful.

The Great God Brown opened in January 1926 at the

Greenwich Village Theater and soon moved to Broadway. Between downtown and uptown it had a surprisingly long run of some eight months. This time Dionysus himself appeared on the stage, the action consisting of his initiation into manhood, his death and his resurrection. The play was set in the social context of the struggle between artist and Philistine, a surface theme with which O'Neill had been concerned from the outset in *Fog*. Here it was given a religious significance as well, the artist representing the seeker after the old, dead God and the Philistine the embodiment of the new, false one. Here, too, there was another, deeper struggle, the inner one between the pagan and Christian psychologies, self-fulfillment and self-denial, the creative and destructive impulses. Both struggles were portrayed in great measure by a complex dramaturgy of masks, and the total effect was confusing enough for O'Neill to offer an explanation of what he was after. This was an impression of the life cycle, though he had been at pains not to let the impression become anything more.

> It was far from my idea in writing Brown that this background pattern of conflicting tides in the soul of Man should ever overshadow and thus throw out of proportion the living drama of the recognizable human beings, Dion, Brown, Margaret and Cybel. I meant it always to be mystically within and behind them, giving them a significance beyond themselves, forcing itself through them to expression in mysterious words, symbols, actions they do not themselves comprehend. And that is as clearly as I wish an audience to comprehend it. It is Mystery—the mystery any one man or woman can feel but not understand as the meaning of any event—or accident—in any life on earth. And it is this mystery I want to realize in the theater . . .[24]

The Birth of Tragedy was extensively quoted in the playbill, the quotes being chosen by O'Neill.[25] And Nietzsche's words emphasized O'Neill's intention not to resolve the mystery or its struggles but to celebrate them. Dionysus first lives, suffers and dies in the person of Dion Anthony. Then after being willed by Dion in the form of his mask to William Brown, he lives, suffers and dies once more. In Brown's death scene the prostitute-mother Cybel and the wife-mother Margaret both chant ecstatic acceptance. Cybel chants acceptance of the bodily reality of godhead, which is what has united Dion and Brown, and Margaret of its masklike human appearance.

> CYBEL. (*gets up and fixes his body on the couch. She bends down and kisses him gently–she straightens up and looks into space–with a profound pain*) Always spring comes again bearing life! Always again! Always, always forever again!—Spring again!—life again!—summer and fall and death and peace again!—(*with agonized sorrow*)—but always, always, love and conception and birth and pain again—spring bearing the intolerable chalice of life again!—(*then with agonized exultance*)—bearing the glorious, blazing crown of life again! (*She stands like an idol of Earth, her eyes staring out over the world*).
>
> MARGARET. (*lifting her head adoringly to the mask–triumphant tenderness mingled with her grief*) My lover! My husband! My boy! (*She kisses the mask*) Good-by. Thank you for happiness! And you're not dead, sweetheart! You can never die till my heart dies! You will live forever! You will sleep under my heart! I will feel you stirring in your sleep, forever under my heart! (*She kisses the mask again. There is a pause*).

This celebration of the mystery of human life was nevertheless one-sided. The Dionysian action took place too much on the stage and not enough in the aesthetic experience of the audience. Cybel's ecstatic acceptance, for example, couldn't be conveyed by her dithyrambic chanting. The chanting was too unnatural, too out of place, too crude as the climax to what on the whole was an extremely sophisticated play with much dialogue that was lean and ironic. Probably no modern play could afford such directly dithyrambic speech, not even in pursuit of a Dionysian communion. However, Cybel's chanting wasn't the main problem. The reliance on masks was more at fault. For all their symbolic qualities, they proved incapable in themselves of stirring the religious emotions. O'Neill complained that the masks looked less symbolic than realistic and should have been twice as large. But evidently he also felt that what had been needed was a unifying chorus. There had been too little rapport between the actors and spectators. A chorus could have done what the individual dithyramb and masks could not. The life of Dionysus had to be expressed in a full ritual of song and dance for the lives of the audience to become one with it.

In *Marco Millions*, which he had begun in 1923 but didn't put into its final form until shortly before production almost five years later, O'Neill had started experimenting with choral groups. Yet he had departed from the life history of Dionysus to tell the story of the God of Success, more a satire than a ritual drama. Marco Polo, the great merchant of the West, gradually loses his soul in taking its immortality for granted and devoting himself wholly to the material world. He brings home from the East valuables worth millions, but by then he is no longer able to imagine his own death and turns into a swine. This kind of satire didn't really lend itself to Dionysian effects, and perhaps no kind of satire would have. There was, however, another side of the play that lent itself readily.

Before Marco leaves the East the Chinese princess who has loved him innocently since her childhood finds him incapable of returning her love. For Marco, blind to his own soul, can hardly love or even recognize another's. The princess then loses her will to live, dying in the prime of her youth and beauty. O'Neill used large choruses to build up the varying moods, making the ritual more elaborate and formal than he had done before. In the last scene he also used masks, though instead of giving them a narrative part in the action he let them serve traditionally as a visual expression or background image of the feeling. They were masks of grief, worn by a chorus of nine in the midst of other ritual groups, all of which echoed the lament of Kublai Kaan for his granddaughter in mournful rhythms of body and voice.

First come the musicians, nine in number, men in robes of bright red. They are followed by the chorus of nine singers, five men and four women, all of them aged, with bent bodies, their thin, cracked voices accompanying the music in queer, breaking waves of lamentation. These are masked, the men with a male mask of grief, the women with a female. All are dressed in deep black with white edging to their robes. After them comes a troupe of young girls and boys, dressed in white with black edging, moving slowly backward in a gliding, interweaving dance pattern. Their faces are not masked but are fixed in a disciplined, traditional expression of bewildered, uncomprehending grief that is like a mask. They carry silver censers which they swing in unison toward the corpse of the PRINCESS KUKACHIN, carried on a bier directly behind them on the shoulders of eight princes of the blood in black armor.

Accompanying the bier, one at each corner, are four priests—the foremost two, a Confucian and a Taoist, the latter two, a Buddhist and a Moslem. Each walks with bent head reading aloud to himself from his Holy Book....

KUBLAI. ...Can words recall life to her beauty? (*To the* PRIEST OF TAO) Priest of Tao, will you conquer death by your mystic Way?

PRIEST OF TAO. (*bowing his head in submission—fatalistically*) Which is the greater evil, to possess or to be without? Death is.

CHORUS. (*in an echo of vast sadness*) Death is.

KUBLAI. (*to the* CONFUCIAN) Follower of Confucius, the Wise, have you this wisdom?

PRIEST OF CONFUCIUS. (*slowly*) Before we know life, how can we know death? (*Then as the* TAOIST, *submissively*) Death is.

CHORUS. (*as before*) Death is.

KUBLAI. (*to the* BUDDHIST PRIEST) Worshipper of Buddha, can your self-overcoming overcome that greatest overcomer of self?

BUDDHIST PRIEST. This is a thing which no god can bring about: that what is subject to death should not die. (*Then as the others, submissively*) Death is.
CHORUS. (*as before*) Death is.
KUBLAI. (*wearily*) And your answer, priest of Islam?
PRIEST OF ISLAM. It is the will of Allah! (*Submissively*) Death is.
CHORUS. Death is. Death is. Death is. (*Their voices die away*).

Marco Millions was produced by the Theater Guild, an outgrowth of the old Washington Square Players, in January 1928. Yet it first passed through the hands of the masters of spectacle, including the team of Morris Guest and Max Reinhardt, who turned down an offer to mount it in collaboration with the triumvirate. David Belasco had it on option for awhile and even entertained elaborate schemes before letting it go. When it finally was done, it received excellent reviews. But audience response was relatively slow and it was placed in repertory with a second play where it had only ninety-two performances over a period of five months. On the other hand, it was appealing enough to last on the road for about two years and in the thirties had several productions abroad. It was also performed by non-professional groups in the States and in 1964 was revived professionally by the Lincoln Center Repertory Company in New York.

Unfortunately, in the Lincoln Center revival the ritual nature of the play was either misunderstood or found too demanding, the choruses being cut down and the masks eliminated altogether. As the satire had badly dated in any case, masks and choruses might not have kept the production from being a failure. But they would at least have made it an interesting failure. For the few compelling moments in the production were the ritualistic ones of choral or near-choral chanting and movement.

In its masks and choruses *Marco Millions* anticipated

Lazarus Laughed, which was completed in 1926. Both works were intended for Macgowan's Theater of Tomorrow. O'Neill subtitled *Lazarus Laughed* "A Play For An Imaginative Theater," and it was his crowning effort to make the theater a place of ritual and religious experience by technically enlarging the dramatic image. He wrote it for a theater that he thought was already at hand, one which Gest and Reinhardt had brought over from Europe with *The Miracle* two years before.

lazarus

The Miracle by Karl Vollmoeller opened at the Century Theater in New York in January 1924 and ran some 250 performances. In the course of touring the country over the next five years it also played at the Cincinnati Music Hall, St. Louis New Coliseum, Chicago Auditorium, Kansas City Convention Hall and Los Angeles Shrine Auditorium, all vast halls or arenas. It was a spectacular miracle play based on Maeterlinck's *Sister Beatrice*, so spectacular, in fact, that the dramatic part of it had to be acted out in pantomime. Its large dimensions made the pantomime essential since a spoken drama could never have held the mass effects together. This aspect of it evidently went unnoticed by O'Neill or else was simply discounted by him at the time he conceived *Lazarus Laughed*.

The world premiere of *The Miracle* had taken place in 1911 under Reinhardt's direction in London. Following this there had been seventeen successful productions on the

Continent in arenas, opera houses, circus buildings and
tents. One had been planned for New York late in 1914, but
the war in Europe had made that impossible. The 1924
production was entirely new, although the Vollmoeller
book and the musical accompaniment by Humperdinck
remained intact. The American impresario Morris Gest
managed and financed it. And one of the first things he did
was to hire the radical American designer Norman-Bel
Geddes.

Geddes was a devotee of the New Stagecraft, and his
collaboration with Reinhardt was spurred by mutual enthusiasm. The plans alone took nine months to prepare,
comprising more than 800 mechanical drawings and half as
many costume designs. The mechanical drawings, which
according to a program blurb numbered more than a sky-
scraper usually required, were for transforming both the
auditorium and the stage of the theater into a cathedral.
When the play was finally presented it made a deep impression. Kenneth Macgowan described it, if only in part, as "an
overpowering lunge into a mystic beauty."[26] Even the wry
Alexander Woolcott, *The New York Herald* critic, couldn't
help being somewhat awed.

> There are high transept windows of such glass as the work-
> ers of Chartres and Carcassonne knew how to make. There are
> high invisible choirs from which the sweet melody of the "Ve-
> nite Adoremus" seems to sift down between the cobwebby
> pillars. There is the thunder of organ music and the air is all
> atremble with chimes.
> But better still, there is the constant shuffle of penitential
> feet, the troops of young folks from the village, the wistful
> procession of the halt and the blind, the sparkle of children
> running in and out of the sunlight into such a temple as was the
> heart of a people in an ancient day. The teeming life of that
> people is renewed in the hubbub of Reinhardt's stagecraft and
> such are the crossways of his theater that before long you, the
> onlooker, are first jostled by and then absorbed into that life.

You accept it. This was ever the theory of his stagecraft. Count-less polysyllabic articles have been written about it in the magazines of small circulations. But the thing works. It works.

Although *The Miracle* was the first wholly successful at-tempt at drama of this kind in the American theater, it wasn't the only attempt. Over thirty years earlier the play-wright Steele MacKaye had designed a 10,000-seat playhouse called the Spectatorium for the performance at the Chicago World's Fair of his spectacle *The World Finder*. The latter, a celebration of Columbus, was a mixture of pantomime, dialogue and songs with choral music by Victor Herbert and interpretative music by Dvorak. Despite being near completion, however, the Spectatorium came to fi-nancial grief in the Wall Street panic of 1893, and *The World Finder* was never performed. MacKaye's son, the poet and dramatist Percy MacKaye, also experimented with a more communal kind of performance or what he called Com-munity Drama. In fact, he originated the civic masque and with it the open-air theater in America. His legitimate play *The Scarecrow* was staged by Reinhardt in one of the more intimate theaters in Berlin in 1914. But his most charac-teristic and famous things, such as *Sanctuary*, *St. Louis* and *Caliban*, were allegorical pageants so elaborate that Reinhardt would have been hard pressed to mount them even in a circus theater.

Caliban, for example, was put on for a couple of weeks at the CCNY stadium in the late spring of 1916 with about 2,500 people reportedly taking part in the production. Among those participating were the Neighborhood Playhouse group, the Washington Square Players, and Robert Edmond Jones, who did most of the designs. The play or masque had been written at the invitation of the New York City committee in charge of commemorating the tercentenary of Shakespeare's death. Using *The Tempest* or what amounted to a sequel as a framework, MacKaye had arranged a series of interludes from Shakespeare's plays together with a mimed historical pageant of the theater extending into the future. O'Neill, who was living in the Village then, conceivably saw this spectacle and found it intriguing, although it was anything but dramatic.

Similar things were being done around this time by others. George Pierce Baker, the teacher of the playwriting course O'Neill attended at Harvard in 1914, wrote one for performance at Plymouth in the summer of 1921 in honor of the tercentenary of the landing of the Pilgrims. But there was a difference of course, between all this and *The Miracle*. Community drama, by MacKaye's own definition, was completely divorced from the commercial theater, which in America meant from the real theater. MacKaye was like O'Neill in seeking to restore to the theater some of its old religious purpose, but with him this took the form of didactic pageantry rather than dramatic celebration.[27] The significance of *The Miracle* was that it proved the dramatic image on the commercial stage could be enlarged without necessarily doing away with the drama.

Actually, the effect this movement had on the theater physically was more important than the drama it produced. Steele MacKaye's Spectatorium was unique in more ways than one. It was to have contained every device of the New Stagecraft, including some of his own invention, from an adjustable proscenium to a cyclorama or dome in back of the stage with a surface of linoleum instead of the usual cloth. After the World's Fair the structure was razed. But there was enough money around to realize the idea on a smaller scale in a playhouse called the Scenitorium, which was successfully exhibited with choral parts from *The World Finder* a short while before MacKaye's death the following

year. Somewhat later Frank Lloyd Wright, in designing a
new playhouse that was to be built in Los Angeles, combined an adjustable proscenium with a concrete and plaster
dome curving out into the lines of the auditorium. Then
Norman-Bel Geddes designed a playhouse without any
proscenium at all. And in 1921, for the 600th anniversary
of Dante's death, he devised a presentation of *The Divine
Comedy* in Madison Square Garden based on the transfiguring effects of light and color. Herman Rosse, with whom
Macgowan was to write *Masks and Demons*, worked out a few
similar ideas, one of which was to turn the Coliseum Building in Chicago into an elaborate theater in the round for the
production of a nativity play. Finally George Cram Cook
designed a theater of many domes that would provide the
playwright with a background of infinity and further the
interplay between the actors and audience.

As it happened, none of these designs was ever realized.
But in 1920 the Provincetown Players—in the person of
Cook—built a concrete and plaster dome for *The Emperor
Jones*, and the technical capability of the American theater
was greatly expanded.[28] The dome reflected light in such a
way that the heavens seemed as much a part of the stage
image as in the Athenian and Elizabethan theaters. For an
O'Neill play to have provided the occasion was more than
coincidence.

Geddes subsequently had his plans for *The Divine Comedy*
published. The book included a foreword by Reinhardt in
which he predicted that Geddes would become the most
important theater man of his day. Geddes was soon to
design a production of *Lazarus Laughed*. Yet O'Neill's miracle play never took its place on the professional stage along
with *The Miracle* largely because there was no Reinhardt at
hand to direct it. Only a Reinhardt could have mounted it as
well as gotten the necessary backing.

O'Neill began working on the play about a year after *The Miracle* ended its run in New York. He finished it some nine months later in the late spring of 1926, by which time Reinhardt had long since returned to Europe and O'Neill's own association with Macgowan and Jones had for all practical purposes dissolved. Experimental Theater, Inc., had been forced by lack of funds to join with Otto Kahn, a philanthropic financier. While Kahn was genuinely interested in the theater and had even been one of the early benefactors of the Provincetown Players, he wasn't that devoted to O'Neill. And O'Neill, for his part, had drawn the image of Success in *The Great God Brown* and *Marco Millions* somewhat in Kahn's likeness. The agreement between the two groups was to follow an experimental policy in an uptown theater with Macgowan in charge. But as Jones went off to Europe from lack of enthusiasm for the merger and O'Neill was hardly ever in town, the experimental spirit was too weak for Macgowan to do very much.

One thing Macgowan did do, however, was try to have *Lazarus Laughed* produced. He corresponded with Reinhardt about it, and there were vain hopes early in 1928 that the latter might stage it in Germany. Meanwhile it had been placed on the Actors' Theater agenda for production in 1927, though when the time came to get it off, not enough money could be raised. Macgowan then accepted an offer from the Chicago Play Producing Company for an opening in Chicago prior to New York. This production, for which Geddes made some very striking expressionistic designs, apparently came close to being realized in the autumn of 1927 before the expense and technical difficulty of it proved too much. There were vague reports a little later that the Theater Guild and the Provincetown Players, reorganized along former lines as of the 1925-26 season, were planning New York productions. With the idea of doing it uptown the Players eventually gave a reading to an audience of prospective backers in 1929, but as with all the other possibilities nothing happened.[29]

The only attempt at staging *Lazarus* that succeeded was by a theater workshop in California. Presumably in despair of a professional production O'Neill gave the play to the Pasadena Community Playhouse. Here things were done on a nonprofit basis with everybody working gratis or for a pittance. In this instance more than 100 people volunteered to take part in the preparations, including students at UCLA and a local art school. The cast numbered well over 150 and there was a paid twenty-two piece orchestra for an original musical score. The whole production, designed by one James Hyde in an abstract style, was put together in just six weeks and opened on April 9, 1928.

O'Neill didn't help much in the direction, although it was his custom to. Probably he would have liked to attend rehearsals, but shortly before they got under way his personal life carried him aboard a ship to Europe with Carlotta Monterey. Yet he did correspond with Irving Pichel, the actor who played Lazarus, and probably with Gilmor Brown, the director. In any event, the idea for the most important aspect of the production, the musical accompaniment for Lazarus' laughter and the dancing of his followers, had been written into the text.

Music had been used in a similar way to support the pantomime and choral movements in *The Miracle*. It was a functional part of Reinhardt's Theater of the Five Thousand and had been foreseen by Macgowan as part of the Theater of Tomorrow. It had even generated Nietzsche's whole conception of tragedy through its ecstatic effect in Wagner's *Tristan and Isolde*. In the drama of Wagner, of course, music was organic and its effect transcended that of the action proper. But the Dionysian spirit of music, of ritual song and dance, was what Nietzsche had intuited to be the origin of classical tragedy. Significantly enough, the last words in Wagner's *Siegfried* are "Laughing at death," an expression of the same spirit or state of mind that possesses Lazarus in O'Neill's play. In a corresponding way the music composed to fit the play supposedly had the tonal qualities and the crescendos of Wagner's. O'Neill and Wagner both tried to write in a Dionysian vein.

Lazarus ran for twenty-eight performances at the Pasadena Playhouse before moving over to the Hollywood Music Box, a much larger theater, for two weeks more. The production was kept together so long on a nonprofessional basis only by virtue of the acclaim it evoked. This acclaim was even enough to bring about a two-week revival at the Playhouse in April of the following year. The great majority of critics praised both the play and the production, especially Pichel's performance as Lazarus. The drama editor of the San Francisco *Chronicle* made the inevitable comparison, saying that "nothing greater in mass acting has been seen in California with the exception of Reinhardt's *The Miracle*," while the local critic from the Pasadena *Star-News* saw it as being in a class by itself. "Not twice in a lifetime will a play-goer experience so vivid an artistic sensation as this production presents . . . [Pichel's] voice falls with haunting cadences; his laughter touches springs too deep for thought."

The Imaginative Theater, for which O'Neill wrote *Lazarus*, was Nietzschean only at a remove. Although the dramaturgy of the play was in the spirit of *The Birth of Tragedy*, that spirit had first been given form in the work of Reinhardt and Macgowan and in O'Neill's own previous experiments. The play itself, however, was Nietzschean in an immediate sense. Its action was inspired directly by *Thus Spoke Zarathustra*.

There were also other sources, specifically the Gospel of St. John for the story of Lazarus' resurrection, and more generally the many religious writings O'Neill had studied. Jung, too, exerted an influence. The book of psychoanalytical theory which O'Neill later described as having interested him most was Jung's *Psychology of the Unconscious*.[30] Some of the mystical poetry Jung illuminated in terms of the libido in that book was from *Thus Spoke Zarathustra*. And in dramatizing Zarathustra's teachings O'Neill undoubtedly had in mind many of their Jungian implications. Yet none of these additional influences made the action of the play any less Nietzschean. Lazarus, after losing the fear of death in his resurrection, returns to life in the body of Dionysus and the mind of Zarathustra.

The resurrected Lazarus is described in the opening stage directions. His body emanates a soft radiance and his head is haloed. He wears no mask, signifying the freedom he now has from the fear of death. His face, "dark-complected, ruddy and brown, the color of rich earth upturned by the plow" is like "that of a statue of a divinity of Ancient Greece . . . in its quality of detached serenity." And he is staring straight ahead as if seeing what no one else in the room can see. There is a suggestion in his appearance that his return to life is two-fold. The color of his skin seems to represent a physical return and his facial expression a spiritual return. The suggestion of a spiritual return is augmented by the light surrounding him and by his not wearing a mask in the midst of over 100 masked figures.

This distinction between the physical and spiritual aspects of the resurrection is necessarily vague, but the total impression is of a change in life rather than of just a continuation or renewal. O'Neill used the device of making Lazarus grow gradually younger partly to emphasize this. Lazarus has been reborn in soul as well as in body, or as one who has overcome himself and is now a higher man. When he tells his neighbors what he has found in the grave, the Nietzschean idea of the play is set forth.

> FATHER. To my son, Lazarus, whom a blessed miracle has brought back from death!
>
> LAZARUS. (*suddenly laughing softly out of his vision, as if to himself, and speaking with a strange unearthly calm in a voice that is like a loving whisper of hope and confidence*) No! There is no death!...
>
> ALL. There—is—no—death?...
>
> ALL THE GUESTS. (*with insistent curiosity but in low awed tones*) What is beyond there, Lazarus?
>
> CHORUS. (*in a low murmur*) What is beyond there? What is beyond?
>
> CROWD. (*carrying the question falteringly back into silence*) What is beyond?
>
> LAZARUS. (*suddenly again—now in a voice of loving exaltation*) There is only life! I heard the heart of Jesus laughing in my heart; "There is Eternal Life in No," it said, "and there is the same Eternal Life in Yes! Death is the fear between!" And my heart reborn to love of life cried "Yes!" and I laughed in the laughter of God! (*He begins to laugh, softly at first—a laugh so full of a complete acceptance of life, a profound assertion of joy in living, so devoid of all self-consciousness or fear, that it is like a great bird song triumphant in depths of sky, proud and powerful, infectious with love, casting on the listener an enthralling spell. The crowd in the room are caught by it . . .*

Lazarus has returned from the grave as a Yea-sayer, as one who affirms life with all its pain, sorrow and death as being worth living. He understands Jesus to have said in raising him, "There is Eternal Life in No, and there is the same Eternal Life in Yes! Death is the fear between!" The No is what Jesus himself represents. It is what O'Neill described at the time he was writing the play—in his explanation of *The Great God Brown*—as "the masochistic, life-denying spirit of Christianity." It rejects life in favor of immortality after death. Lazarus' revelation, however, is that this saying of No to life implies the saying of Yes to it.

Just as there is Eternal Life in immortality after death, there is also Eternal Life in life itself by virtue of its endlessly recurring nature.

The essence of both attitudes is the acceptance of physical death. This acceptance is what frees one from death, at least in a psychological sense. For the fear of physical death, which results when there is no acceptance, becomes a fear of life, a fear of what leads to death, and the fear of life becomes in turn a death in life. Death is consequently a living death proceeding from fear, the fear between Yes and No. Now that the endlessly recurring nature of life has been revealed to him, Lazarus is able to accept death. And as this has liberated him from his fear of death, he has been liberated at the same time from his fear of life. His spirit is naturally one which loves life, and it is to this spiritual state he has returned.

Benjamin De Casseres, the American poet and a personal friend of O'Neill's, once spoke of the play as "Hellenism battering down Buddhism, or at least fusing with it—for in the great spiritual dimension of Lazarus' laughter, Yea and Nay are one."[31] But the fusion of Nietzsche's Hellenism that O'Neill made was less with Buddhism than with Christianity. De Casseres' Nietzschean bias perhaps made him overlook this. For such a fusion constituted a departure from Nietzsche's view that Hellenism and Christianity were irreconcilable, a view which O'Neill had more or less adhered to a year earlier in *The Great God Brown*. Nietzsche, summing up in *Ecce Homo* the opposition of his philosophy to the existing morality of Western culture, finally asked, "Have you understood me? *Dionysus* versus *Christ* . . . ."

Yet O'Neill's fusion of the two outlooks wasn't a compromise with Christian morality. By *Christ* Nietzsche meant not Jesus himself so much as the Church of Peter and Paul. In fact, the Jesus of the Gospels and of *Lazarus* is really more

Nietzschean than Christian. At the same time the influence of Jesus on Lazarus endows Lazarus with compassion on top of the Dionysian hardness Nietzsche called for. As a result Lazarus is also more of a universal savior than Nietzsche could ever have believed in. Nevertheless, in the course of the action he assumes the form of the Dionysus perceived by Nietzsche in Greek tragedy. And he reveals his wisdom in Apollonian images, which is to say with the voice of Zarathustra. In the first act Lazarus tells the crowd that man must become something more than he is if he is to be saved from himself.

> LAZARUS. . . . You forget! You forget the God in you! You wish to forget! Remembrance would imply the high duty to live as a son of God—generously—with love!—with pride!—with laughter! . . . Why are your eyes always fixed on the ground in weariness of thought, or watching one another with suspicion? Throw your gaze upward! To Eternal Life! To the fearless and deathless! The everlasting! To the stars! (*He stretches out his arms to the sky—then suddenly points*) See! A new star has appeared! It is the one that shone over Bethlehem! (*His voice becomes a little bitter and mocking*) The Master of Peace and Love has departed this earth. Let all stars be for you henceforth symbols of Saviors—Sons of God who appeared on worlds like ours to tell the saving truth to ears like yours, inexorably deaf! (*Then exaltedly*) But the greatness of Saviors is that they may not save! The greatness of Man is that no god can save him—until he becomes a god!

O'Neill was familiar with *Thus Spoke Zarathustra* in translation as far back as 1906 when he was only eighteen. And while at Harvard eight years later he worked his way through it in the original. He told De Casseres in 1927 that the book had influenced him more than any other, though he sometimes thought that both his life and work were pitiful contradictions of it. By that time he was in the habit of reading it over every year or so, and during one reading

he copied out a great many passages particularly meaningful to him. He also knew some of it by heart, even if imper-
fectly. For one misquoted passage, undoubtedly written
down from memory, appears in some notes he made for
Lazarus prior to doing a first draft. According to Agnes
Boulton, the book was a sort of Bible to him and in the latter
part of their marriage he kept it by his bedside. Most likely
this was when he was at work on the play. In any case, his
devotion to Nietzsche then was both passionate and of long
standing.[32] In "Zarathustra's Prologue" he first found the
idea of the higher man.

> And Zarathustra spoke thus to the people:
> "*I teach you the overman.* Man is something that shall be over-
> come. What have you done to overcome him?
> "All beings so far have created something beyond them-
> selves; and do you want to be the ebb of this great flood and
> even go back to the beasts rather than overcome man? What is
> the ape to man? A laughing-stock or a painful embarrassment.
> And man shall be just that for the overman: a laughing stock or
> a painful embarrassment. You have made your way from
> worm to man, and much in you is still worm. Once you were
> apes, and even now, too, man is more ape than any ape . . . .
> "Man is a rope, tied between beast and overman—a rope
> over an abyss. A dangerous across, a dangerous on-the-way, a
> dangerous looking-back, a dangerous shuddering and stop-
> ping.
> "What is great in man is that he is a bridge and not an end:
> what can be loved in man is that he is an *overture* and a *going
> under.*[33]

Zarathustra, like Lazarus, is a Yea-sayer, one who affirms
life as having value for its own sake in spite of all suffering.
He tells the heaven above him, "But I am one who can bless
and say Yes, if only you are about me, pure and light, you
abyss of light; then I carry the blessings of my Yes into all
abysses. I have become one who blesses and says Yes . . ." He
laughs at death, the psychological death-in-life of the fear

between. One of his disciples interprets a dream for him as meaning that "like a thousandfold children's laughter Zarathustra enters all death chambers, laughing at all the night watchmen and guardians of tombs and at whoever else is rattling with gloomy keys." And in the form of a parable Zarathustra describes the birth of the higher man from out of the life-and-death struggle of the individual with himself—

> no longer human—one changed, radiant, *laughing*! Never yet on earth has a human being laughed as he laughed! O my brothers, I heard a laughter that was no human laughter; and now a thirst gnaws at me, a longing that never grows still. My longing for this laughter gnaws at me ...

Lazarus is the incarnation of this vision of Zarathustra's. He is even Zarathustra himself after the prophet has passed through the three metamorphoses of the spirit leading to the higher man. It is necessary for the spirit to become in turn like a camel, like a lion and like a child. It must first weigh itself down with all the old values, then seek the prey of its own freedom from them, and finally accept life as it is in order to create something new. After his first "going under," or going down, from the mountain of his solitude Zarathustra finds that he still isn't enough like a child to fully accept life as it is. He says, "The child is innocence and forgetting, a new beginning, a game, a self-propelled wheel, a first movement, a sacred 'Yes.'" But only on reascending for the second time can he pronounce this sacred Yes. And there are many more years of struggling with his spirit on the mountain before he receives the sign of its last metamorphosis and is ready to go down again. The journey Lazarus makes is essentially just such a third and final down-going. His resurrection picks up where Zarathustra's metamorphosis leaves off.

O'Neill was well aware of the distinction Nietzsche made between becoming like a child in the Christian sense and in the Dionysian sense. The Christian becoming meant a rejection of life while the Dionysian meant an acceptance.[34] O'Neill had already dramatized the Christian in *All God's Chillun Got Wings* as a psychological regression to an earlier state, a movement backwards away from life. At the same time he had let the regression, which is suffered by his heroine, bring a spiritual revelation to his hero. This was an attempt to transform the outer defeat of the characters into an inner triumph. Yet the hero's revelation was Christian also, constituting a submission rather than an overcoming and failing to have the desired effect. In *Lazarus* there is no psychological regression, and the spiritual revelation has already taken place in Lazarus' grave before the curtain rises. The Jungian implications of Nietzsche's distinction serve to make this clearer, O'Neill having been equally well aware of them.

To Jung the symbolic return to the womb had two meanings on the level of individual psychology. It was an expression of the desire to return to the state in which one existed in the womb, in effect a desire for psychological death. Simultaneously, it was an expression of the desire to enter into a new state just as one first entered into life from out of the womb, in effect a desire for psychological rebirth. The first meaning corresponds to the Christian sense of becoming like a child, the second to the Dionysian.

So if Lazarus' grave is understood as his psychological womb, his resurrection in the spiritual likeness of a child may be taken to be a psychological rebirth. Like Zarathustra he gives birth to a new and higher form of being from out of himself. And he does this by virtue of the revelation he has of the Eternal Recurrence of life, which takes the form of his being brought back to life by Jesus. When he enters a square in Athens in the second act, he is mistaken by the people for Dionysus. They deck him out and prostrate themselves before him as though he were the god reborn, but he tells them what happened to the man Lazarus in his grave.

> LAZARUS. ...Then, of a sudden, a strange gay laughter trembled from his heart as though his life, so long repressed in him by fear, had found at last its voice and a song for singing. "Men call this death," it sang. "Men call life death and fear it. They hide from it in horror. Their lives are spent in hiding. Their fear becomes their living. They worship life as death!".... And here the song of Lazarus' life grew pitiful. "Men must learn to live," it mourned. "Before their fear invented death they knew, but now they have forgotten. They must be taught to laugh again!" And Lazarus answered "Yes!"... Thus sang his life to Lazarus while he lay dead! Man must learn to live by laughter! (*He laughs*).

Lazarus echoes here the words of Zarathustra, "...you higher men, *learn* to laugh!" The phrase "Lazarus laughed" was used by O'Neill as the title of the play for the sake of contrast with the "Jesus wept" of John 11:35. The pain of life causes the Nay-saying Jesus to weep with sorrow, but the very existence of life regardless of its pain causes the Yea-saying Lazarus to laugh with joy. As it happened, O'Neill had done some reading for the psychology of Lazarus' laughter in Bergson and Freud. Only he had found their views too rationalistic, or at least too limited in scope, for his purpose, laughter in Bergson being mainly a social corrective and in Freud a discharge of eased tension. Strictly speaking, the Freudian view did apply. But O'Neill was really more interested in the spirituality than the psychology of laughter. And Lazarus' laughter ended up just as much pure Nietzsche as it had begun, a sheer overflow of joy in life itself.[35]

Lazarus' faith in Eternal Recurrence is also pure
Nietzsche, or rather another echo of Zarathustra. At the
beginning of his last period of solitude Zarathustra lets his
eagle of pride and his serpent of wisdom tell him what he
has come to believe—

> that all things recur eternally, and we ourselves too; and that
> we have already existed an eternal number of times, and all
> things with us. You teach that there is a great year of becoming,
> a monster of a great year, which must, like an hourglass, turn
> over again and again so that it may run down and run out
> again; and all these years are alike in what is greatest as in what
> is smallest; and we ourselves are alike in every great year, in
> what is greatest as in what is smallest.
> "And if you wanted to die now, O Zarathustra, behold, we
> also know how you would then speak to yourself . . . .
> " 'Now I die and vanish,' you would say, 'and all at once I am
> nothing. The soul is as mortal as the body. But the knot of
> causes in which I am entangled recurs and will create me again.
> I myself belong to the causes of the eternal recurrence. I come
> again, with this sun, with this earth, with this eagle, with this
> serpent—not to a new life or a better life or a similar life: I
> come back eternally to this same, selfsame life, in what is
> greatest as in what is smallest, to teach again the eternal recur-
> rence of all things, to speak again the word of the great noon of
> earth and man, to proclaim the overman again to men.' "

He will return to the selfsame spiritual life, though not to
the selfsame bodily one. For when the cyclical flow of time
renews itself in every great year of becoming, the spirit of all
life's forms is also renewed. Zarathustra's belief in this is
crucial because it signifies that life has at last been fully
accepted as is. At that point hope in an evolutionary perfection of man, of the last man, is wholly supplanted by the
necessity of the individual's perfection of himself, of the
overman.

To Lazarus the Eternal Recurrence implies that the spirit
will return to its more elemental forms as though to a

universal womb and then be reborn from out of that womb. It also implies, however, that in the course of eternal life the spirits of the smallest men as well as the greatest may take on a higher form. Zarathustra spoke only to those great enough in spirit to pass through the three metamorphoses, but Lazarus bears his message to the world at large.

> LAZARUS. . . ."Once as squirming specks we crept from the tides of the sea. Now we return to the sea! Once as quivering flecks of rhythm we beat down from the sun. Now we reenter the sun! Cast aside is our pitiable pretense, our immortal egohood, the holy lantern behind which cringed our Fear of the Dark! Flung off is that impudent insult to life's nobility which gibbers: 'I, this Jew, this Roman, this noble or this slave, must survive in my pettiness forever!' Away with such coward-ice of spirit! We will to die! We will to change! Laughing we lived with our gift, now with laughter give we back that gift to become again the Essence of the Giver! Dying we laugh with the Infinite. We are the Giver and the Gift! Laughing, we will our own annihilation! Laughing, we give our lives for Life's sake!" (*He laughs up to heaven ecstatically*) This must Man will as his end and his new beginning! He must conceive and desire his own passing as a mood of eternal laughter and cry with pride, "Take back, O God, and accept in turn a gift from me, my grateful blessing for Your gift—and see, O God, now I am laughing with You! I am your laughter—and You are mine!"

Zarathustra functions as a prophet, Lazarus as a messiah. The fusion by O'Neill of Hellenism with Christianity accounts for the difference. The journey Lazarus makes in his second life leads to his martyrdom on the spear of Caligula even as he is being burnt alive at the stake. His death has an affinity with both the crucifixion of Jesus and the ritual sacrifice of the Year-Daimon Dionysus. The ritual sacrifice of Dionysus in primitive societies generally took the form of a slaying of his corresponding totem animal, after which the animal was eaten so the tribe might partake of its godhead. The equivalent for Lazarus is his death on the spear, a substitute for the sacrificial knife. The crucifixion of Jesus is inseparable in religious mythology from the cross of wood, which Jung had identified in *Psychology of the Unconscious* as the Tree of Life. The equivalent of this for Lazarus is his being burnt at the stake.[36] In a stage direction to the death scene O'Neill calls it "the feast and sacrifice of Life, the Eternal."

At the time of his resurrection Lazarus is about fifty. Growing gradually younger, he reaches the palace of Tiberius in Capri looking only twenty-five. His increasing youth signifies his psychological rebirth. Through his belief in Eternal Recurrence he has passed through the third metamorphosis and become in spirit like a child. But more especially, his increasing youth signifies the process of Eternal Recurrence itself. Lazarus grows younger in his second life by way of returning to his metaphysical life source, personified by Miriam. Although her children have already died before the action of the play begins, she is an abstract figure of motherhood, much like Margaret in *The Great God Brown*. Hers is the womb through which the mortal life of the individual spirit passes on its way to and from the universal womb of eternal life. Ironically, her mortal nature doesn't allow her to understand this, and Lazarus' return to the womb of eternal life appears to her like his death. So as he grows younger, she for love of him grows older. In the third act she begs him to let her bite into a piece of poisoned fruit offered by Pompeia.

MIRIAM. (*to* LAZARUS—*requesting meekly but longingly*) May I accept, Lazarus? Is it time at last? My love has followed you over long roads among strangers and each league we came from home my heart has grown older. Now it is too old for you, a heart too weary for your loving laughter. Ever your laughter has grown younger, Lazarus! Upward it springs like a lark from a field, and sings! Once I knew your laughter was my child, my son of Lazarus; but then it grew younger and I felt at last it had returned to my womb—and ever younger and younger—until, tonight, when I spoke to you of home, I felt new birth-pains as your laughter, grown too young for me, flew back to the unborn—a birth so like a death! (*She sobs and wipes her eyes with her sleeve—then humbly, reaching out for the fruit*) May I accept it, Lazarus?

Only at the moment of death does she affirm Lazarus' faith in Eternal Recurrence by crying out, "Yes! There is only life!" And when Lazarus himself dies, he reaffirms his faith. The last thing he says is "There is no death!" following which his voice is heard in "a faint dying note of laughter that rises and is lost in the sky like the flight of his soul back into the womb of Infinity." However, Lazarus' faith isn't enough to save man. The message he brings back from the grave is forgotten as soon as his laughter is no longer heard. The tragedy of man is that he forgets. The new God which man must find to replace the old, dead one is to be found only in himself, and such a discovery requires a higher level of spiritual life than he is generally capable of. The failure of Lazarus as a savior is a failure of the Christian element in the play, a failure of the desire to be a savior. The Hellenistic element is what succeeds. Life is accepted as is.

O'Neill gave all this as Dionysian a form as he thought the modern stage would allow. The success of *The Miracle* in New York had led him to believe the professional theater could also be an Imaginative Theater. But the dramatic part of *The Miracle* was acted out in pantomime, leaving only a lyrical effect to the voice. And a successful production of *Lazarus* would have had to combine the effects of spoken and lyrical drama. In other words, the dithyrambic or rhapsodic passages recited by Lazarus and the crowds would have had to prove equally dramatic or integral to the action, which they were quite unlikely to do.

Still the Pasadena production was put together in only six weeks, and though unprofessional it must have been fairly exciting. So the problem for Broadway was seemingly more the money than the technical difficulties involved. The Theater Guild's presentation of *Marco Millions* in 1928 at least had a critical success, but no one with the resources ever cared to take on the problems of the laughter, masks and ritual groups of *Lazarus Laughed*. In a note for a limited edition of his works brought out in 1934-35 O'Neill could only say, "The cost of mounting such an elaborate play has deterred the New York commercial theatre from risking the gamble." At the same time he described the Pasadena production as successful and imaginative.

The play calls for a cast of at least 180, even with actors taking several roles. That many people appear on the stage at one time, including main characters, secondary figures, small choruses of seven and large crowds of forty-nine. O'Neill's intent, not carried out in Pasadena for lack of space, was for the large crowds to move in and out of the audience with the individual characters and choruses remaining on stage. The choruses on stage have the function of transmitting the action to the crowds, and the crowds of transmitting it to the audience. The idea here is to expand and intensify the emotional impact of the action, giving the audience the sensation of participating in it directly. This sensation has the effect of making the action appear universal in scope rather than particular or limited to any time and place. Paul Green, the American folk playwright, quotes O'Neill as telling him not long after finishing *Lazarus* that he was trying to write plays in which the "whole environment of the piece—stage and auditorium, actors and spectators—should be emotionally charged." According to Green, O'Neill wanted the audience of *Lazarus* to get "caught up enough to join the responses—the laughter and chorus statements even, much as Negroes do in one of their revival meetings."[37] The reference to Negro revival meetings sounds like Green's own addition, but O'Neill was at least after a comparable unity of the spectators and actors.

Toward this end he devised a system of masks behind which the individual characteristics of the actors would be hidden. The masks worn by the crowds and secondary figures are face-size, those worn by the choruses double-size, and those by the four main characters apart from Lazarus half-size. All in all the masks total more than 550, changing as they do to express different ethnic qualities in the course of Lazarus' journey. They also express psychological type and period of age. O'Neill later explained that one of his aims was for the masks, their effect heightened by the lighting, to give the audience a visual sense of the crowd as a collective entity. Moreover, he had the very practical desire of keeping the play's historical illusion from being shattered by the local looks and accents of stage supers. He hoped that masks would disguise both the appearance of the supers and the familiar tones of their speech, especially their Third Avenue vowel sounds in the case of the New York theater. Masks would also make the actors participate more in the drama with their bodies to make up for their loss of facial expression.[38] Presumably he thought such an increase in physical movement would add to the overall ritual effect.

At one point in O'Neill's preoccupation with getting a professional production he conceived of a version where only Lazarus himself would appear in the flesh and everything else would be shown on film in the background. He even went so far as to think this version would add to the mood of the play by revealing Lazarus as the only person truly alive in a world of marionettes. The idea was undoubtedly born of desperation. It would have canned the ritual,

so to speak, and O'Neill's understanding had always been
that the ritual had to be created anew for every
performance. For better or worse the masked crowds were
built into the action. So unless the play were to be completely rewritten, they had to be there moving in and out of
the audience.

As for the laughter, O'Neill himself was never too sure of
the best way to do it. In the Pasadena production Irving
Pichel succeeded in using his own voice with a musical
accompaniment. But in a letter to Barrett Clark in early
1944 O'Neill suggested an even closer relationship between
the laughter and music.

> Recently—and not for the first time—I have tried to get the
> Guild interested in a Lazarus production—that is, in a cut,
> condensed version with masks omitted. Choruses, a choir,
> small parts almost entirely cut out, crowds done by off-stage
> choral effect, etc. Simplest way to explain my idea is, you
> remember the opera, Boris Gudinoff? Well, along that line,
> but not opera as far as main characters are concerned, except
> that Lazarus' laughter becomes transformed into music. (I
> believe in the Pasedena production they tried to do a little of
> what I mean.) However, it is foolish to think of it. Not a chance.
> And, after all, I can't blame the producers. Who could do
> inspiring choral music for such a production? I don't know.
> Who could direct it? I can't answer that one either. Above all,
> who could play Lazarus? Since Chaliapin died, I can't think of
> anyone. He could have done it—and how!—for he was a mag-
> nificent actor, a tremendous personality on the stage. He sang,
> but he could also give speech the quality of music—and that's
> exactly what Lazarus must do.

In a second letter that year he elaborated on the idea of
the laughter being transformed into music. The music
would first spring from the laughter, accompany it, rise
above it, and then become pure music with no voice left.
With an important difference this was the technique used in

an amateur production at Fordham University in 1948.
The difference was that, instead of growing out of the
laughter, the pure music was substituted for it to begin
with. Eight performances were given in Fordham's well-
endowed, if conventional, theater. The preparations were
on a smaller scale than in Pasadena but were just as much in
earnest. There was an original musical score with new sets,
masks and costumes, and O'Neill took part in an advisory
capacity. However, it all turned out disenchanting enough
for the critics to condemn the play with a vengeance. *The
Miracle* had been forgotten. The only critic who had any
appreciation of what O'Neill had tried to do was from the
New York World-Telegram. He wrote, "The total result, for
anyone familiar with the written intent of the play, is somewhat like listening to a group of people read the libretto of
'Parsifal.' " *Siegfried* or *Die Götterdämmerung* would have
suited the comparison better, but the remark points up the
static and anticlimatic effect that had to result from the lack
of laughter.

O'Neill also approved a university production in the
open-air, Greco-Roman theater at Berkeley in 1950. The
laughter was again muted, remaining only in its negative
aspect. The choruses, scaled down to a total membership of
twenty, laughed mockingly in disbelief of Lazarus, who had
the effect of transforming their laughter into a joyful silence. Music then came in, conveying Lazarus' ecstasy, now
shared for the moment by the choruses. According to
Travis Bogard, "The effect, surprisingly, worked well, and
although it fell far short of O'Neill's sense of what the
chorus and the laughter could accomplish, the production
was valid."[39] The open-air theater might have made a difference. But at the very least this production, and for that
matter the Fordham one, allowed the characterizations of
Lazarus, Tiberius and Caligula to emerge in the manner

O'Neill had envisioned in his letters to Clark and even earlier in his conception of *The Iceman Cometh*.

After Pasadena the only staging of the play as written took place in Mexico in 1934. Here, too, everything was done on an amateur basis, the participants being mainly students and local workers. Yet there was an added element. The preparations, which lasted more than seven months, reportedly had a religious atmosphere similar to what characterizes those for a passion play or native Indian ritual drama. The latter of these was and possibly still is the most popular form of drama in Mexico, which might explain the enthusiasm *Lazarus* was able to evoke with its masks and dancing. Other plays of O'Neill's have also had an appeal to what amounts to a more primitive dramatic instinct. *The Hairy Ape*, for example, was performed in 1936 by a group of Bantus in Johannesburg, South Africa. And as the theater of a country in the throes of a radical social change is apt to be more Dionysian than elsewhere, O'Neill had a series of triumphs in the Russia of the early twenties.

In 1927 Nemirovitch-Dantchenko, co-founder with Stanislavski of the Moscow Art Theater, was in New York and arranged with O'Neill for the Moscow company to do *Lazarus*. However, the Stalinization of the Russian theater shortly after found the play lacking in social realism. There was also the possibility about this time of a production in the Schauspielhaus in Frankfurt. This was the one that held out the hope of Reinhardt directing. But for reasons that were more professional than political nothing materialized here either. The play only reached the stage when the spirit of production was inhibited by neither ideology nor commerce, in other words when it was wholly communal.[40] And so *Lazarus* was never done in the American professional theater, though that was the theater for which O'Neill wrote it and for which as an American he naturally had to write all his plays.

Shortly after it was finished he told Barrett Clark that it was the most successful thing he had ever done. If it really wasn't the most successful, it was at least the thing that sprang most wholly from his ideals both of life and the theater. In 1929 when he married Carlotta Monterey in Paris, the inscriptions on the rings they exchanged made up a line from Lazarus' Eternal Recurrence speech. The one he gave her said, "I am your laughter," while the one she gave him said, "—and You are mine!" *Lazarus* remained closest to him of all his plays up to the completion of *The Iceman*. In the meantime he had written *Mourning Becomes Electra*, which he realized was his greatest achievement for the theater as it existed. But he didn't have the emotional attachment to that play which he had to *Lazarus* and then transferred to *The Iceman*.

In the summer of 1940 he wrote to Lawrence Langer, the chief director of the Theater Guild, that *The Iceman* was one of his best, perhaps the best. It undoubtedly fulfilled his ideal of the drama in the same way *Lazarus* did. Yet his hope that *Lazarus* would eventually be produced in the professional theater was still alive at the time of his letters to Clark in 1944. And the fact that he participated in an advisory capacity in the Fordham production, which came about a year after *The Iceman* ended its Broadway run, indicates that he was gratified by even an amateur attempt. His commitment to *Lazarus* was very deep, and the writing of *The Iceman* was essentially a transposition of the earlier play into a form the professional theater could stage.

One good reason O'Neill never suggested any connection between the two was simply that to do so would have been a professional blunder. This was a consideration he never failed to take seriously after what had happened to *Dynamo*.[41] Following the closing of that play after fifty performances in 1929 O'Neill had gotten off a letter to Langner about it. He expressed regret at having divulged it as the first part of a projected trilogy, feeling he had been misinterpreted both as to the form and meaning of the trilogy and that this misinterpretation had affected the play's reception. He also felt that the enormous success of *Strange Interlude* had prejudiced the chances of whatever play of his came next, a barrier he was convinced only *Lazarus* could have overcome. In any case, he soon announced that he had dropped his plans for the trilogy, the other two parts of which were to be called "Without Ending of Days" and "It Cannot Be Mad." But *Days Without End*, written in 1932-33 and produced in January 1934, was originally conceived as the second part of the trilogy. And this time O'Neill didn't say anything, at least not publicly.

Days Without End was badly received on its own and ran only fifty-seven performances, though its surface theme of salvation through Catholicism subsequently made it a great success at the Abbey Theater in Dublin. Yet the virtue of O'Neill's silence was that it kept everybody's attention on the drama itself, which he was probably most anxious to do later for *The Iceman*. Not only might a production of *The Iceman* lose in originality and power if the play were compared beforehand to *Lazarus*, but if the relationship between the two were known the earlier play would never be produced. If *The Iceman* were a failure, no one would ever think of risking *Lazarus*. And if *The Iceman* were a success, it would always offer a cheaper and surer way of putting on the same thing. A revival of *The Iceman* would always be preferable to an original production of *Lazarus*.

Both trilogy plays, *Dynamo* and *Days Without End*, were in keeping with O'Neill's idea of the theater as a place of ritual and religious experience. But while they had to do directly with the religious experience, the ritual accompanying the experience was greatly reduced. This was because they dealt with religion as such, with formal religion, rather than with human experience that was religious. The question of faith was posed not in a Dionysian but an orthodox framework, which was aesthetically inhibiting. The plays were also damaged, however, by an undercurrent of mocking guilt that O'Neill let escape from his personal life. At least he failed to provide the detachment or aesthetic distance his conscious aims demanded.

In his letter to George Jean Nathan about *Dynamo* O'Neill said that the trilogy as a whole would attempt to dig at the roots of the modern sickness, at the death of the old God and the failure of the new. Similarly, in a letter to De Casseres around the same time he suggested that the trilogy's overall title might be "God is Dead! Long Live—What?" *Dynamo*, as the first of three projected plays, was a statement of the problem. O'Neill described it to Nathan as "a symbolical and factual biography of what is happening in the American (and not only American) soul right now." But it was much more of a sardonic comment on what was happening, in fact so sardonic it offered the audience little to sympathize with.

The problem was dramatized as a corruption of the religious instinct by science. This complemented *Marco Millions* with its theme of the corruption of the spirit by materialism. Yet here the corruption was total. Although the worship of the old God had derived from a primitive fear of lightning, the worship of the new God was based on nothing but the revelation of lightning as electricity. And though the manifestation of the old had been in fire and brimstone, the manifestation of the new was in nothing more human than a dynamo.

The idea for using the dynamo as an image of godhead may have been suggested by an episode in *The Education of Henry Adams*. There Adams related visiting the Great Exposition of 1900 in St. Louis and being almost mystically impressed by the dynamo as a symbol of infinite force, one before which he even felt an instinct to pray. But whether O'Neill read this or not, he visited a power house near his home in Ridgefield, Connecticut, sometime before writing the play and was similarly impressed, especially by the hypnotic whirring of the dynamos. Later he suggested that the set designer make a trip up to get an idea of what the plant was like since the scenic scheme and sound effects he wanted were taken from it. Philip Moeller, the director, finally arranged for the whole cast to pay a visit in the hope everyone would get a better feeling for the atmosphere of the play and for what O'Neill was trying to do.

Actually, this wasn't the first time godhead was characterized by O'Neill as electricity. In *Strange Interlude*, the play he wrote just before, Nina says, "...our lives are merely strange dark interludes in the electrical display of God the Father!" Before that, in *Marco Millions*, Kublai says, "My hideous supicion is that God is only an infinite, insane energy which creates and destroys without other purpose than to pass eternity in avoiding thought." God in this sense is Schopenhauer's universal will, the ultimate cosmic energy in which all spirit and all matter, animate and inanimate, have their source. And when, as in *Marco Millions* and *Dynamo*, man worships the inhuman forms of the will, he inevitably destroys himself.

The corruption of the religious instinct in *Dynamo* was characterized as a festering incest wish, which served to suggest a sickness that was basic and widespread. The infected adolescent hero worships the dynamo, a false mother, and is driven to his death in an incestuous electrocution. Even the figure of Mother Earth, the true mother, fails to heal the infection and prevent his destruction. For, like Nature in the modern world, her appeal has become domesticated, sentimental and dreamy. In the last act the hero, or anti-hero, Reuben Light, tells her in the person of Mrs. Fife of his faith in Dynamo. It is the spirit of Lazarus fixated and diseased.

REUBEN. (*leans against her gratefully, his head almost on her shoulder, his eyes half closed*) Yes. You're like her—Dynamo—the Great Mother—big and warm— (*With a sudden renewal of his unnatural excitement, breaks away from her*) But I've got to finish telling you all I've come to know about her—how all things end up in her! Did I tell you that our blood plasm is the same right now as the sea was when life came out of it? We've got the sea in our blood still! It's what makes our hearts live! And it's the sea rising up in clouds falling on the earth in rain, made that river that drives the turbines that drive Dynamo! The sea makes her heart beat, too!—but the sea is only hydrogen and oxygen and minerals, and they're only atoms, and atoms are only protons and electrons—even our blood and the sea are only electricity in the end! And think of the stars! Driving through space, round and round, just like the electrons in the atom! But there must be a center around which all this moves, musn't there? There is in everything else! And that center must be the Great Mother of Eternal Life, Electricity, and Dynamo is her Divine Image on earth! Her power houses are the new churches! She wants us to realize the secret dwells in her! She wants some one man to love her purely and when she finds him worthy she will love him and give him the secret of truth and he will become the new saviour who will bring happiness and peace to men! And I'm going to be that saviour . . .[42]

When *Days Without End* was produced, it appeared to be O'Neill's solution of the problem as stated in *Dynamo*. The modern sickness of soul was to be cured by a return to orthodox faith, which for the hero as for O'Neill was the Catholicism of his childhood. But O'Neill was never wholly satisfied with this, and the affirmation of Catholicism isn't to be taken at face value. In fact, as Carlotta later admitted, "He felt he had ruined the play and that he was a traitor to himself as a writer. He always said the last act was a phony and he never forgave himself for it." One of his regrets was that he had altered his earlier idea of the clergyman who saves the hero from a nonsectarian figure to a priest. And even before that he had switched from a country doctor to the nonsectarian figure. This might imply an affirmation of formal religion in general, if not Catholicism. Yet such an affirmation isn't to be taken at face value either. The clergyman, whether Catholic or simply Christian, is actually less a man of the Church and dogma than of God and faith.

O'Neill had apparently reverted to Catholicism against his will. Indeed, even his earlier idea of salvation through the nonsectarian figure seems something of an unwilling reversion, a reversion to the very old God pronounced dead by Nietzsche long since. In the beginning stages of work on the play he had thought of "On to Hercules" as a possible title, which suggests that his original conception led up to Nietzsche's overman theme, a call for a spiritual Hercules. This conception changed so much that seven drafts, including four complete versions, were required prior to rehearsals. And the endings ranged from despair and suicide in the first draft to faith and regeneration in the seventh.

Perhaps an explanation for his turning back in midstream lies in his being under such great tension during his first years with Carlotta, tension presumably arising from guilt over the failure of his marriage to Agnes and his having abandoned his two children. In any case, some conflict erupted here, and he was unable to find a suitable ending for the play because of it. On the one hand, there appears to have been a deep-rooted urge to submit and gain some form of parental approval; on the other, an equally deep-rooted urge to rebel and be independent, or at least seek his needed approval in another manner. The title reflects the conflict. It has two meanings, both of which he intended—days that are without purpose from rebellion and disbelief, days that are without death from submission and belief.

Once the urge to submit had won out, assuming this is what happened, he began to make concessions to Church dogma such as leaving unclear in the dialogue that the heroine's first husband was divorced. As a reward he hoped for official Catholic acceptance. He did get a big Catholic acceptance, of course, but it wasn't official. The Church wanted him to say that the first husband had died, and he couldn't do that. He was divorced twice himself, and Carlotta three times. In his reversion he was encouraged by some Jesuit priests with whom he had a number of discussions, and seemingly by Carlotta too. In another sense she was very involved in the play, the heroine being modeled after her. This made O'Neill's indecision even greater, and much to his regret he took the easy way out, submitting to the Church and to his life with Carlotta both. Normally his personal drives gave force to the intellectual purpose in his work, but in this instance and in the trilogy as a whole he was incapable of controlling and shaping them.[43]

However, *Days Without End* is still part of his religious theater. He called it a "modern miracle play,"[44] considering it a partial equivalent of the Faust legend. The central dramatic device was a double personification of the hero. The character of John was the inner man or Faust and the character of Loving the outer man or Mephistopheles. In his "Memoranda on Masks," written while he was at work on the play, he had asked if Faust and Mephistopheles weren't really one and the same. Loving was the Mephistophelian personality or mask of John, the actor in the role wearing a mask that reproduced John's features distorted by a mocking scorn. Yet O'Neill was never really interested in masks or the split personality device simply for the sake of psychological insight. Speaking in the Memoranda of how he would like to change his use of the masks in *The Great God Brown*, he said it was "the more superficial meaning that people wear masks before other people and are mistaken by them for their masks." He would make the masks more symbolic of the abstract theme, in other words use them more effectively in the celebration of the life cycle.

The last scene in *Days Without End* takes place before the crucifix in a church, an attempt to transform the stage into an altar by putting an altar on the stage. There John is freed from the disintegrating influence of Loving by his affirmation of faith. But more than the beliefs or dogma that he affirms, the act of affirmation itself is what brings about the miracle. He is spiritually reborn as a whole person. And like Lazarus he sings in triumph over psychological death, "Love lives forever! Death is dead! . . .Life laughs with God's love again! Life laughs with love!"

In October 1933 O'Neill had written Langner that

> this play, like *Ah Wilderness!* but in a much deeper sense, is the paying of an old debt on my part—a gesture toward more comprehensive, unembittered understanding and inner freedom—the breaking away from an old formula that I had enslaved myself with, and the appreciation that there is their own truth in other formulas, too, and that any life-giving formula is as fit a subject for drama as any other.

The old formula he referred to probably consisted of the Nietzschean ideas of Eternal Recurrence and the overman. After *Lazarus Laughed* they never appeared, at least overtly, in any of his plays. Yet in his Nobel Prize letter a few years later he reaffirmed his faith in Nietzsche. And the Dionysian spirit had actually been assuming a variety of forms all the while. The diseased experience of *Dynamo* and the dogmatic experience of *Days Without End* both had a certain amount of ecstasy about them. O'Neill's purpose in his religious plays, regardless of their framework, was always to celebrate life by way of an emotional or spiritual communion.

Even *Ah, Wilderness!*, which has no real place in the theater he tried to create, may be understood on this basis. O'Neill wrote it in 1932 in between drafts of *Days Without End*. He awoke one morning and found he had dreamed the whole scenario. He had also been thinking consciously of writing something to be called "Nostalgia" along the same lines. The title he chose was a reference to *The Rubáiyát of Omar Khayyám*, from which the "Wilderness" quatrain among others was quoted in the first act. The play turned out to be a huge popular success, running on Broadway with George M. Cohan in the role of the father for almost 300 performances. It was a comedy of boyhood with the quality of a traditional *Saturday Evening Post* cover, and in its way quite affecting.

O'Neill later described the play as "a sort of wishing out loud,"[45] meaning that it was how he would have liked his boyhood to be. By his own admission *Days Without End* was a wish-fulfillment also, and the two are linked together if only for that. Lionel Trilling, one of O'Neill's more perceptive early critics, once dismissed *Ah, Wilderness!* as "the satyr play that follows the trilogy."[46] He was thinking at the time of its having followed in production on the *Mourning Becomes Electra* trilogy. Actually, it was the satyr play, however domesticated, following on the *Dynamo* trilogy. The trouble was that neither the trilogy nor the satyr play was Dionysian enough.

The next thing O'Neill completed after *Days Without End* was *The Iceman Cometh*, though six years had passed in the meantime. The old formula of Eternal Recurrence and the overman was by then just another illusion, and the ecstatic acceptance of life in the abstract had become an ecstatic despair of it in the flesh. But for this very reason the ritual of celebration was more dramatic than ever before. Unfortunately, the original production in 1946 wasn't as effective as it might have been, and it took an off-Broadway revival ten years later for the play to be fully realized on the stage as intended. Thirty years after the writing of *Lazarus Laughed* the American theater was finally made for awhile into a modern temple of Dionysus. This O'Neill accomplished by cutting the old play down to size and resetting it in a contemporary idiom.

Lazarus entering the banquet hall of Tiberius' palace—premiere of *Lazarus Laughed*, **1928 in Pasadena**

Irving Pichel as the original Lazarus

Harry Hope's birthday party—premiere of *The Iceman Cometh*, 1946 on Broadway, with James Barton (far left) as Hickey

Jason Robards, Jr. as Hickey in the 1956 off-Broadway revival

hickey

O'Neill wrote his second letter to Barrett Clark about a revision of *Lazarus* in December 1944, which was some five years after he had completed *The Iceman*. But he had most likely thought of revising *Lazarus* in the manner described to Clark when he first conceived of *The Iceman*. In fact, his original idea for the later play was evidently to write something new in the exact dimensions of a revised *Lazarus*. For *The Iceman* is essentially the same as the other in both its action and main characters, though it is distinct in its naturalistic setting and pessimistic mood. Actually, its pessimistic mood couldn't be more directly opposed to the mood or outlook in *Lazarus*. Yet just this change in outlook was probably one of the things that made O'Neill write a whole new play instead of simply rewriting the old. Another was that new material was insistently at hand in his still vivid impressions of saloons like Jimmy the Priest's and the Hell

Hole together with the people he had met there and elsewhere in the early days.

O'Neill's main concern, however, was always aesthetic
rather than philosophic or autobiographical. In *The Iceman*
he wasn't so much interested in philosophizing or reminisc-
ing about life as in celebrating the very fact of life itself. His
purpose was to offer up an image of life as he saw it for
embodiment in a ritual act. The play with all its hopeless
despair was intended to provide the same kind of aesthetic
experience in the theater as *Lazarus* with its ecstatic acceptance. Accordingly, it has to be understood less as a
philosophic statement than as a religious communion. And
for this reason it is seen most clearly in its relation to
Lazarus, in which the same basic subject of life and death
and the ritualistic form are much more obvious. O'Neill
repeated in his December letter to Clark many of the things
he had said the previous February.

> The story of my cut version of "Lazarus Laughed" is fable.
> It's true I've thought of different ways it might be cut and
> simplified—for example, cut my complicated mask
> scheme—no double-size mask idea for Chorus—all crowds
> done by off stage effects—cuts in the repetitious chants and all
> these given to the Chorus—many of the minor characters cut
> out—concentration on Lazarus, Tiberius, Caligula, etc. with
> chorus background—music to sustain Lazarus' laughter and
> that of others, as if this music sprang from their laughter, went
> along with it, dominated it, and finally became pure music with
> no voice or voices left. Well, you get the idea. Take all the
> pageantry of my immense "Imaginative Theatre" stadium out.
> Make it simple, all to be put on in a modern large theatre, the
> symbolic story of Lazarus' brief second life on earth, and the
> message he brought back from the tomb.

The Iceman was probably conceived in the very image of
Lazarus as later outlined here for revision. It has none of the
pageantry of the Imaginative Theater and can be mounted

on any modern stage. It has no mask scheme, no large crowds and no ecstatic singing and dancing. However, the celebratory ritual is still effected by means of a chorus, a repetitive rhythm in the dialogue and what amounts to an archetypal pattern in the action. Off-stage crowds aren't called for by the plot, and so there are no off-stage effects. Similarly, Lazarus' laughter has no place in a naturalistic setting, and the idea of music as a supporting device doesn't apply. Yet there is an equivalent for Lazarus' laughter in the exuberant salesmanship of Hickey, which serves as a like device for stimulating the movement of the action. And the rhythmic structure of the dialogue gives the play a corresponding musical element. The story is told without any abstract symbolism and its message despairs of rather than accepts life, but it is still about the second life on earth of one who has been reborn as a savior and comes to save man from himself.

The action doesn't immediately appear to be the same as the earlier play's, for on the surface it is expressed in terms of a conflict between illusion and reality. But its life-and-death basis is gradually made clear by what happens to the characters involved in the conflict. By following O'Neill's suggestions for cutting the cast of *Lazarus* it is possible to arrive at the cast of *The Iceman*. He probably didn't arrive at the latter in exactly this way, but the way in which he did couldn't have been far removed—"many of the minor characters cut out—concentration on Lazarus, Tiberius, Caligula, etc. with chorus background." This may be safely taken to mean cutting all the secondary figures and possibly the relatively minor characters of Miriam and Pompeia. If one assumes that in *The Iceman* the residents and habitués of Harry Hope's saloon (apart from Hickey, Don Parritt and Larry Slade) form the chorus background, the only secondary or minor characters are the two detectives who appear in the last act. In that case Pompeia also has to be included in the cutting, while Miriam is made into the off-stage figure of Hickey's wife. Lazarus, Tiberius and Caligula are then left to be transposed into the three main characters of Hickey, Parritt and Larry respectively. And the concentration is entirely on them with a chorus background.

Hickey, like Lazarus, has already experienced a psychological rebirth by the time the action begins. This is implied when Cora relates in the saloon how she and Chuck have just seen him standing outside on the next corner. She quotes him in her dialect as saying, "Tell de gang I'll be along in a minute. I'm just finishin' figurin' out de best way to save dem and bring dem peace." She takes it jokingly, as does everybody else, but at the same time she says he seemed different somehow. Almost as soon as he arrives Hickey lets it be known Cora was right. He has changed and is evidently quite serious about bringing everybody peace. The most immediate effect of his rejuvenation is that he no longer feels the need to drink. Unlike Lazarus, he doesn't reveal exactly how he came to experience what he did until the last act. This adjustment in the action was required by the nature of what Hickey then reveals. For the moment he says only that he has finally had the courage to face himself and do what he had to for the sake of all concerned. It is this which has enabled him to find an inner peace, a peace he wants to help all his old friends find too.

> HICKEY. ...Of course, I was only kidding Cora with that stuff about saving you. (*Then seriously*) No, I wasn't either. But I didn't mean booze. I meant save you from pipe dreams. I know now, from my experience, they're the things that really poison and ruin a guy's life and keep him from finding any peace. If you knew how free and contented I feel now. I'm like a new man. And the cure for them is so damned simple, once you have the nerve. Just the old dope of honesty is the best policy—honesty with yourself, I mean. Just stop lying about yourself and kidding yourself about tomorrows.

When Hickey does reveal the exact nature of his experience, the peace he has felt up to then is seen to have been based on a self-deception. Instead of having faced himself he had unknowingly accepted the lie of another pipe dream. Yet the journey he has taken from the bedroom of his home in Astoria to Harry Hope's saloon in downtown Manhattan is as messianic a journey as Lazarus' from his grave in Bethany to Tiberius' palace in Capri. In both Hope's saloon and Tiberius' palace life is a living death. There man's sickness of soul is manifest and there Hickey and Lazarus come in their capacity as saviors.

Lazarus doesn't enter the palace of Tiberius until the third act, prior to which all the scenes have had the cumulative effect of leading up to it. Hickey enters the saloon in the very first act, but not until his coming has been made equally climactic by the mock invocations of various members of the chorus. Willie Oban, for example, says to Larry, "Let us join in prayer that Hickey, the Great Salesman, will soon arrive . . . Would that Hickey or Death would come!" In Tiberius' palace the living death proceeds from a fear of physical death giving rise to a fear of life. Lazarus attempts to release men from their fear of life by revealing the process of Eternal Recurrence and making them accept death as part of it. He fails because men are ultimately incapable of exchanging their own egos for a faith in a life beyond themselves. In Hope's saloon the living death also proceeds from a fear of physical death and a fear of life, though here the former doesn't give rise to the latter.

The fear of life in Hope's saloon arises directly from life itself, which is to say from reality. Man's nature is such that he is bound to suffer, to experience life as pain, as pain that sooner or later becomes unbearable. The fear of physical death arises no less directly from life or reality. Man's nature is such that he fears extinction no matter how painful his life may be. The result is that eventually reality brings him to the point where he is caught between his fear of life and his fear of death. He then has no choice but to escape reality in the illusion of a pipe dream, at which point he enters into a state of psychological death. He withdraws into the illusion of a pipe dream because there he can experience no pain. The worst he can experience there is the appearance of pain. The world of the pipe dream is all appearance, all make-believe, and in it nothing is ever felt—in illusion the emotions are buried, the real personality entombed. So man must ultimately choose between psychological and physcial death. And if the pipe dream that is psychological death is shattered, no choice is left but physical death since life itself is unlivable.

Hickey's understanding of this is distorted by his self-deception. He believes that the peace he feels comes from an acceptance of reality when it actually comes from his unconscious escape from it. Ironically, he sees the escape of a pipe dream as just what prevents everybody from finding peace. To him the trouble is that men have false ideas of themselves which give rise to burdens of guilt because of the impossibility of living up to these ideas. He attempts to release men from their guilt by revealing their self-images to be false and making them accept themselves as they are. He fails because men are unable to accept a condition in which there is no hope of living without pain.

Hickey is apparently concerned solely with this question of illusion and reality. Lazarus, on the other hand, is concerned solely with the question of life and death. And the difference suggests that any relationship between them involves nothing more than the parallel of their messianic attempts and failures. Yet Hickey's concern manifests itself directly in terms of life and death. For in the world of *The Iceman* illusion is the equivalent of life and reality the equivalent of death. Even though Hickey's understanding is distorted, Larry sees everything quite clearly. In the opening dialogue he says to Rocky, "The lie of a pipe dream is what gives life to the whole misbegotten mad lot of us, drunk or sober." It is the life of psychological death which the pipe dream gives, but that is better than nothing. He indicates this when he describes Harry Hope's to Parritt shortly after.

> LARRY. (*with a sardonic grin*) What is it? It's the No Chance Saloon. It's Bedrock Bar, The End of the Line Café, The Bottom of the Sea Rathskeller! Don't you notice the beautiful calm in the atmosphere? That's because it's the last harbor. No one here has to worry about where they're going next, because there is no farther they can go. It's a great comfort to them. Although even here they keep up the appearances of life with a few harmless pipe dreams about their yesterdays and tomorrows, as you'll see for yourself if you're here long.

Larry, too, is guilty of a self-deception. Despite the fact he can see everybody else's pipe dreams for what they are, he can't see his own. Like Hickey, he believes he has accepted reality, which in his case means that, having found life as it is to be unlivable, he is now only waiting to die. After thirty years' devotion to the Anarchist Movement and the idea that life could be something better, he had to admit to himself the attempt to change men was hopeless since they didn't really want to change and would always be greedy. From then on he was through with the Movement and with everything else as well. Or as he tells Rocky, "So I said to the world, God bless all here, and may the best man win and die of gluttony! And I took a seat in the grandstand of philosophical detachment to fall asleep observing the cannibals do their death dance."

Larry's withdrawal from the experience of life is a withdrawal from pain. He believes he neither cares about life anymore nor fears death, implying that since he has no fear of death he needn't retreat from it to the painless illusion of a pipe dream. His only interest is in keeping his indifference, but this is the heart of his self-deception. For though he insists on his indifference to both life and death, he still cares about the one and fears the other. In the second act Hugo, who is being taunted by Hickey, arouses Larry's sympathy. And Larry angrily asks Hickey if he has no decency or pity.

> HICKEY. (*quizzically*) Hello, what's this? I thought you were in the grandstand. (*Then with a simple earnestness, taking a chair by* LARRY, *and putting a hand on his shoulder*) Listen, Larry, you're getting me all wrong. Hell, you ought to know me better. I've always been the best-natured slob in the world. Of course, I have pity. But now I've seen the light, it isn't my old kind of pity—the kind yours is. It isn't the kind that lets itself off easy by encouraging some poor guy to go on kidding himself with a lie—the kind that makes his lying hopes nag at him and reproach him until he's a rotten skunk in his own eyes. I know all about that kind of pity. I've had a bellyful of it in my time, and it's all wrong! (*With a salesman's persuasiveness*) No, sir. The kind of pity I feel now is after final results that will really save the poor guy, and make him contented with what he is, and quit battling himself, and find peace for the rest of his life.

The peace Hickey preaches is of a strangely negative kind. He doesn't ask men to accept themselves so their love of life will be restored. He simply believes they just won't care about either life or death anymore and will be protected from pain and fear by their indifference. This is the very indifference Larry imagines he already feels. Hickey repeats his gospel a few minutes later at Harry's midnight birthday party. He talks of the guilt that pipe dreams breed and how he himself used to suffer from it. Then he says, "But you can all see that I don't give a damn about anything now. And I promise you, by the time this day is over, I'll have every one of you feeling the same way!" He has no hope of regenerating anyone, just of making them all feel indifferent to what they really are. In the next act he at last provokes them into trying to live up to their pipe dreams. When Harry leaves the saloon for the first time in twenty years, Rocky expresses amazement and watches through the window. Harry stops immediately outside, and Rocky says disgustedly, "Aw, he's stopped. I'll bet yuh he's comin' back." Here Hickey finally makes his intention clear by replying, "Of course, he's coming back. So are all the others. By tonight they'll all be here again. You dumbbell, that's the whole point."

While having a pipe dream of his own in which he hides from reality, Hickey still brings reality with him to Hope's saloon. Consequently, everyone there has his pipe dream shattered and is plunged into despair along with Hickey himself. At the climax of this process Hickey, prompted to explain exactly how he found the peace he claims, inadvertently reveals his self-deception. He tells the story to relieve himself of his increasing doubt about the nature of his experience. The despair of Harry and the others, after they have been made to take a good look at themselves, has made him wonder if he wasn't all wrong about both himself and them. Before leaving his home in Astoria he had shot his sleeping wife Evelyn through the head. Yet he believes this to have been an act of love, the only way he could release her from the pain of her love for him.

In a long monologue he talks about how he had only brought his wife misery by his whoremongering on the road as a traveling salesman and his drunken binges twice a year at Harry Hope's. She had always forgiven him, even when he once infected her with gonorrhea. But this had only made him feel guilty about not having lived up to her idea of him. Whenever he saw how hurt she was, he would promise not to be unfaithful or go on a binge again. Still, at the crucial moment, he could never help himself. And all the while his guilt had increased to the point where it was almost unbearable. He says that as Harry's birthday approached he began to realize he wouldn't be able to keep his promise not to go. He sensed that everything was finished, that this time he wouldn't have the courage to come back. He saw he could never be what she wanted him to be since only in a place like Harry's was he ever really at peace. When he went to the bedroom just before leaving to tell her the marriage was over, she was asleep. Even if she had been awake, however, he couldn't have told her. She would only have taken it to mean he no longer loved her, which would have been more painful than anything else. Then it occurred to him that if she never woke up, she would never have to know. So he killed her out of love for her. He goes on to describe how all his guilt seemed to be lifted off him, but here his unconscious feelings come out through a slip of the tongue.

> HICKEY. (*obliviously*) And then I saw I'd always known that was the only possible way to give her peace and free her from the misery of loving me. I saw it meant peace for me, too, knowing she was at peace. I felt as though a ton of guilt was lifted off my mind. I remember I stood by the bed and suddenly I had to laugh. I couldn't help it, and I knew Evelyn would forgive me. I remember I heard myself speaking to her, as if it was something I'd always wanted to say: "Well, you know what you can do with your pipe dream now, you damned bitch!" (*He stops with a horrified start, as if shocked out of a nightmare, as if he couldn't believe he heard what he had just said. He stammers*) No! I never—!

With this the nature of Hickey's experience becomes clear. He actually killed his wife out of hatred for all the guilt she made him feel. And he never accepted himself as he was but unconsciously took refuge from his real motive in believing he only wanted to bring her peace. Moreover, he was aware and even content that the same kind of peace he brought her was now waiting for him. In the birthday party scene he says, "I knew when I came here I wouldn't be able to stay with you long. I'm slated to leave on a trip." At the beginning of the last act he calls the police from off-stage to turn himself in for murder. Then as he is arrested he remarks to one of the detectives, "I should have phoned you from the house right afterwards." He has evidently been anticipating his own death in the electric chair, though still feeling the need to deceive himself about his motive in the meantime.

As soon as his illusion is shattered Hickey fully accepts death as the only escape possible. He tells the detective, "I want to go to the Chair," explaining he hasn't "got a single damned lying hope or pipe dream left!" The life-and-death basis of the action—along with the play's assumption that life is unlivable—comes into sharp focus here. Not only does the illusion-and-reality conflict emerge as a life-and-death struggle, but the life-and-death struggle itself is seen to have been a contest between two forms of death. Hickey had brought physical death with him to the stronghold of psychological death, or what Larry calls "the Palace of Pipe Dreams."

When Willie Oban invoked Hickey, he unknowingly invoked Death. Hickey is Death. His old joke about his wife being in the hay with the iceman comes to be understood as her being in the arms of Death. The iceman, Hickey and Death are one and the same. Larry has an increasing sense of this throughout the play. He suggests it at one point without realizing it by asking Hickey, "Your iceman joke finally came home to roost, did it?" When Hickey later reveals that his wife is dead, Larry exclaims, "Be God, I felt he'd brought the touch of death on him!" The birthday party is said by Rocky to have turned out more like a funeral. Larry refers to it as a wake. And then shortly afterwards he puts everything together in telling Rocky to give him a drink on Hickey, " . . .I'd get blind to the world now if it was the Iceman of Death himself treating! . . . What made me say that, I wonder. (*With a sardonic laugh*) Well, be God, it fits, for Death was the Iceman Hickey called to his home!"

The reality of death hidden in Hickey has its effects even before he reveals it. The illusion which gives Larry the appearance of life is that he isn't afraid to die. But Hickey strips him of this appearance by making him admit to himself he is. When Harry and the others return from their forced excursion into reality, they have been stripped of their appearance of life almost literally. Hugo says, "Vhat's matter, Harry? You look funny. You look dead. Vhat's happened? I don't know you. Listen, I feel I am dying, too." A minute later Rocky says, "Jees, Larry, Hugo had it right. He does look like he'd croaked." And Larry tells Hickey bitterly, "It's the peace of death you've brought him."

Just before Hickey goes off with the detectives, however, he frees everybody from the claim of death he has made on them. He tells Harry that he has been insane ever since killing Evelyn. "Yes, Harry, of course, I've been out of my mind ever since! All the time I've been here! You saw I was insane, didn't you?" This is also a last-ditch attempt to escape from himself again, and now quite knowingly. For he has seen that believing reality to be acceptable is insane. Emotionally, reality won't sell. Hugo says soon after. "I don't feel I am dying now. He was selling death to me, that crazy salesman." Harry then announces the general reprieve by declaring that the liquor, which had seemed like dishwater without pipe dreams to accompany it, has its old kick back again. "It was Hickey kept it from—Bejees, I know that sounds crazy, but he was crazy, and he'd got all of us as bughouse as he was." With the exception of Larry and Parritt they all escape into illusion once more, into the sanity or relative sanity of mere psychological death.

For Larry and Parritt no escape is possible. Like Hickey, they have irretrievably lost the life-and-death struggle, a struggle at bottom with themselves. As Larry is no longer able to believe in his indifference to things, he has no choice but to take part in them, which means more of his old pain. Parritt, who serves as a foil to both Hickey and Larry, has badgered Larry from the beginning to listen sympathetically to what he has to say. Despite Larry's refusal he has told him about his life with his mother in the Movement, revealing that it was he who betrayed her to the police. Now his guilt and self-loathing finally make him confess that he did it out of hatred for her, and Larry is compelled by the pity and disgust he feels to condemn him. Parritt then kills himself by jumping off the fire escape, which as he has sensed all along is his only way out. And Larry is brought face to face with the life and death he has always feared.

LARRY. (*in a whisper of horrified pity*) Poor devil! (*A long-forgotten faith returns to him for a moment and he mumbles*) God rest his soul in peace. (*He opens his eyes—with a bitter self-derision*) Ah, the damned pity—the wrong kind, as Hickey said! Be God, there's no hope! I'll never be a success in the grandstand—or anywhere else! Life is too much for me! I'll be a weak fool looking with pity at the two sides of everything till the day I die! (*With an intense bitter sincerity*) May that day come soon! (*He pauses startledly, surprised at himself—then with a sardonic grin*) Be God, I'm the only real convert to death Hickey made here. From the bottom of my coward's heart I mean that now!

Being face to face with reality again, he is now sincere in his wish to die. To confront the world as it is, and oneself as one is, can ultimately result only in horror and disgust. And the natural consequence of this is a longing for death, if not immediate suicide. Were men capable of a higher form of spiritual life by which they could overcome reality, they wouldn't have to escape their pain in death. But as it is, death in one form or another is the inevitable result. Such is the implied message of *The Iceman Cometh*, and it is the same as the more explicit one of *Lazarus Laughed*.

The two plays are alike in their action and the characters of Hickey and Lazarus. Both Hickey and Lazarus attempt to save man from himself and fail, the worlds in which they take their messianic journeys being similarly set between the polarity of life and death. The only difference between these messiahs is faith. Lazarus' belief in Eternal Recurrence enables him to accept life as it is. Hickey, being incapable of any such belief, rejects life as it is. Lazarus' acceptance of pain and death makes life livable. He even accepts men's failure to remember what he has taught them, by which that failure becomes livable too. And while he fails to save them, he at least redeems them by his martyrdom. Hickey, on the other hand, doesn't redeem them. Suffering from the same sickness of soul he tries to cure, he can only make things worse. When he departs, life is even more unlivable than before. Where Lazarus transforms reality by faith, Hickey increases the general despair of it. Lazarus can laugh at reality, Hickey is driven to sell it. Theirs is the difference between a higher man and an ordinary modern one.

Lazarus' faith sets him apart from Hickey regardless of the identical pattern of their attempts and failures. Despite his faith being as psychological in its workings as Hickey's self-deception, it gives him a transforming mystical quality. Yet if Lazarus were stripped of this life-giving faith, he would appear exactly like Hickey. He, too, would be a bringer of death. In the second act of *Lazarus* a whole multitude of followers is slain, and in the third act Miriam dies. In each instance Lazarus affirms death with his Yea-saying laughter as a part of the life cycle. But if the eternally creating life cycle were revealed to be only a pipe dream, these deaths would be unjustified and cruel, if not insane. Lazarus and Hickey would be one and the same. And Lazarus' motivating love would be a form of Hickey's motivating hatred.

Lazarus and Hickey are really antagonists rather than protagonists. Although each of them exists in a state of psychological death and then experiences a rebirth, this occurs before the action of the play begins. And though the action takes them to the point of physical death, they aren't affected by what happens in any significant way. They remain more or less unchanged in what is the most important element in the action, the attitudes of the characters toward life and death. Both of them are catalysts. They affect all the spiritual and bodily life around them while remaining unaffected in return. Their movement toward physical death is entirely predetermined by the state of their inner beings prior to the first act. This is suggestive of the extent of the connection between the two plays. Not only are Lazarus and Hickey essentially alike in themselves but in their relationships to all the other characters.

They both directly bring about the deaths of their wives. Lazarus allows Miriam to bite into the poisoned fruit out of compassion for her. Hickey shoots Evelyn through the head in her sleep, mistaking his hatred for just such a compassion. Each time it is the pain of life that begs for a release in death. Miriam begs Lazarus herself while Evelyn begs Hickey in Hickey's own mind.

The deaths of Tiberius and Parritt are indirectly brought about. As a result of Lazarus' effect on Caligula and Tiberius, Caligula kills Tiberius. As a result of Hickey's effect on Larry and Parritt, Larry sends Parritt to kill himself. Lazarus, laughing at the death Tiberius has devised for him, makes Tiberius love him and accept death himself. Tiberius then renounces all Caesars as idols of fear. And Caligula, whom Lazarus has also made love him, strangles Tiberius in a fit of jealousy and rage. Hickey, shattering everyone's pipe dreams including his own, makes it easier for Parritt to see himself as he really is. Larry, whom Hickey has also made see himself, then insinuates in his outburst of pity and disgust that Parritt should jump off the fire escape.

The interrelationship of the three main characters in each play is exactly the same. Hickey and Larry together bring about the death of Parritt just as Lazarus and Caligula bring about the death of Tiberius. And Larry and Parritt both provoke Hickey into revealing his self-deception, which is the equivalent act of Caligula and Tiberius slaying Lazarus. As soon as Hickey lays eyes on Parritt he senses there is something between them. This something is later seen to be the hidden hatred and guilt each of them feels. Hickey refuses to admit this to himself, but his intuitive sense of it is one of the things which eventually disturb him into making his *lapsus linguae*. Right before telling his story he says that it was he who killed Evelyn, at which point the following exchange ensues.

> LARRY. (*bursts out*) You mad fool, can't you keep your mouth shut! We may hate you for what you've done here this time, but we remember the old times, too, when you brought kindness and laughter with you instead of death! We don't want to know things that will make us help send you to the Chair!
> PARRITT. (*with angry scorn*) Ah, shut up, you yellow faker! Can't you face anything? Wouldn't I deserve the Chair, too, if I'd— It's worse if you kill someone and they have to go on living. I'd be glad of the Chair! It'd wipe it out! It'd square me with myself!
> HICKEY. (*disturbed–with a movement of repulsion*) I wish you'd get rid of that bastard, Larry. I can't have him pretending

there's something in common between him and me. It's what's in your heart that counts. There was love in my heart, not hate.

His bond of hatred with Parritt and Larry's recognition of him as Death are equally disturbing to Hickey. Along with his failure to bring peace to Harry and the others, they are what finally make him give up the psychological ghost. Caligula and Tiberius each have a hand in Lazarus' death. Caligula stabs him with a spear while he is being burnt at the stake by order of Tiberius. Then after Tiberius and Lazarus have experienced death in the one play and Parritt and Hickey, to all intents and purposes, in the other, Caligula and Larry remain alone to experience the effect of all that has happened. In this sense they are the real protagonists. They are the only ones who undergo a significant change in the course of the action and are left with it at the end. Caligula is just as fearful of death as when he first appears, but now at least he is aware of it. He alone retains the possibility of remembering what men forget. Correspondingly, Larry says of himself that he is "the only real convert to death that Hickey made."

Lazarus and Hickey also have a similar effect on their respective choruses. They leave them basically unchanged, no wiser for what they have experienced. The crowds and choruses in *Lazarus* forget the faith in Eternal Recurrence that Lazarus has brought back with him from his psychological grave. As soon as his laughter is no longer heard they return to the immediacy of their own egos. The fourteen individual figures who comprise the chorus in *The Iceman* forget the hatred and death Hickey has brought them from out of the depths of his unconscious. As soon as he pleads insanity they return to the comfort of their old dreams.

Like Hickey and Lazarus, the other characters who parallel one another correspond in their personal motives as well as in what happens between them. Parritt's main concern is his relationship with his mother, a relationship of exactly the same nature as between Tiberius and his mother. Tiberius suffers from the guilt he feels at having caused his mother's death. He tells Lazarus how Livia's obsession with making him Caesar poisoned his child's love for her and how later he revenged himself by depriving her of her power and the will to live. He says, "I hated that woman, my mother, and I still hate her!" Parritt has also caused the death of his mother. By betraying her and the Movement to the police he has murdered her in just as subtle and cruel a way, for she will lose her will to live by being shut off in prison from the freedom she so passionately craves. Further, he has betrayed her for the same reason as Tiberius revenged himself on Livia. As he says in the last act, "It was because I hated her." The Movement was everything to her just like the role of Caesar to Livia. Earlier he complains to Larry, "She was never true to anyone but herself and the Movement." The story he slowly but surely tells is of an unloved child who revenges himself on his mother. It is directly parallel to the story Tiberius tells. Both mothers suffer the same fate at the hands of their sons, who suffer themselves as a result. And to make the parallel of mother and son more striking, the presence of a father is totally lacking in each case.

Caligula and Larry are equally alike in their motives. However, their motives are impersonal rather than personal. Both figures are characterized by a lack of any human attachment. Caligula's past history has to do with the army camps where he was born and spent his childhood. Crassus, a Roman general, addresses him at one point as "camp-brat," and Caligula himself is fond of singing an old camp song that contains the lines, "A Roman eagle was my daddy,/ My mother was a drunken drabby."

He is attached only to the ambition of becoming Caesar, the
incarnation of death. Larry's only attachment is also to
death, though he desires none but his own. His past history
has to do with the Movement, to which he devoted all the
active years of his life. Parritt's mother was his mistress at
one time, but she was more or less part of the Movement.
Parritt characterizes her as being inseparable from it, and
Larry's relationship with her doesn't in itself motivate him
in any way. It serves merely to connect him with Parritt just
as Caligula is connected with Tiberius by being his heir.

So the three main characters in the *The Iceman* are like
those in *Lazarus* both in their individual make-up and their
interrelationship. And the minor characters, too, are much
the same in each play. If one allows for the transposition of
Miriam into an off-stage figure who is already dead when
the action begins, Evelyn is her direct counterpart. Just as
Miriam is the personification of motherhood even though
her children are dead, Evelyn is an embodiment of maternal love even though she is childless. Hickey relates that she
felt toward him like a loving mother toward her wayward
child—not understanding but all-absorbing. This is
Miriam's feeling toward Lazarus. In both instances it con-
trasts with the egoistic love of the other mother figure in the
play, Tiberius' and Parritt's.[47] As for the minor characters
of Moran and Lieb, the two detectives who arrest Hickey,
they are simply called for by the particular plot situation.
Yet they too play a parallel role, corresponding to the
Roman soldiers who take Lazarus on his journey to Caesar.

All the other characters make up the chorus, in which
body they are the equivalent of the many crowds and
choruses in *Lazarus*. Each of them has an individual identity
and is characterized by a distinct pipe dream. At the same
time they have a more significant identity as a member of
the group, their experiences of illusion and reality being

essentially the same. For most of the play they function as a chorus in a contrapuntal way, then in the latter part they combine into a single entity. When Larry suggests in the birthday party scene that Hickey's revelation consists of having found his wife to be sick of him, "a chorus of sneering taunts begins, punctuated by nasty, jeering laughter." The chorus here is in counterpoint.

> HOPE. Bejees, you've hit it, Larry! I've noticed he hasn't shown her picture around this time!
> MOSHER. He hasn't got it! The iceman took it away from him!
> MARGIE. Jesus, look at him! Who could blame her?
> PEARL. She must be hard up to fall for an iceman!
> CORA. Imagine a sap like him advisin' me and Chuck to git married!
> CHUCK. Yeah! He done so good wid it!
> JIMMY. At least I can say Marjorie chose an officer and a gentleman.
> LEWIS. Come to look at you, Hickey, old chap, you've sprouted horns like a bloody antelope!
> WETJOEN. Pigger, py Gott! Like a water buffalo's!
> WILLIE. (sings to his Sailor Lad tune)
> "Come up," she cried, "my iceman lad,
> And you and I'll agree—"
> (They all join in a jeering chorus, rapping with knuckles or glasses on the table at the indicated spot in the lyric)
> "And I'll show you the prettiest (Rap, rap, rap)
> That ever you did see!"
> (A roar of derisive, dirty laughter. But HICKEY has remained unmoved by all this taunting. He grins good-naturedly, as if he enjoyed the joke at his expense, and joins in the laughter).

As the play approaches its climax the unity of the individual characters increases. In the last act Parritt asks Rocky sarcastically why Larry doesn't take a hop off the fire escape, and Rocky's reply is echoed by everybody as if with a single voice.

ROCKY. (*dully*) Sure. Why don't he? Or you? Or me? What de hell's de difference? Who cares? (*There is a faint stir from all the crowd, as if this sentiment struck a responsive chord in their numbed minds. They mumble almost in chorus as one voice, like sleepers talking out of a dully irritating dream, "The hell with it!" "Who cares?" Then the sodden silence descends again on the room.*)

Taken together, they are like the crowds and choruses of the earlier play in their ritual effect as well as their part in the action. In fact, their ritual effect is precisely what makes the relationship between the two plays significant. For O'Neill transposed the aesthetic idea of the one play to the other mainly through this effect. Just as the crowds and choruses in *Lazarus* celebrate the life struggle in the abstract, the chorus in *The Iceman* celebrates it on an individual level. This is probably one reason O'Neill allowed the chorus to be more in the foreground of the main characters than in the background. It was the only ritual device as such he left himself in cutting away the excesses of the Imaginative Theater, and the idea of celebration demanded as outright a use of it as possible.

In sum, O'Neill derived *The Iceman* from *Lazarus* in almost every aspect of its action and characters, virtually writing the first play over in minor key. Perhaps he did this under a compulsion to set what he had come to feel against what he had felt, a need to throw the evolution of his feelings into high relief. But more clearly, he wanted to realize in the theater at hand what he had been unable to realize in the nonexistent Imaginative Theater. Once again this was a celebration of life by means of its embodiment in ritual forms, by means of singing and dancing about it. The underlying aesthetic idea was that only through ritual could the audience be made to experience a Dionysian communion with life itself. And that only in such a communion would the pain and death of life appear justified. It was an idea that had its source in *The Birth of Tragedy*, an idea that assumed the theater to be a place of ritual and religious experience.

While the singing and dancing in *Lazarus* would dominate any performance of the play, the ritual forms in *The Iceman* are hardly even apparent. They comprise the action rather than accompany it. Yet they are ritual forms nevertheless, they are the very same singing and dancing. The singing is done mainly by the chorus, but the main characters also join in by virtue of the musical structure of the dialogue. Some of the singing is simply of songs. Willie Oban renders his bawdy Sailor Lad ballad in the first act and again in part in the birthday party scene. Hope's favorite song, "She's the Sunshine of Paradise Alley," is played on the piano and sung by Cora when he appears for the party, prior to which she and Joe rehearse it in the background throughout the latter half of the act. Hugo also sings for an instant at one point. And at the final curtain everybody lets go with his own favorite to celebrate his escape from Hickey.

> HOPE. . . .Bejees, let's sing! Let's celebrate! It's my birthday party! Bejees, I'm oreyeyed! I want to sing! (*He starts the chorus of "She's the Sunshine of Paradise Alley," and instantly they all burst into song. But not the same song. Each starts the chorus of his or her choice.* JIMMY TOMORROW's *is a "A Wee Dock and Doris";* ED MOSHER's, *"Break the News to Mother";* WILLIE OBAN's, *the Sailor Lad ditty he sang in Act One;* GENERAL WETJOEN's, *"Waiting at the Church";* MCGLOIN's, *"Tammany";* CAPTAIN LEWIS's, *"The Old Kent Road";* JOE's, *"All I Got Was Sympathy";* PEARL's *and* MARGIE's, *"Everybody's Doing It";* ROCKY's, *"You Great Big Beautiful Doll";* CHUCK's, *"The Curse of an Aching Heart";* CORA's, *"The Oceana Roll";* while HUGO *jumps to his feet and, pounding on the table with his fist, bellows in his guttural basso the French Revolutionary "Carmagnole." A weird cacophony results from this mixture and they stop singing to roar with laughter. All but* HUGO, *who keeps on with drunken fervor.*)

HUGO.
>Dansons la Carmagnole!
>Vive le son! Vive le son!
>Dansons la Carmagnole!
>Vive le son des canons!

These songs alone don't constitute a celebratory ritual. To be sure, by themselves they are more of a mockery of celebration. Yet embedded as they are in a structure of dialogue with a pattern of repetition, they contribute to an overall rhythmic effect which does make for celebratory ritual. The pattern in the dialogue consists of the same things being said over and over, both by the main characters and the figures in the chorus. Lawrence Langner has told that during a rehearsal for the Theater Guild production in 1946 he requested his assistant to count up the number of times a certain point was repeated. It was eighteen. Langner then complained of this to O'Neill, who replied in a particularly quiet voice that he had intended it to be repeated eighteen times. Eighteen was an exaggeration. But Hickey makes his point about pipe dreams, for example, and Hugo repeats his line about how cool it is beneath the Babylonian willow trees more times than are necessary to get them across. O'Neill intended the repetition for its rhythmic, musical quality. This is why he told Nathan prior to the opening, "If there are repetitions, they'll have to remain in, because I feel they are absolutely necessary to what I am trying to get over."

Actually, O'Neill had used this device in most of his earlier plays. As far back as 1922 he had been aware that "rhythm is a powerful factor in making anything expressive. People do not know how sensitive they are to rhythm. You can actually produce and control emotion by that means alone."[48] Later, however, he had complained that the productions had seldom allowed the rhythm to come through. The original production of *The Iceman* evidently didn't allow it to come through either. And when the play was revived off-Broadway at the old Circle in the Square, the musical element in the dialogue was discovered to be the key to interpreting it successfully. José Quintero, the director, subsequently described his experience with this.

> My approach in directing *The Iceman Cometh* was different from that used in any play I had ever done. It had to be, for this was not built as an orthodox play. It resembles a complex musical form, with themes repeating themselves with slight variations, as melodies do in a symphony. It is a valid device, though O'Neill has often been criticized for it by those who do not see the strength and depth of meaning the repetition achieves.
>
> My work was somewhat like that of an orchestra conductor, emphasizing rhythms, being constantly aware of changing tempos; every character was a different instrument, every character advanced a different theme. The paradox was that for the first time as a director, I began to understand the meaning of precision in drama—and it took a play four and one-half hours long to teach me, a play often criticized as rambling and overwritten.[49]

In this sense the dialogue has the ritualistic effect of singing. *Lazarus*, at least in its choral passages, is equally characterized by repetition and variation. But as the device here expresses rather than accompanies the action, it is much more successful dramatically. And all that is obviously dithyrambic or rhapsodic in the earlier play is here naturalistic and wholly believable.

The dancing element in *The Iceman* is even less apparent than the singing. It is contained in the underlying movement of the action as against the verbal expression of it, a movement which forms the archetypal pattern of a journey from life to death and then back to life again. Such a pattern is archetypal by virtue of its being one of the recurring images in the religious mythology of various peoples.[50] In *Psychology of the Unconscious* Jung had tried to show that these images stemmed from man's primary emotions, and O'Neill perhaps made use of the journey pattern in the belief it would help recall those emotions. Just like the singing, this pattern of action was derived from *Lazarus*, though here it was formed beneath the surface.

The journey takes Hickey from his rebirth to his death, which is to say from birth to death generally. Then at the climactic point another birth following on death is suggested. In *Lazarus* this rebirth process was symbolized by Lazarus' increasing youth. But in *The Iceman* Hickey's lack of faith doesn't allow for a regeneration through him. The suggestion of the rebirth process is made, however ironically, by the return of the chorus to the world of illusion. As the nature of man is such that life is unlivable, he can only return to an appearance of life. Yet he returns nevertheless. Even though life is a dance of death, psychologically and physically, it is still eternal. The dancing of Lazarus and his followers is a dancing about life, while the dancing of Hickey and his followers is life itself. The physical movement in the earlier play is a psychological movement in the later, and in the modern theater the effect of psychological ritual is incomparably greater.

With *The Iceman* O'Neill was finally able to celebrate life in wholly dramatic terms. The surface action beneath which the process of birth, death and rebirth is hidden evokes an immediate response of its own, but through this response a more intuitive level of understanding is opened up. Notwithstanding the total despair of life in the play, the experience of life it affords an audience in the theater leads beyond despair. The action can be experienced on some deeper level where all that happens, all that exists in the world, is felt to be justified. Life, with its manifold suffering, is accepted and renewed through a celebratory experience of it. For a celebratory experience, a participation in ritual, a singing and dancing about life, exorcises all pain and the fear of death, magically invoking more life.

O'Neill realized in *The Iceman* his idea that the American theater should be equivalent in function to the Theater of Dionysus. He achieved a reconciliation of the two artistic principles which Nietzsche called the Apollonian and the Dionysian in a manner consistent with the facilities of the modern stage. The play embodied the Apollonian artistic principle of individual experience on its surface and the Dionysian artistic principle of communal experience in its depths.

In speaking of Greek tragedy Nietzsche remarked that the actions of the heroes were more meaningful than their words. The reason for this lay in the limited powers of the tragic poets to express in words what was mythic. When writing the plays, they had necessarily relied on less conscious powers—"The structure of the scenes and the intuitively created images reveal a deeper wisdom than the poet himself can put into words and concepts . . ." O'Neill's attempt to achieve a Dionysian effect in *The Iceman* was probably more conscious than intuitive. He derived all the essential parts of the play from *Lazarus* where the attempt was undoubtedly more conscious. And he generally was in the habit of trying to evoke emotional responses by ritual means rather than "through words or mere copies of real actions," as he had once phrased it.[51] Even so, what he did consciously was motivated by what he felt intuitively, and his intuition went deeper than his consciousness. For there is still more in the heart of the play than can be reached by intellectualizing about its words and dramaturgy.

Most likely this is equally true of the two plays which *The Iceman* resembles, Ibsen's *The Wild Duck* and Gorki's *The*

Lower Depths. While the philosophical similarities don't really explain how the three plays came to be alike in ways that are more than philosophical, in ways that are aesthetic, there seem to be similarities on the intuitive level which do. But to fully understand the aesthetic nature of *The Iceman* one must look back to *Lazarus* and *The Birth of Tragedy.* What O'Neill was after in all his plays with a Dionysian emphasis was the experience Nietzsche had considered to be a function of tragic myth. In fact, the words of Nietzsche's describing this aspect of tragic myth were among those selected by O'Neill to appear in the program to *The Great God Brown.*

> The substance of the tragic myth is first of all an epic event involving the glorification of the fighting hero: but how does it come about that the essentially puzzling trait, the suffering of the hero, the most painful victories, the most agonizing contrasts of motives, in short, the exemplification of the wisdom of Silenus [that the best thing for man is not to be born, and the second best is quickly to die[52]], or, in esthetic terms, the ugly and unharmonious, are always represented anew in such countless and popular forms, and precisely at the most youthful and exuberant age of a people, unless there is really a higher delight experienced in all this? . . .
>
> Here it becomes necessary to raise ourselves with one daring bound into a metaphysics of Art. Therefore I repeat my former proposition that only as an esthetic phenomenon may existence and the world appear justified: and in this sense it is precisely the function of tragic myth to convince us that even the ugly and unharmonious is an artistic game which the will plays with itself in the eternal fullness of its joy.

oedipus

In his ritual dramas O'Neill was primarily concerned with the religious experience of life. But in his other plays he was primarily concerned with its tragic experience. In the 1925 letter to his genteel admirer Arthur Hobson Quinn he wrote that "where the theater is concerned, one must have a dream, and the Greek dream in tragedy is the noblest ever!" The other plays were attempts to restore that dream to the new theater he was creating. Earlier he had said, or at least implied, that the tragic hero would have to represent mankind as a whole.

> The struggle of Man to dominate life, to assert himself and insist that life has no meaning outside himself; where he comes in conflict with life, which he does at every turn; and his attempt to adapt life to his own needs, in which he doesn't succeed, is what I mean when I say that Man is the hero.[53]

However, he never really made clear what he meant by

tragedy itself. He thought that to the Greeks tragedy "brought exaltation, an urge toward life and ever more life. It roused them to deeper spiritual understanding and released them from the petty greeds of everyday existence."[54] He thought that through tragedy they gained the experience of suffering—or pathos—and, with the release of that suffering, transcendence over it. Yet the Greek form of tragedy was somewhat different from play to play, and nothing O'Neill ever said dealt with its mechanics.

In the Quinn letter, though, he did indicate that the essential thing to his mind was the fate element. For he referred to "the Force behind—(Fate, God, our biological past creating our present, whatever one calls it—Mystery certainly)." His own dream of tragedy, then, meant finding an equivalent for Greek fatalism, presumably as that fatalism was manifested in the *Oresteia* and *Oedipus Rex* where just such a "Force behind" as he referred to played a dominant role. Moreover, the fact he considered God as a possibility points up that the equivalent had to endow man's defeat in the life struggle with some divine significance. Without such an equivalent any pathos he could evoke would be limited.

The mythological gods who were the source of man's fate in the ancient Athenian world were, of course, long dead. And the modern world lacked any divine source of its own. The biblical God and His absolute values were equally dead, while science and materialism had failed to take their place. Yet O'Neill's search for an equivalent was still a search for God, or at least for some source of fate comparably divine. The critic Joseph Wood Krutch once quoted him as remarking, "Most modern plays are concerned with the relation between man and man, but that does not interest me at all. I am interested only in the relation between man and God."[55] The remark isn't to be taken altogether literally, but it does reveal the extent to which he was seeking out an ultimate scheme of things.

Eventually he came to believe that man was the source of his own fate and possessed in himself whatever godhead there was. But he always thought of life as "one eternal tragedy, of Man in his glorious, self-destructive struggle to make the Force express him instead of being, as an animal is, an infinitesimal incident in its expression." Whether the Force was external as in the earlier plays or internal as in the later made no difference. In all the plays an attempt was made to give man's defeat in the life struggle a significance such that, directly or indirectly, he would be able to triumph over it. There had to be cause for exulting in the defeat, though at the very end the only triumph O'Neill found possible was in the phenomenon of the defeat being rendered with all its pathos in a work of art.

It was shortly before the founding of the Provincetown Players that the writings of Freud and Jung began to make an impression in America. *The Interpretation of Dreams* was published in an English translation in 1913, first bringing psychoanalysis to the attention of the layman, particularly in Greenwich Village and Provincetown. The interest grew in 1916 with Jung's *Psychology of the Unconscious*, and Freud's *Totem and Taboo* heightened it further two years later. However, there were already enough amateur psychologists around early in 1915 for George Cram Cook and Susan Glaspell to write *Suppressed Desires*, a one-act satire on everybody's obsession with everybody else's complexes. The Provincetown Players produced it that summer in the Wharf Theater and twice more the following summer, the second time on a review bill along with O'Neill's *Bound East for Cardiff*. Psychoanalysis as such had nothing to do with O'Neill's play, but Freud and Jung were to have a great influence on him in the years to follow.

Despite the obviousness of that influence O'Neill saw fit to disavow it on a number of occasions. One of these was in October 1929 when he answered a letter about it from a graduate student at Northwestern University. He denied any direct influence on his work whatsoever.

There is no conscious use of psychoanalytical material in any of my plays. All of them could easily be written by a dramatist who had never heard of the Freudian theory and was simply guided by an intuitive psychological insight into human beings and their life-impulses that is as old as Greek drama. It is true I am enough of a student of modern psychology to be fairly familiar with the theories of Freud and his school, and to have realized the Freudian implications inherent in the actions of some of my characters while I was portraying them; but this was always an afterthought and never consciously was I for a moment influenced to shape my material along the lines of any psychological theory. It was dramatic instinct and my own personal experience with human life that alone guided me.

I most certainly *did not* get my idea of Nina's compulsion [in *Strange Interlude*] from a dream mentioned by Freud in "A General Introduction to Psychoanalysis." I have only read two books of Freud's, "Totem and Taboo" and "— and the Pleasure Principle [Beyond the Pleasure Principle]." The book that interested me the most of all those of the Freudian school is Jung's "Psychology of the Unconscious" which I read many years ago. If I have been influenced unconsciously it must have been by this book more than any other psychological work. But the "unconscious" influence stuff strikes me as always extremely suspicious! It is so darned easy to prove! I would say that what has influenced my plays the most is my knowledge of the drama of all time—particularly Greek tragedy—and not any books on psychology! . . .

As for the various presentations of God in my plays, I don't see exactly to what you refer, but perhaps it will clear the matter up when I explain that my childhood training was strict Roman Catholic and that, off and on, of late years I have studied the history and development of all religions with immense interest as being—for me, at least—the most illuminating "case-histories" of the inner life.[56]

To be sure, the study of religion had taught him a great deal about the inner life. This was particularly true of the teachings of Christ and Buddha, who seemed to him to have said very much the same thing. About six years earlier, in his scenario for *Marco Millions*, he had described Kublai as studying their teachings and being "impressed with the essential identity of their truth but amazed by the contradictory manner in which their truth becomes distorted in human life, the dogma of religion." Their truth had to do with self-overcoming, and it was close enough to Nietzsche's truth for O'Neill to keep the hero of *Lazarus Laughed* fairly biblical without compromising the Nietzschean idea of the play. In the ritual plays generally O'Neill was more influenced by Nietzsche and his own religious studies than by psychoanalytical theory. Yet it required no great turnabout for him to leave Buddha, Christ and Nietzsche for Freud and Jung in the tragedies. What was needed wasn't a change in thought but a shift in emphasis.

O'Neill made another denial two years later in a letter to Barrett Clark. Answering the latter's criticism of *Mourning Becomes Electra*, he protested that "critics . . .read too damn much Freud into stuff that could very well have been written exactly as is before psychoanalysis was ever heard of." He stated he had read no more than four books by the psychoanalytical school. And he added that "Jung is the only one of the lot who interests me. Some of his suggestions I find extraordinarily illuminating in the light of my own experience with hidden motives."

So by late 1931 he had read just four books of psychoanalytical theory, at least two by Freud and one by Jung. If the fourth book wasn't *Wit and Its Relation to the Unconscious*, which would have made three by Freud, he was at least familiar with that book as a result of his interest in the psychology of laughter for *Lazarus*. Another book by

Freud he conceivably read for *Lazarus* was *Group Psychology and the Analysis of the Ego*, a copy having been in his library in Bermuda in 1925.[57] But whatever the fourth book, which could have been read anytime before his 1931 letter to Clark, the one that made the greatest impression was *Psychology of the Unconscious*. He evidently read this before writing *The Emperor Jones* in 1920, for in that play he was well aware of the idea of the collective unconscious. *Totem and Taboo* was evidently read before 1924 when he wrote *Desire Under the Elms*, for there he was well aware of Freud's account of the primal family. *Beyond the Pleasure Principle* could have been read anytime before his October 1929 denial, which is to say before the writing of *Morning Becomes Electra*. Yet most likely it was read relatively early in the twenties and influenced him in a general way. He disclaimed all this, but there were good reasons.

For one thing, it would have been a blunder to admit it, just as it would have been a blunder to say anything about the relationship between *Dynamo* and *Days Without End* and later between *Lazarus* and *The Iceman*. At the time of the letter to Clark, for instance, *Mourning Becomes Electra* was in rehearsal, and O'Neill was presumbaly anxious to guard against any categorically Freudian interpretation of that play. Such an interpretation, particularly if he shared in it in any way, might have had a stifling effect on the spontaneous response he was after in the theater. As it was, there was enough preoccupation with the psychological content for the letter he had written to the student at Northwestern to be published shortly after the play opened.

Such an interpretation would have been misleading besides. For the imputation by the critics was of a predominantly, if not wholly, Freudian influence, while he actually felt closer to Jung. To all appearances the psychology of *Mourning Becomes Electra* was Freudian, but there was a less obvious element that was Jungian and at least as vital. Jung's influence on O'Neill had mostly to do with the relationship between individual psychology and the godhead in religious mythology. And as the search for inevitability was in reality a search for godhead, Jungian insights were at the heart of most of the plays. One of the things O'Neill undoubtedly resented in the criticism of too much Freud was the implication of his being a rationalist. To have acknowledged any Freudian influence at all would have been to direct the audience away from the religious nature of what he was trying to do.

Similar reasons prompted him to make all his disavowals. It was necessary to guard against any academic suggestion of his being a textbook borrower and any mindless chatter about Freud, sex and O'Neill in the popular press. At the same time he perhaps didn't realize he had been influenced as much as he had. Or else he managed to avoid lying about it by allowing the discussion to remain on a superficial level. For the suggestions were usually of some specific borrowings, and the influence on him was fairly general. Denying any use of Freud in *Desire Under the Elms*, he remarked, "I respect Freud's work tremendously—but I'm not an addict." As far as it went what he said was the truth, and it had the virtue of keeping his imagination from being fingered by those with little or no imagination.

He was telling the truth in much the same way when he wrote that he had never been influenced to shape his material along the lines of any psychological theory. While undergoing some analysis himself—enough, for example, to know at first hand what an Oedipus complex was—he was never interested as a dramatist in any of the therapeutic aspects of analysis. If he was aware of the analytical explanation of his characters' behavior, he didn't motivate his characters for the sake of analyzing them on the stage.

Psychoanalytical theory really interested him only in its religious aspects, its concern with primal causes and the essential nature of life, which is where all his diverse influences came together. So in a therapeutic or scientific sense he didn't consciously shape his material along the lines psychoanalysis suggested, though in a religious sense he did.[58] A passage in *Beyond the Pleasure Principle*, first published in translation in 1922, crystallized what he was then in the process of dramatizing in his plays.

> What psycho-analysis reveals in the transference phenomena of neurotics [that the latter repeat in one form or another their repressed traumatic experiences] can also be observed in the lives of some normal people. The impression they give is of being pursued by a malignant fate or possessed by some extraneous power; but psycho-analysis has always taken the view that their fate is for the most part arranged by themselves and determined by early infantile influences.[59]

O'Neill didn't accept this in its entirety, at least not for the moment. The phenomenon of a traumatic experience repeating itself became an integral part of *Strange Interlude*, written in 1926-27. At first, however, the idea of early infantile influences being all-determining probably seemed too rigid for his purposes. While most of the major characters in his plays of the twenties were motivated in their actions by early experiences, these experiences usually belonged to a later period of development than the infantile. More importantly, they didn't lead inevitably to the characters' final defeat.

It was only with the writing of *Mourning Becomes Electra*, begun in 1929 and completed two years later, that O'Neill fully accepted the Freudian idea of fate. Both the concept of motivating infantile influences and the phenomena of repetition were worked into a cause-and-effect pattern of inevitability spread over several generations. And as these influences and the experiences they determined had been found by Freud to be of an Oedipal nature, the cause-and-effect pattern in the play was Oedipal. Yet such a pattern of inevitability wasn't in itself tragic. The tragedy lay in a spiritual triumph over the inevitable, which was another problem altogether.

O'Neill read further in *Beyond the Pleasure Principle* a highly speculative hypothesis dealing with the nature of man's instincts. The instincts were defined as all the forces in the mental apparatus originating in the interior of the body. Freud saw these forces as generally conservative or passive since they tended to return to an earlier state of existence and ultimately to the inanimate or death. Yet the sexual instincts, and the instincts of self-preservation in their guarding of the reproductive process, were active forces, tending rather to create new life. Accordingly, there was an opposition in the organism between life instincts and death instincts, an opposition that was a basic factor in human neurosis and even in normal human behavior. Life was largely determined by the conflicting functions of the inherited instincts. And when O'Neill wrote in 1925 of "our biological past creating our present," he must have been thinking partly of this. But he equated the phenomenon with mystery, indicating that he didn't wholly accept it on a biological basis. In fact, he was more inclined toward the Jungian explanation of this determining opposition or ambivalence, and especially of man's struggling to free himself from it.

To Freud man had no innate urge to struggle for freedom from his inherited state. The propensity for such a struggle wasn't part of his inheritance. The conditions in which pursuit of a higher level of development might take place were always present, but the pursuit itself rarely materialized. And when it did, the individual in whom it materialized was only driven by a repressed sexual instinct seeking in disguised form a gratification that was unattainable.

To Jung, though, man's struggle to free himself was neither an accident of development nor physically motivated. In *Psychology of the Unconscious* he presented a theory of ambivalence on a wholly psychological basis.[60] Where Freud made a biologically rooted distinction between life or sexual instincts and death or ego instincts, Jung thought of all man's instincts as comprising one body of psychic energy. This energy or libido was characterized by an inner opposition that was similarly between life and death tendencies. But as the conflict was entirely psychological, it allowed man to struggle more meaningfully against his inherited fate. For the psychological life tendency was simultaneously a striving toward perfection; it sought a higher level of development by its very nature. This view of Jung's approached the mystical and even corresponded to the Nietzschean idea of the overman. According to Jung, the libido of man is "always in advance of his consciousness; unless his libido calls him forth to new dangers he sinks into slothful inactivity . . . instead of striving with desperate courage towards the highest."

Both psychoanalytical theories found their way into O'Neill's plays, entering mainly in the form of the Oedipus complex. The Freudian version of the complex entered on a materialistic level, the Jungian on an idealistic or spiritual level. O'Neill reconciled the two by assuming a spiritual whole greater than the sum of its materialistic parts.

His grasp of the Freudian version probably came in large part from *Totem and Taboo.* In this book Freud delved into the nature of the clans or totems comprising primitive societies. With anthropological studies of the rituals and the taboos that surrounded the sacred totem animal serving as a point of departure, he was led to conclude that "the beginnings of religion, ethics, society, and art meet in the Oedipus complex . . . the nucleus of all neuroses so far as our present knowledge of them goes."[61] By Oedipus complex, of course, he meant the son's fixated incestuous desire for his mother and fixated jealous hatred of his father accompanied by guilt on both accounts due mainly to the incest taboo. In the case of a female child, or an Electra complex, the feelings toward the parents were reversed.

Building on his earlier writings,[62] Freud made clear here that the incest taboo was as significant in the life of civilized man as it had been in the life of primitive man. For in his development the civilized individual apparently passed through stages comparable to all those in the historical development of the race, beginning with the experience of the incestuous primal horde or family. Both the child and the neurotic, who was held at some point in his development at the level of the child, were in their inner life like the primitive in his outer life. And since the infantile years of development corresponded to the life of primitive man, the Oedipal phase of it and any ensuing complex constituted an inheritance from the physical or biological past.

In effect, society demanded the repression or at least sublimation of what were sexual or life instincts, while it encouraged the dominance of what were ego or death instincts, the ego instincts making for guilt and restraining the sexual. As a result there existed an Oedipal condition that was universal and inescapable. If the individual matured enough to free himself from his incest wish, he wouldn't be driven to do the forbidden and suffer the consequences. But even then he wouldn't be fully happy. Man could never be fully happy because of the conflict between his physical nature and his social needs. The greatest cultural achievements—including religion, philosophy and art—were but substitute gratifications of physical desires, which in civilized or for that matter any society had no possibility of complete attainment. So while the individual might not meet a personal Oedipal fate as a prisoner of the incest wish, he still had to meet a racial or cultural one as an ex-prisoner. The defeat of the life forces by the death forces was inevitable.

This view of Freud's, if only by reason of its absolute determinism, was very appealing to O'Neill. But even for O'Neill's special purposes, not to say generally, it had its limitations. For one could believe that life was an equivalent of the sexual instincts and death of the ego instincts only in the most abstract, biological sense. In addition, the struggle between the two sets of instincts as the basis for everything man achieved tended to reduce man's stature rather than enlarge it.[63]

In *Psychology of the Unconscious* Jung, too, traced the Oedipus complex historically. Only his concern was more with its symbolic presence in religious mythology and poetry than with its physical presence in primitive society. Like Freud, he thought of it as the dominant factor in life, as the source of man's fate. But, unlike Freud, he didn't distinguish between the sexes and make women subject to a corresponding Electra fate. In the Jungian scheme women were subject to the Oedipal fate in the same way men were, the daughter taking a male attitude toward the mother. This was possible because the offspring's incestuous desire for the mother was psychological rather than biological. It didn't "aim at cohabitation but at the special thought of becoming a child again, of turning back to the parent's protection, of coming into the mother once more in order to be born again."

The Oedipal conflict in Jung consisted of this simultaneous longing for death and renewed life in the womb of the mother. The mother was a symbol of both the death and renewed life, and the longing for her was ambivalent. In support of this Jung found that the image of the mother divinity in religious mythology had a dual aspect. On the one hand, she appeared in a demonic or destructive form; on the other, in a benevolent or life-giving form. He also found that in each case the image was a projection from out of the depths of the human unconscious. In fact, the source of all the gods was man's own incestuous libido, which had projected them in the course of history. The duality of the mother image emanated from an Oedipal ambivalence rooted in every individual. When the libidinal energy available to the individual wasn't enough for struggling against the realities of the external world, his ambivalence entered a critical state. At that point the incestuous longing for the depths overcame him and he descended into himself either to die or be reborn.

> When the libido leaves the bright upper world, whether from the decision of the individual or from decreasing life force, then it sinks back into its own depths, into the source from which it has gushed forth, and turns back to that point of cleavage, the umbilicus, through which it once entered into this body. This point of cleavage is called the mother, because from her comes the source of the libido. Therefore, when some great work is to be accomplished, before which weak man recoils, doubtful of his strength, his libido returns to that source—and this is the dangerous moment, in which the decision takes place between annihilation and new life. If the libido remains arrested in the wonder kingdom of the inner world, then the man has become for the world above a phantom, then he is practically dead or desperately ill. But if the libido succeeds in tearing itself loose and pushing up into the world above, then a miracle appears. This journey to the underworld has been a fountain of youth, and new fertility springs from his apparent death.[64]

O'Neill made more use of Freudian than of Jungian

insights into the individual Oedipus complex. Yet he was greatly impressed by the Jungian belief that, whatever the personal cause and effect, the Oedipal experience of the race as represented by the gods was inherited by the individual in his unconscious mind. In Freud the individual had a memory only of his own Oedipal experience, but in Jung he had a memory of the collective racial experience. This belief in a collective unconscious shaped the idea of fate in both *The Emperor Jones* and *The Hairy Ape*. But, more importantly, it encouraged the development of an archetypal characterization and an Oedipal symbolism in the plays generally, a characterization and symbolism that suggested the patterns of religious mythology.

In myths Jung had found all the Oedipal figures—a restrictive, vengeful father as well as a dualistic mother and a striving hero-son.[65] The symbolism O'Neill evolved on the basis of Jung's findings had the purpose of enlarging the scope of the fate suffered by his characters, especially his more contemporary or civilized characters. Appearing like a projection from out of the characters' collective unconscious, the symbolism reflected the eternal life-and-death struggle of the race underlying their individual struggles. O'Neill thought that either an archetypal characterization or mythic symbolism was indispensable in giving the individual's defeat in the life struggle a divine significance. In 1925 he wrote of the theater that it "should give us what the church no longer gives us—a meaning. In brief, it should return to the spirit of Greek grandeur. And if we have no Gods, or heroes to portray we have the subconscious, the mother of all gods and heroes."[66]

So just as Nietzsche supplied the godhead for the ritual plays, Jung supplied it for the tragedies. And it was an essential part of the tragedies. The exultation O'Neill wanted seemingly depended on a triumph over the inevitable defeat of death, on a spiritual rebirth or resurrection. The rebirth in the ritual plays could be taken for granted as part of the life cycle in the abstract. In the tragedies, however, it had to issue out of the individual struggle itself.

At first O'Neill sought to equate the rebirth with a climactic change in the personality of the main character or characters, though only in *Desire Under the Elms* did this come close to having a tragic effect. Very soon he also tried giving the characters a heroic dimension by having them partake of godhead on a symbolic level. Where the characters failed to experience a final triumph themselves, they could still move the audience to one by what they had attained in the course of their defeat. To the extent that the characters had approached the highest, the audience could experience a final triumph. O'Neill never expected the audience to understand the symbols in a play as projections from out of the characters' collective unconscious. In fact, he discouraged any understanding like that by playing down the psychoanalytical influence. The idea was rather for the symbols to evoke an intuitive response within the audience's own unconscious. Such at least was implied in the Quinn letter when he said,

> it is possible—or can be—to develop a tragic expression in terms of transfigured modern values and symbols in the theatre which may to some degree bring home to members of a modern audience their ennobling identity with the tragic figures on the stage.

O'Neill came to rely more and more on this symbolic experience by the audience for the effect of rebirth. Growing pessimistic over the years, he ceased to believe in the reality of personal triumph. The individual could wrestle with God, or with himself, but never win. So while the mechanics of inevitability took shape from Freud, the tragedy of it took shape from Jung. The psychological fate of man was dramatized in many ways, and on the surface the plays had different themes. There were struggles to belong, to realize an ambition or ideal, to find fulfillment in love—struggles made ultimately futile by an all-determining past. But underneath there was always the struggle for life itself, or for life in the fullest sense, which alone offered the consolation of the heroic.

Finally O'Neill abandoned even this. In the end the only triumph he could allow was the aesthetic. For he also ceased to believe in the reality of symbolic triumph. And independently of his pessimism, he realized that tragic exultation demanded a greater release of pathos, which meant intensifying the suffering of the characters rather than finding a direct or indirect means for them to win out over it.

The earliest plays were necessarily written with little, if any, awareness of psychoanalysis and the Oedipus complex. Still O'Neill was preoccupied from the very start with finding both an equivalent for the Greek sense of fate and a way of overcoming that equivalent. And as the way of overcoming changed from the personal to the symbolic, the equivalent changed from an external force to an internal. In the process psychoanalytical elements were absorbed until they were dramatized quite openly, a development that was only natural since O'Neill apparently intuited them before he consciously made use of them. In the four one-acters of the "S.S. Glencairn" cycle, for example, the psychoanalytical elements were anticipated in his treatment of the sea.

The earliest of the four, *Bound East for Cardiff*, was written in 1914. It had a very simple plot of a badly injured sailor being comforted by his friend and then dying. The injured sailor, Yank, is in great pain and knows he is going to die. But he tells his friend Driscoll that he isn't sorry about it, for his life on the sea has been miserably hard and lonely. And he muses about how for the past year he had been thinking of a life on a farm where he would never smell the sea or see a ship. At the same time the Glencairn is making its way through a heavy fog that has been on the sea ever since they left port about five days before, and every minute or so the ship's foghorn can be heard. As Yank gets weaker he imagines he sees the fog down in the seamen's forecastle where he is lying in his bunk. Then he dies, immediately after which a member of the crew comes in and says the fog has cleared.

The play manages to suggest that man's life is a struggle against a mysterious force and his only release from the pain of the struggle is in death. The sea acts as a symbol of this force and the fog as a symbol of its mystery. The foghorn serves as a constant reminder that defeat in the struggle is inevitable. Underlying Yank's desire for a life on the land is a desire to escape his fate as represented by the sea. As in all the early plays the inability to escape is less a matter of fate than of circumstance. Yet the fact that he dies at sea and is to be buried there is more than mere irony. It implies that there is no escape. The sea isn't really archetypal or psychoanalytical here. But in a general way O'Neill took it for granted as a mother symbol. At first he even called the piece "Children of the Sea," borrowing the title from Conrad.[67] And later he entertained the idea of writing an autobiographical play to be called "Sea-Mother's Son."

The other three Glencairn plays were written in the winter of 1917. One of them, *In the Zone*, turned out to be the most commercial of all the one-acters, holding the stage for years in the vaudeville circuit. Yet O'Neill always considered *The Moon of the Caribbees*, one of the others, as his best. To him *In the Zone* was conventional and sentimental, while *The Moon of the Caribbees* suggested "the impelling, inscrutable forces behind life." Actually, *In the Zone* also suggested inscrutable forces, however circumstantially they manifested themselves. In the four Glencairn plays, and in one-acters such as *Ile* and *Where the Cross Is Made*, these forces had an all-determining influence on the lives of the characters. Only occasionally was there a suggestion that they were rooted in individual past experiences, anticipating the Freudian influence in the later plays. But invariably they were symbolized by the maternal sea, anticipating the later Jungian influence. *The Long Voyage Home*, the fourth play of the cycle, takes place in a London waterfront dive. Olson, who is about to return to his home in Sweden after many hard years on the sea, is drugged, rolled and shanghaied aboard a ship bound around Cape Horn and known for its slave-driving treatment of the crew. And in *The Moon of the Caribbees* Smitty says drunkenly to the donkeyman, "We're poor little lambs who have lost our way, eh, Donk? Damned from here to eternity, what? God have mercy on such as we! True, isn't it, Donk?" They are all children of the sea, a womblike sea from which there is no escape.

O'Neill's first full-length plays, discounting those dating from his apprentice years, were *Beyond the Horizon, The Straw, Gold* and *Anna Christie*. In all of these, written over a stretch from early 1918 to the summer of 1920, the fate equivalent worked out as mere circumstance, though there was always a suggestion of something more inevitable. The external force consistently verged on the internal without ever becoming it.

Beyond the Horizon, dealing with the frustration of the life goal, was very much in the vein of the one-acters. But the full-length form and a touch of Schopenhauer in the narrative gave it a greater scope. The Schopenhauer also set it off from other treatments of the horizon theme, popular at the time. O'Neill's characters are led to seek their happiness in ways totally opposed to their natures. And their visions of love and success turn out to be illusions, mirages, deceptions of an irrational power wasting and destroying them. Robert's fulfillment lies in making voyages to exotic places across the sea. Yet he ends by spending his whole life on the farm. His brother Andrew's fulfillment lies in the sowings and reapings of the farm, but he ends by dissipating himself abroad. In the death scene, however, Robert cries out triumphantly, "It isn't the end. It's a free beginning—the start of my voyage! I've won to my trip—the right of release—beyond the horizon!" The trouble is that his triumph has more shadow than substance.

The Straw was essentially a love story. But it took place for the most part in a tuberculosis sanatorium and so had its life and death equivalents. O'Neill knew the psychology of patients in a sanatorium at first hand. The tubercular hero Stephen Murray and most of the other characters came straight out of his own experience, though the story itself didn't. While the real heroine died soon after O'Neill left the sanatorium, the stage heroine was allowed to cling to a hope of recovery inspired by the hero's love. This suggested the triumph of life in the struggle. Yet Murray described the love as a hopeless hope, implying that the chances were only illusory and would soon give way to death. As in *Beyond the Horizon* the ending was an unsuccessful and rather callow attempt to have the characters win out spiritually over the outer defeat.

The next play, *Gold*, was an old-time, treasure-hunting potboiler with the irony of the buried treasure chest being filled with worthless trinkets. O'Neill was writing feverishly at this time, perhaps overly anxious for wide recognition. In fact, *Gold* was but a full-length version of *Where the Cross Is Made*, which he had written only to be represented on the opening Provincetown bill two seasons before. The full-length play was basically the same as the one-acter except that more emphasis was placed on the determinism of the individual past. The whole Bartlett family was shown being drawn into the circle of retribution for a psychological crime committed by the father. Out of greed for the supposed treasure he had allowed two members of his shipwrecked crew to be murdered on a desert island. From then on he was haunted by the furies of his own conscience while making his wife and children suffer in turn from his guilt-fed and finally insane lust for the gold. The false gold was a symbol of the values of materialism, which corrupted and led to death. But corruption and death ensuing from false values weren't inevitable. And Captain Bartlett's fate had more to do with the circumstance of his crime than with the nature of his being. In other words, *Gold* was melodrama.[68] Still the idea of relentless guilt was to serve well in the development of the Oedipal fate.

In *Anna Christie* O'Neill again struck the ambiguous note of love and hope, this time provoking a good deal of criticism as a result. The play gave the impression of having a happy ending, an impression he was at a loss to correct. In a long letter to *The New York Times* he said he would have been false to his characters if he had made the last act unhappy in the obvious and conventional way expected by everyone. Yet he insisted the ending was still far from happy since there had never been a more sentimental, futile way of defying fate than Burke and Anna agreeing to get married.[69] Actually, the play does suggest that unhappiness and death will hold sway before long, though the suggestion is diluted by the sentimentality and comedy. O'Neill again used the sea as a symbol of the inescapable defeat awaiting the characters and placed more emphasis than previously on the individual or family past as the cause. The

influence of the sea was made to extend over three generations as a hereditary force or simply something in the blood.
Nevertheless, the fate of the Christopherson family appeared to be more an environmental or even accidental
sequence of events than anything else. Its workings were
those of a force still imposed mysteriously from without
rather than emanating from within.

Perhaps O'Neill was thinking with dissatisfaction of this
as well as the ending when he omitted *Anna Christie* from a
selection of nine plays for a Modern Library volume in
1932. He also omitted *Beyond the Horizon*, beginning the
selection chronologically with *The Emperor Jones*. These
omissions were made despite the fact that *Beyond the Horizon*
and *Anna Christie* had won the Pulitzer Prize for the 1919-20
and 1921-22 seasons respectively.

The Emperor Jones was the first play to make the external
forces internal. While the fate it dramatized wasn't Oedipal,
it conjured up some of the unconscious forces on stage.
And from this innovation to the dramatizing of the Oedipal
fate—in *Desire Under the Elms*—O'Neill had only a short
distance to go. The idea for the play came from a story
about the recent President Sam of Haiti.[70] The story was to
the effect that he had fashioned a silver bullet to kill himself
with if he were ever overthrown. With a good deal of
braggadocio O'Neill's character, an American Negro who
has set himself up as emperor over a tribe of bush Negroes
in the interior of a West Indian island, has done the same.

In the opening scene Brutus Jones learns that the natives
are about to revolt, and he sets out along a planned escape
route through the Great Forest. Yet during the next six
scenes he only wanders in a circle. It is night and he loses his
way in the darkness, but more so it is a psychological night
and the darkness is within his own mind. With each scene he
sinks further and further into the hidden experiences of his

soul, projecting them outwards as hallucinations. They are the racial experiences of his collective unconscious as well as his individual experiences, and finally he regresses to an image of a primitive witch doctor conjuring up a crocodile god. At each level of regression he fires one of the six bullets in his revolver at the hallucinatory figures, the last bullet being the silver one he has saved for his own death. He is then right back where he started from, the point at which he entered the psychological forest seeking to escape from his primitive self. The relationship of internal and external is suggested among other things by the beating of a tom-tom as if it were the beating of Jones' pulse. It begins in the middle of the first scene with his decision to escape and continues to his death in the last scene, accelerating gradually from a normal rate to a completely hysterical one.

The symbol of fate here is the silver bullet, which, like the false treasure in *Gold*, stands for the values of materialism that corrupt and lead to death. On the surface the Negro Jones is what white America has made him. His purpose in having set himself up as emperor was to exploit his subjects, and he tells Smithers in the first scene that he has managed to put away a fortune in a foreign bank. Fittingly enough, the bush Negroes kill him with silver bullets they have made out of melted-down money. But, unlike the false treasure in *Gold*, the silver bullet also stands for a separate destruction from within. In fact, the materialism of the outside world is only what calls up this other, more inevitable destruction.

Jones' real death is the one that occurs when he fires his own silver bullet at the crocodile god. It is his regression to the inner primitive world from the outer civilized one. He regresses to the primitive because he isn't in harmony with the civilized, its materialism being alien to the crocodile-god or religious nature of his unconscious self. His inability to belong to the civilized is implied by his having killed both a colored man and a white man as well as having escaped from a chain gang in the States. And he can belong to the primitive only in death since it is impossible to exist physically in the past. Yet it isn't only Jones who doesn't belong. It is man at large who is alienated by the civilized world from his real self and in the unconscious existence of that self bears his fate within him.

Like all the early plays, *The Emperor Jones* had its limitations. But it was an original and brilliant piece of theater, and it became the first big popular success of the Provincetown Players. A month after its opening at the Macdougal Street playhouse in November 1920, they took it uptown for what turned out to be a long run of over 200 performances. Another O'Neill play, *Diff'rent*, was also transferred uptown soon afterwards. O'Neill had finished this one immediately after *The Emperor*, the Players presenting it late in December. Its theme made it a success, if only commercially, in its own right, and it was given at the same theater in daily matinees through the spring. It was a melodramatic treatment of the effects of sexual frustration, a matter of particular appeal in the early twenties. In writing it O'Neill digressed somewhat from his development of the fate motive. Yet *Diff'rent* was the first play in which he attempted to make use of the Puritan outlook on life as a deep-rooted psychological force. He was later able to bring this off, at least in the context of the time, in *Desire Under the Elms* and *Mourning Becomes Electra*, in both of which the Puritanism played an Oedipal role. *Diff'rent* was also the first play in which he made use of the South Sea Islands as the antithesis of Puritanism, the former symbolizing life and the latter death.

Early in 1921 O'Neill wrote *The First Man*, which foreshadowed the dramas with a ritual or religious emphasis he was to turn out subsequently. Then, after starting

The Fountain, he put together *The Hairy Ape* in a single month, having developed the plot to some extent years before in a short story that was never published. *The Hairy Ape* paralleled *The Emperor Jones* in both form and content. In eight scenes Yank proved the white counterpart of the Negro Jones. But it was much more complex, and though O'Neill waited until it had been long closed he saw fit to offer an explanation.

> [Yank] was a symbol of man, who has lost his old harmony with nature, the harmony which he used to have as an animal and has not yet acquired in a spiritual way. Thus, not being able to find it on earth nor in heaven he's in the middle, trying to make peace, taking the "woist punches from bot' of 'em." This idea was expressed in Yank's speech. The public saw just the stoker, not the symbol, and the symbol makes the play either important or just another play. Yank can't go forward, and so he tries to go back. This is what his shaking hands with the gorilla meant. But he can't go back to "belonging" either. The gorilla kills him. The subject here is the same ancient one that always was and always will be the one subject for drama, and that is man and his struggle with his own fate. The struggle used to be with the gods, but is now with himself, his own past, his attempt "to belong."[71]

Actually, the theme of belonging had been set forth much more explicitly this time. What was only implied in *The Emperor Jones* was verbalized in two long speeches in the first scene by Paddy and Yank, the representatives of the past and present respectively. Paddy, who is equated with fog, longs for the days when "a ship was part of the sea, and a man was part of a ship, and the sea joined all together and made it one." The sea is the harmony that he, or man generally, had with nature in the past but now has lost. It is even the psychology of that past life, an image of the unconscious depths. And the fog is an image of the longing for those depths. On the other hand Yank, who is equated with steel, doesn't long for anything. He prides himself on being "de new dat's moiderin' de old! . . . smoke and express trains and steamers and factory whistles." He feels his primitive self to be one with the outside world. In the next six scenes, though, he finds like Brutus Jones that he doesn't belong to the outside world after all. His primitive self isn't steel but only a prisoner in a steel cage. The zoo scene at the end is a literal setting of this cage just as the scenes in the firemen's forecastle and the jail are figurative settings of it. The mechanized world deprives man of contact with nature and of true dignity in his labor. And having slain the old God without providing a new, it also deprives him of a meaning for his life as a whole. He can't feel any psychological or spiritual belonging to it. Nor can he return physically to the primitive world left behind.

Accordingly, Yank suffers a psychological death at the hands of civilized society and a physical death at the hands of the gorilla with whom he changes places in the zoo. By the sheer force of his primitive self, equivalent to modern man's unconscious, he is led to attempt what Paddy merely longs for, the fulfillment of that self in the outer world. And to attempt such a fulfillment means inevitable destruction. The irony is that the outer world he struggles against to the psychological death is a world of his, or man's, own making. It is only after his physical death, as in the final stage directions, that "the Hairy Ape at last belongs." Yet even then he doesn't belong to the outer world but, like Paddy and his namesake Yank in *Bound East for Cardiff*, to the inner world of the fog and the sea.

At the same time *The Hairy Ape* was O'Neill at his most radical and on its surface America's first proletarian drama. In fact, its supposed revolutionary fervor was what made many New York theatergoers overlook its flaws, expecially the rather facile, schematic ending. The Russians, too, had no doubt about O'Neill's radicalism. More than *Anna Christie*, *All God's Chillun Got Wings* and *Desire Under the Elms*, all of which were popular in Russia through the twenties, *The Hairy Ape* was the play that made O'Neill a great favorite there. When he and Nemirovitch-Dantchenko met in New York in 1927, the latter said happily, "You are one of us, you are a Russian." Yet it really wasn't so. Dantchenko told him how successful his plays were, but O'Neill remarked somewhat drily that he hadn't received any royalties. His radicalism was more philosophical than revolutionary, more along anarchist than strictly Marxist lines. In fact, his radicalism was already in another sphere altogether. And Yank's problem in *The Hairy Ape* couldn't be solved by a revolution even if there had been one forthcoming. As he says toward the end, "Aw, hell! What does dat get yuh? Dis ting's in your inside, but it ain't your belly. Feedin' your face—sinkers and coffee—dat don't touch it. It's way down—at de bottom." When O'Neill spoke for himself, he put it in Nietzschean terms.

> ...as we progress, we are always seeing further than we can reach. I suppose that is one reason why I have come to feel so indifferent toward political and social movements of all kinds. Time was when I was an active socialist, and, after that, a philosophical anarchist. But today I can't feel that anything like that really matters. It is rather amusing to me to see how seriously some people take politics and social questions and how much they expect of them. Life as a whole is changed very little, if at all, as a result of their course. It seems to me that, as far as we can judge, man is much the same creature, with the same primal emotions and ambitions and motives, the same powers and the same weaknesses, as in the time when the Aryan race started toward Europe from the slopes of the Himalayas. He has become better acquainted with those powers and weaknesses, and he is learning ever so slowly how to control them. The birth-cry of the higher men is almost audible, but they will not come by tinkering with externals or by

legislative or social fiat. They will come at the command of the imagination and the will.[72]

The perfection of the individual was always more important than the liberation of the masses. Still he considered the United States the most reactionary country in the world and in a passive way remained in favor of a complete social revolution. During the thirties, however, he lost whatever expectation he had of the Bolsheviks making such a revolution. In fact, he even planned to write a play about Robespierre by way of paralleling and satirizing what had happened in Russia. In 1946 at a rehearsal for *The Iceman* he again described himself as a philosophical anarchist. And among his unwritten plays at the time was one about Errico Malatesta, the Italian anarchist who had died after a long and active career in 1932. Then in a mass press interview prior to the opening O'Neill declared America to be a great failure, explaining that "we've squandered our soul by trying to possess something outside it, and we'll end as that game usually does, by losing our soul and the thing outside it too."[73]

All God's Chillun Got Wings, first conceived as a one-acter at the request of George Jean Nathan for publication in *The American Mercury* magazine, was completed at much greater length in December of 1923. It was produced by Experimental Theater, Inc., the following spring, causing a small furor in the meantime when word spread that it was a treatment of a mixed marriage. The news provoked a barrage of ranting and threatening letters. As usual these proved to be from idle cranks and perverts, and the play opened without violence. Yet O'Neill found that the sensational publicity had hurt "since it put the whole theme of the play on a false basis and thereby threw my whole intent in the production into the discard."

His intent wasn't to preach integration but to combine the racial unconscious with the individual past. On stage *The Emperor Jones* and *The Hairy Ape* had turned out more exciting than exulting. The heroes had been unable to triumph over their defeats. And the racial unconscious had been too abstract as a motivating force for the defeats to have a deep emotional effect, to evoke a tragic pathos. If a psychological fate were to be exulting as well as acceptable, it had to be worked out on the individual level of experience.

O'Neill wrote *All God's Chillun* in two acts of several scenes each. The scenes in the first act present the conflicting environmental or individual influences on the two main characters, Jim Harris and Ella Downey, from the time they are eight until they are married some fourteen years later. But the fact that Jim is Negro and Ella white made O'Neill put a sociological rather than a psychological emphasis on these influences. The scenes in the second act, dramatizing the conflict in the marriage itself, bring in the inherited racial influences. These are symbolized by an African religious mask, which is made to stand out conspicuously in the setting of the Harris flat. The setting itself is supposed to shrink from scene to scene so the mask with its primitive character will appear to grow.

Under the influence of the mask the conflict is revealed as a deeply rooted racial one, at least for Ella. She hates what is Negro in Jim and loves only what is white, the white being the civilized surface and the black the unconscious depths. For the inferiority she really feels toward others and her consequent self-hatred make her murderously jealous of what is proud and untamed in him. In the end she defeats his ambition to be a lawyer, bringing about his failure in the civilized world out of her need to keep the Negro in him down. Then thinking she has proven herself superior and laughing without restraint, she plunges a knife through the mask right in front of him. Yet in violating what is Negro in him she totally succumbs to what is unconscious in herself and regresses to an earlier state of being. Unlike Brutus Jones and Yank, she doesn't return to the primitive but to a corresponding state of childhood, which has the similar effect of being a psychological death. Jim, on the other hand, is intended to experience a psychological rebirth in submitting to the fate of the stabbed mask. Resigning himself to his defeat and to Ella's regression, he has a revelation of Christian humility. But as the revelation is more a submission than an overcoming, it fails to bring about a rebirth or triumph in the tragic sense. And in O'Neill's next play he made sure to do away with the humility while making the individual influences proceed more inevitably from the racial.

Desire Under the Elms was written in the winter and spring of 1924 and produced in November. It also caused a small furor, though not until it had moved from the Greenwich Village Theater to Broadway, where it subsequently ran for a year. The furor this time was over the openly sexual content, and as with *All God's Chillun* it obscured for the moment O'Neill's underlying intent. The District Attorney ordered the play withdrawn as part of a semi-official morals campaign that had gotten under way. Macgowan refused to withdraw it but agreed to put it on trial in accord with a play-jury plan requiring a three-fourths vote for conviction. Some other plays also came under attack and were placed before the jury, including Maxwell Anderson and Lawrence Stallings' *What Price Glory?* and John Howard Lawson's *Processional*. With the exception of the District Attorney himself, who was clearly guilty of bullying, ignorance and all-around Philistinism, everybody involved was exonerated. But *Desire* was subsequently banned in Boston and England. And in Los Angeles the next year a road company was arrested for obscenity and had to perform for the court, being let off by virtue of a hung jury—eight guilty and four not guilty.

O'Neill's intent wasn't sex but incest. He told Walter Huston, who acted the part of Ephraim, that he had dreamed the whole play. Yet as with the dreamed scenario of *Ah, Wilderness!* later on, this was no doubt after some conscious preoccupation with the theme. For by now he had been taken with the idea that the tragedy of man lay in his Oedipal nature. Accordingly, the characters in the play were those of the primal family. And the action consisted of a struggle between the father and the son for the mother, a struggle of mythic proportions.

The image of fate was the farm with its stone walls, its earth and elm trees, and its house. The stone walls corresponded to the father, the earth and trees to the mother or mother-imago, and the house to the hero-son filled with longing for the maternal depths. The inside of the house, in which most of the action took place, was like an image of the hero's psyche. Jung had described the tree in mythology as predominantly a mother symbol, and O'Neill characterized it as such in the setting.

The action of the entire play takes place in, and immediately outside of, the Cabot farmhouse in New England, in the year 1850. The south end of the house faces front to a stone wall with a wooden gate at center opening on a country road. The house is in good condition but in need of paint. Its walls are a sickly grayish, the green of the shutters faded. Two enormous elms are on each side of the house. They bend their trailing branches down over the roof. They appear to protect and at the same time subdue. These is a sinister maternity in their aspect, a crushing, jealous absorption. They have developed from their intimate contact with the life of man in the house an appalling humaneness. They brood oppressively over the house. They are like exhausted women resting their sagging breasts and hands and hair on its roof, and when it rains their tears trickle down monotonously and rot on the shingles.

The stone wall here represents the Puritanical and repressive aspect of the farm. Peter, one of the elder sons, says to his brother Simeon in the opening dialogue, "Here—it's stones atop o' the ground—stones atop o' stones—makin' stone walls—year atop o' year—him 'n' yew 'n' me 'n' then Eben—makin' stone walls fur him to fence us in!" The hardness of the stones is the hardness of the father and of God the Father as well. At one point the father, Ephraim, says, "God's hard, not easy! God's in the stones! Build my church on a rock—out o' stones an' I'll be in them. That's what He meant t' Peter!" According to Jung, God the Father was a later projection out of the human unconscious than the mother-imago and represented the modern external world as against the primitive internal one. In a parallel way Ephraim is believed by Eben, the hero-son, to have stolen the farm from Eben's mother, who was Ephraim's second wife and has been dead for some time when the action of the play beings. This incident in the past is all-motivating on the individual level of the action. Eben wants to regain the farm that he believes belonged to his mother and is now rightfully his. The stones of the father are the hard outer world that has fenced in the fertile inner one of the mother and son.

The life-giving aspect of the farm is represented by the earth and the elms. Abbie, Ephraim's new wife, is fertile like the earth and maternal like the elms. In the second act she tells Eben how she feels the sun "burnin' into the earth—Nature—makin' thin's grow—bigger 'n' bigger—burnin' inside ye—makin' ye want t' grow—into somethin' else—till ye're jined with it—an' it's your'n—but it owns ye, too—an' makes ye grow bigger—like a tree—like them elums." And then, in the scene where she seduces Eben, she takes the place of his mother, at which point the incestuous longing for the depths overwhelms him.

A grim, repressed room like a tomb in which the family has been interred alive [the room of Eben's mother, unopened since her death] . . .

ABBIE. When I fust come in—in the dark—they seemed somethin' here.

EBEN. (*simply*) Maw.

ABBIE. I kin still feel—somethin' . . . .

EBEN. It's Maw.

ABBIE. At fust I was feered o' it. I wanted t' yell an' run. Now—since yew come—seems like it's growin' soft an' kind t' me. (*Addressing the air–queerly*) Thank yew.

EBEN. Maw allus love me.

ABBIE. Mebbe it knows I love yew, too. Mebbe that makes it kind t' me . . . .

EBEN. . . .She was kind. She was good.

ABBIE. (*putting one arm over his shoulder. He does not seem to notice–passionately*) I'll be kind an' good t' ye!

EBEN. Sometimes she used t' sing fur me.

ABBIE. I'll sing fur ye!

EBEN. This was her hum. This was her farm.

ABBIE. This is my hum! This is my farm!

EBEN. He married her t' steal 'em. She was soft an' easy. He couldn't 'preciate her.

ABBIE. He can't 'preciate me!

EBEN. He murdered her with hardness.

ABBIE. He's murderin' me!

EBEN. She died. (*A pause*) Sometimes she used to sing fur me. (*He bursts into a fit of sobbing*).

ABBIE. (*both her arms around him–with wild passion*) I'll sing fur ye! I'll die fur ye! (*In spite of her overwhelming desire for him, there is a sincere maternal love in her manner and voice–a horribly frank mixture of lust and mother love*) Don't cry, Eben! I'll take yer Maw's place! I'll be everythin' she was t' ye! Let me kiss ye, Eben!

The fate the farm embodies is Oedipal. The hard part of

stones is the Oedipal father, the fertile part of earth and elms the Oedipal mother. When Eben goes up the road earlier to see Min the whore. whom his father and both his brothers have already had, he says, "She's like t'night, she's soft 'n' wa'm, her eyes kin wink like a star, her mouth's wa'm, her arms're wa'm, she smells like a wa'm plowed field . . ." Before Abbie arrives Min is the mother. In his love for Abbie, which is psychological rather than physical incest, Eben is absorbed, as it were, into the womb of the farm. He is possessed by the farm instead of the other way round, for Abbie at this point is the mother-imago in its demonic appearance. She desires the farm as a material possession, which is her motive for first desiring Eben, and in such a desire she is the demonically possessive mother. However, Eben also desires the farm as a material possession. He still wants to possess it in the way that Ephraim does. He isn't only his mother's son but his father's. This is why Simeon and Peter and then Abbie describe him at various times as the "dead spit 'n' image" of Ephraim, while Ephraim says that he is the "dead spit 'n' image" of his mother. The hero contains both the father and mother in himself.

The hero-son's struggle with the father comes from his infantile longing for the mother. But whenever Ephraim is lonely, he goes down to the maternal cows in the barn, where it is warm and he finds peace. He, too, has an infantile longing for the mother, try as he may to repress it by heeding a stern God. The demonically possessive mother has the father and son equally in her grip.

The irony is that only when Abbie attempts to prove her love for Eben by killing the child she has had by him does she become the benevolent and life-giving mother. For then Eben finally delivers himself from his incest wish and his desire for the farm. The death of their child brings about the death of the child in himself, and he is psychologically reborn out of the womb. The Jungian hero overcame the demonic mother not by overpowering her but through renunciation or sacrifice of the incest wish. In realizing and accepting his share of the guilt Eben frees himself from his infantile longing, the sacrifice of which amounts to a heroic rebirth. And the rebirth is tragic in view of the additional irony that, to be reborn out of the womb of psychological death, he has to accept physical death or a long imprisonment amounting to the same. In fact, the rebirth is tragic for Abbie and Eben together, the mother and son, both of whom suffer the outer defeat of death but triumph over it inwardly.

Actually, Ephraim's fate is also tragic, if not the most tragic of all. While he fails to enter into a new state of mind through his defeat, his individual pathos or suffering is greater than Eben's or Abbie's. He does no more than affirm his old hardness, but in his hardness is the will to endure life's hardness. He will suffer now even more than before. His tragedy is one of pathos alone. In this play O'Neill was still aiming more at the characters' sensation of triumph than at the audience's sensation of it, more at the philosophical or psychological tragedy on stage than at the aesthetic tragedy out front. He was aiming to make his characters exult first and his audience second. Yet the aesthetic tragedy, where the triumph resides simply in the fullest release of the characters' suffering, was to be his great achievement with *Long Day's Journey*. And the figure of Ephraim is an early, submerged instance of that kind of tragedy.

O'Neill intended the fate of the Cabots to issue simultaneously from the individual past and an unconscious or universal source. The killing of the child instead of the Oedipal father was perhaps a flaw. At the same time it was perfectly believable as a substitute act for what was both psychologically and physically more forbidding. And if it wasn't really inevitable, its very irrationality gave it that appearance in the acting. The result was a drama that has become an American classic by virtue of its mythic quality. But up until the climax, where the pathos is introduced or at least felt for the first time, *Desire Under the Elms* remains somewhat distant from the audience. For in its attempt to reach the tragic emotions it undercuts the audience's self-consciousness too radically. The tragic effect, whether of the lovers' renunciation or the father's final loneliness, is inhibited by the characters being essentially archetypes.

In *Strange Interlude*, begun two years later, O'Neill shifted the emphasis back toward the individual past, focusing on a psychological complex rising out of particular rather than general experience. There were to be no archetypes. And to release the tragic effect more fully than the ordinary climax allowed, he sought to make the pathos cumulative. The search for a tragic inevitability was now heading him full speed in the direction of the drawn-out narrative. Already when writing *Chris Christopherson*, the forerunner of *Anna Christie*, he had the notion a prose play was by nature, and should resemble in its workings, the skeleton of a novel. That notion was now reinforced. He even noted for *Strange Interlude* that the only difference between a play and a novel was in the amount of detail, a difference in selection.

So his emphasis was on the individual psychology of a struggle having a novel's scope. And along with the desire to evoke more pathos, such an emphasis prompted him to explore the inner thoughts of his characters through an elaborate device of asides or interior monologues cast in varying rhythms. Joyce's use of stream of consciousness in *Ulysses* may have encouraged him in this also. In any case, what he came up with was a dramatic or melodramatic intimacy lasting about five hours. Indeed, one frustrated woman novelist was jealous enough to sue him for plagiarism, though the suit ended with her having to pay costs. *Strange Interlude* ran for eighteen consecutive months on Broadway. There were six performances a week, starting at 5:30 in the afternoon with a dinner recess in between the two parts into which the play was divided. O'Neill originally expected that one performance would have to be spread over two successive evenings, but rehearsals proved this unnecessary.

The action of *Strange Interlude* takes place over a period of twenty-five years. It begins shortly after a shattering incident in the life of Nina Leeds at the age of twenty and ends with its repetition when she is forty-five, during which time almost everything that happens to her is shaped by it. The incident is the loss in the war of her fiancé, Gordon Shaw. This loss is meant to be traumatic in a clinically Freudian sense, Nina feeling an overwhelming guilt for not having married him or at least given herself to him before he left. The reason for both Gordon's forebearance and hers lies in the influence her father, acting out of selfish motives, had on them at the time. But the loss has the effect of bringing about Nina's psychological birth, for it awakens her to her father's real motives. At that point she ceases to think of herself as the girl who is his daughter, thinking instead only of the need to fulfil herself as the woman who should have been Gordon's wife and the mother of his children. Subsequently, Ned Darrell, a neurologist, states that this incessant need of hers derives from the initial guilt she feels. O'Neill readily assumed a modern theater audience would understand the complex and accept it as the basis for all that follows.

The repetition of the incident brings about Nina's psychological death, for then the cycle has been completed

from unfulfillment to fulfillment and back to unfulfillment. She regresses to childhood, returning to her
psychological father in the person of Marsden, himself an
Oedipal figure for whom Nina is a mother as well as a
daughter. Everything in the generation of years between is
the struggle for the fulfillment and against the unfulfillment. Yet the final defeat is inevitable, or intended to be,
since the very struggling against it issues from a past failure
that must repeat itself.

The embodiment of fate here is Gordon Shaw. And apart
from some help the Gordon fate gets from arbitrary circumstance, it proceeds directly from the psychology of life
on the individual level. Nina isn't the only one who is subject
to it. With varying effect the men whose lives are related to
hers are subject to it also. This is especially true of Darrell,
her lover and the father of her son born in Gordon's imag.
When he refuses toward the end to help her keep from
losing her son to Madeline Arnold, the Nina of the next
generation, he tells her, "I was only a body to you. Your first
Gordon used to come back to life. I was never more to you
than a substitute for your dead lover! Gordon is really
Gordon's son!" Then in watching the finish of the crew
race, in which the whole struggle against Nina's Gordon
psychology is symbolized, he can't help openly protesting
for a moment by rooting against her son's shell. He protests
in behalf of all the victims, the unwilling ones like Marsden
and himself as well as the willing ones like Evans, Nina's
husband. But Evans reacts as if betrayed, and Darrell is
forced to say, "Slip of the tongue! I meant Gordon! Meant
Gordon, of course! Gordon is always meant—meant to win!
Come on, Gordon! It's fate!"

The would-be inevitability of the Gordon fate ensues
wholly from the Freudian psychology of the characters. Yet
such a fate has nothing inherently heroic or of divine sig-

nificance in it, and O'Neill tried to make up for this by placing the striving of the characters in a larger, even ultimate, framework. Seen in this framework, the pattern of events beginning with the death of Gordon Shaw is an episode or interlude in a cosmic pattern of events. The struggle between the characters' invididual needs for love and accomplishment appears as an emanation or surface reaction of the psychologically deeper struggle between life and death. And the cosmic pattern of this latter struggle O'Neill expressed in the Jungian terms of a mother god and a father god, the mother representing the life of the internal world and the father the death of the external. In the second act Nina says to Marsden,

> NINA. ...The mistake began when God was created in a male image. Of course, women would see Him that way, but men should have been gentlemen enough, remembering their mothers, to make God a woman!. But the God of Gods—the Boss—has always been a man. That makes life so perverted, and death so unnatural. We should have imagined life as created in the birth-pain of God the Mother. Then we would understand why we, Her children, have inherited pain, for we would know that our life's rhythm beats from Her great heart, torn with the agony of love and birth. And we would feel that death meant reunion with Her, a passing back into Her substance, blood of Her blood again, peace of Her peace!

In the fourth act, feeling herself at the height of fulfillment after conceiving Darrell's child in the image of Gordon, she consequently thinks of God as a mother and of herself as being suspended in the tide of the sea, " ... suspended in the movement of the tide, I feel life move in me, suspended in me ... no whys matter ... there is no why ... I am a mother ... God is a mother." All life is contained within her as in the maternal sea. Then in the next act Darrell, who has run away, returns to her, and her fulfillment reaches its height in the external world through her possession of Evans, him and Marsden. She thinks to herself, "Why, I should be the proudest woman on earth! . . . I should be the happiest woman in the world! . . . Ha-Ha . . . only I better knock wood . . . before God the Father hears my happiness!"

The racing scene takes place twenty years after, by which time the cyclic interlude is nearing its end. Darrell and Nina no longer love each other, while Gordon is about to leave her. And as the crews approach the finish line it is God the Father who is triumphant. In her jealousy Nina thinks, "I hear the Father laughing! . . . O Mother God, protect my son! . . . let Gordon fly to you in heaven! . . . quick, Gordon! . . . love is the Father's lightning! . . . Madeline will bring you down in flames! . . . I hear His screaming laughter! . . . fly back to me!" The interlude is completely over in the last act. Evans is already dead, Gordon flies away just like Gordon Shaw, and Darrell, about to return to his surface dabbling as a scientist, says goodbye for the last time, leaving Nina and Marsden in the death and peace of the psychological womb as when it all began.

> NINA. (*with a strange smile*) Strange interlude! Yes, our lives are merely strange dark interludes in the electrical display of God the Father! (*Resting her head on his shoulder*) You're so restful, Charlie. I feel as if I were a girl again and you were my father and the Charlie of those days made into one. I wonder is our old garden the same? We'll pick flowers together in the aging afternoons of spring and summer, won't we? It will be a comfort to get home—to be old and to be home again at last—to be in love with peace together—to love each other's peace—to sleep with peace together—! (*She kisses him—then shuts her eyes with a deep sigh of requited weariness*)—to die in peace!

The characters' defeat in the life struggle comes more directly from their individual psychology in *Strange*

Interlude than in any of the previous plays. Yet the death of Gordon Shaw that sets the struggle off is more a stroke of bad luck than of fate. And the insanity in Sam Evans' family, which first makes Nina take Darrell for her lover in order to have a healthy baby, is simply a matter of circumstance, not a coming to pass of what is already within. Even Nina's Gordon Shaw obsession lasting through twenty-five years is perhaps unjustified since the painful experience of his death, its only basis, happens relatively late in her life.

These lapses of inevitability in the plot are more than academic because they act against a build-up of pathos. The melodramatic acts against the tragic. The pathos is also lessened by the purely aesthetic lapses in the technique. The interior monologues are too profuse and on the whole too prosaic for a tragic effect. They aren't really interior enough. For this reason O'Neill cut back on their use and then discarded them altogether in the plays to follow. The failure of plot he corrected by returning to the mythic, or the psychoanalytical source of the mythic. In the second part of *Strange Interlude* he had dramatized in great detail a painful experience in the life of the young Gordon at the age of eleven. He had also let Darrell explain to Nina in clinical terms why the boy hated him. In *Mourning Becomes Electra* he made a much greater use of the early childhood experience, going back further than eleven to the very first years, and more indirectly a greater use of such explanations as Darrell's. The result was the bringing of the idea of an inevitable fate to its mechanical perfection.

electra

It was just around the time he was starting on *Strange Interlude* that O'Neill decided to undergo psychoanalysis himself. Not long before then both he and Agnes had taken part in a study of marriage being made by Dr. Gilbert van Tassle Hamilton, a friend of Kenneth Macgowan's. Hamilton's study, financed by a research grant, had consisted of interviewing 100 married men and 100 married women about the motives at work in their marriages. Approximately half of those interviewed were married to each other and almost all were in the professions or the literary world. In return for their cooperation Hamilton had offered free advice in his capacity as a psychoanalyst to anyone who desired it when the interviews were over. An additional grant at that time had enabled him to offer six of the people an intensive, if short, analysis. One of these six was O'Neill, who took him up on the offer in the winter of 1926.

O'Neill had actually been paying sporadic visits to a New York psychiatrist for the past two years. The arrangement had been very informal—he had gone merely to talk over problems as they happened to arise. With Hamilton he was more serious. He had the primary motive of saving himself from alcoholism, and probably the secondary motive of saving his marriage. Yet his sessions with Hamilton lasted only six weeks, for he then left with Agnes for Bermuda. And though he was on the wagon for the rest of his life with just two falls, the analysis couldn't have gone very deep. His insight into things was no doubt made sharper, but six weeks was too short a time for him to be affected much, whether personally or as a playwright.

On the other hand, he probably wouldn't have been too influenced in his work even if the sessions had gone on longer. A more extensive analysis might have had other therapeutic results in his private life. However, the scientific idea of therapy would have remained opposed or at least foreign to the aesthetic idea of an inevitable fate. The idea of fate was really independent of therapy since therapy couldn't change death and the emotions of death. And more relevant to the question of psychological fate, therapy couldn't change life very much either. Perhaps in his own case O'Neill's resistance was at fault, but in most other cases the natural limitations of therapy were at fault. Even when the therapy was extensive, significant change in the life pattern was rare. In any event O'Neill's pattern, his underlying dependency, soon led to the break-up of his marriage. Within a year he had abandoned his wife and children for Carlotta. By then he had finished *Strange Interlude*, and of the several tormented characters in the play the one he had shown suffering most was the neurologist, the scientist, Ned Darrell.

O'Neill's flight to Europe with Carlotta failed to ease the

tension under which he lived. There was no escape from his
conflict in flight. In fact, the tension proved so unabating it
eventually led him astray in his work, causing him to take
further flight in the wish-fulfillments of *Days Without End*
and *Ah, Wilderness!* before he finally got the better of it.
After a short stay in London and six months in southern
France, he and Carlotta embarked on a tour of the Far East.
On this trip an earlier idea for a possible play on the Electra
theme recurred to him. In Bermuda in the spring of 1926
he had asked himself if he could "get modern psychological
approximation of Greek sense of fate into such a play,
which an intelligent audience of today, possessed of no
belief in gods or supernatural retribution, could accept and
be moved by?"[74] At the time he had been trying to persuade
Macgowan to do Hugo von Hofmannsthal's *Electra*, which
he probably liked for its plumbing of the Dionysian depths.
Hofmannsthal's treatment might have been what first
made him think of using the myth himself. At the very least
it added to his preoccupation with the Greeks, which finally
became so strong he began studying ancient Greek in the
vain hope of being able to read the old tragedies in the
original in three or four years.

The trip with Carlotta was hectic. At one point
O'Neill—already resenting the claims of his new love while
feeling guilty about the claims of his old—began gambling
feverishly, hit the bottle again and wound up in a hospital
with a temporary nervous breakdown. Twice he drove Carlotta into leaving him, their romance all but over. Still,
drawn back together by their mutual need, they returned
united to southern France. This was toward the end of
January 1929, and by April of that year he felt ready to
begin working out the idea of the Electra play in detail. In
early March the findings of Hamilton's study had been
published in a book by both himself and Macgowan entitled

What Is Wrong With Marriage. Presumably O'Neill would have liked not to be reminded of his relationship with Agnes right then. But either Hamilton or Macgowan sent him a copy, and he was persuaded enough by the findings to make use of them in his character sketches and plot outline.[75]

The book was actually written by Macgowan, who based it on Hamilton's statistical results. The latter had written a book for professional readers called *A Research in Marriage: Report of Findings*, which Kinsey was later to acknowledge as a forerunner of his own researches. Macgowan's book was at first intended to be a paraphrase of Hamilton's for the layman. Yet it ended up as more of a personal interpretation with the following conclusion.

> Looking back over this research we are struck with an immense pessimism. It is not over the institution of marriage. It is merely despair over the way in which the sins of the fathers are visited upon the children, and the children, growing up, inevitably repeat the process. Again and again we see the misery of maturity driving men and women to teach their children exactly those things which will perpetuate the misery when the children themselves grow up. In this respect the family circle seems a vicious circle. It seems indeed the greatest vicious cricle ever conceived; for its circumference has become the straight line of descent from parent to child world without end.

The pattern of psychological cause and effect found in the marriage relationship no doubt struck O'Neill as having an even greater significance. If marriage was subject to a determining force, so were all emotional relationships and consequently life itself. This was really nothing new, but it reinforced his idea of inevitability with the family as the starting point. The cause-and-effect pattern in marriage came down to the way men and woman were motivated in their marriage choices by their childhood experiences.

In a chapter entitled "Oedipus Rex" Macgowan analyzed the findings that of 17 men who had married women physically like their mothers, 16 or 94% were happy, while of 60 who had married women physically unlike their mothers, only 20 or 33% were happy. There was a similar discrepancy, though not as great, in the happiness of men whose wives were like and unlike their mothers psychically. Macgowan assumed that the unconscious desire of the man was to marry a woman physically and psychically like his mother but that his conscious desire was to marry someone unlike her. On the one hand, the man wanted to retain the security of his childhood; on the other, to achieve his emotional independence. The result was an ambivalence in his feelings that affected his relationship with his wife and brought unhappiness. And the conscious desire to achieve independence was almost as inevitable as the unconscious desire not to. In breaking down the statistics another way the same thing appeared. The married sons who still had ambivalent feelings toward their mothers were far less happy than those who had resolved them either positively or negatively. The frustration of the unconscious desire for the mother was more evident in the physical than psychic categories because the conscious marriage choice was usually based on the woman's physical qualities.

In a chapter entitled "The Tragedy of Electra" Macgowan analyzed the corresponding statistics for the women. These were much less striking than for the men, but the conclusions he was led to draw were similar. The figures argued against the idea that the father was to the daughter as the mother to the son. Yet they bore out the importance of the childhood experiences in determining the capacity for marital happiness later on. This was particularly evident, for example, in cases where the father of the girl had been constantly belittled in her eyes by her mother. The girl was likely to make a bad marriage and belittle her own husband in turn.

Macgowan explained that under normal circumstances the woman was like the man in unconsciously desiring a mate like the parent of the opposite sex physically or psychically or both. And just as the man tended to bring about his own unhappiness by frustrating that desire, so did the woman. However, the woman didn't feel the same conscious need for emotional independence from her father as the man from his mother. Her unconscious desire was frustrated by her equally unconscious fear of incest, which drove her to someone unlike her father.

What most interested O'Neill in this was the way in which the unconscious image of the opposite parent was related to the physical likeness or unlikeness of the mate. More than likely he found many of the statistics unconvincing and many of Macgowan's explanations questionable. But the suggestion that the essentially psychic image tended to be expressed physically made a great impression, especially as he himself was one of the subjects of the study. Macgowan related elsewhere in the book how both the men and women, especially the former, indicated that they would like to change the physical appearance of their mates to be more like those of their mothers and fathers respectively. These changes had to do with height, the color of the eyes and the color of the hair. And the color of the hair was the physical characteristic which came to symbolize the cause-and-effect pattern of psychic incest in *Mourning Becomes Electra*.

O'Neill married Carlotta in July 1929, three weeks after Agnes had divorced him. He worked steadily in France for almost the next two years, and in the spring of 1931 he and Carlotta came back to America. The production of the trilogy opened at the Guild Theater some five months later.

His original intention had been for the three plays to be given separately in a weekly rotation. But with all the cutting he ended up doing in rehearsals a *Strange Interlude* type of schedule was possible. There were performances six evenings a week starting at 5:00 with an hour recess for dinner after "Homecoming," the first of the three plays. Yet where *Strange Interlude* had run over 400 performances, *Mourning Becomes Electra* ran only 150. One reason may have been the Depression. Another was that the trilogy, set at the end of the Civil War in New England, lacked *Strange Interlude*'s direct contemporary appeal. O'Neill had overshot the mark in the opposite direction and made the aesthetic distance too great again. Nevertheless, he had approximated the Greek sense of fate in terms a modern theater audience could accept. And highbrow, middlebrow and lowbrow critics alike proclaimed the trilogy a masterpiece.

Many of the critics assumed O'Neill had adapted Aeschylus' *Oresteia*. Yet this wasn't exactly the case. O'Neill was generally attracted to Aeschylus and, as with Robespierre and Malatesta, planned at one time to write a play about him. The elements he took over from the *Oresteia*, however, were only structural, namely its trilogy form and the basic outline of its plot. And the plot outline he followed only up to a point.[76] The last play of the *Oresteia* dramatizes the reconciliation of the opposing social forces set in motion by the deeds of the past. But "The Haunted" dramatizes a further extension of the determining effect of the past on the lives of the individual characters in the present. As O'Neill remarked in a letter to Robert Sisk, the Theater Guild press agent at the time, *Mourning Becomes Electra* "stems directly from my past work."

In the *Oresteia* the fatal events go back to when Thyestes seduced his brother Atreus' wife. Atreus drove him into exile, but Thyestes returned and sought sanctuary at the divine altar, where he was granted immunity from ever having his blood spilled in his native land. As a result Atreus took the revenge of slaying all of Thyestes' children except the youngest and serving them up to him at a banquet. When Thyestes knew he had eaten the flesh of his own children, he vomited it out and laid a curse on Atreus' whole race. Then Atreus sent him with his remaining son Aegisthus into banishment again. Agamemnon was a son of Atreus, and Aegisthus later took revenge on him for what had been done to his father. During the Trojan War he became the lover of Clytemnestra, the absent Agamemnon's wife and queen. For Aegisthus' sake, and even more for reasons of her own, Clytemnestra decided to kill Agamemnon on his return home. And it is shortly before his return—on the night the signal is received of the taking of Troy—that the action of the trilogy begins.

In *Mourning Becomes Electra* the events go back to when Abe Mannon, Atreus' counterpart, drove his brother Dave into exile. Consumed with jealousy over his brother's mistress Marie Brantôme, a French Canadian nurse taking care of his own young daughter, Abe put both Dave and Marie out of the house. The ostensible reason was to protect the family from the scandal of her being pregnant and his brother having to marry her. After they were thrown out Dave did marry her, and she gave birth to a boy named Adam. Abe then tore down the house to make room for a new one—with the Greek temple front fashionable at the time—because he didn't want to live where the Mannons had been disgraced. He also forced his brother to sell him his share in the family shipbuilding business for a fraction of what it was worth. In the following years Dave was driven to commit suicide, and at the age of seventeen Adam ran away to sea. Abe's daughter had died meanwhile, the sole inheritor of the estate at his death being his son Ezra. After seventeen more years Adam returned for the first time, although he had occasionally written to his mother and sent her money. He found her dying from illness and starvation. She told him that when she had become too sick to work, not knowing where he was, she had written to Ezra Mannon for a loan. Ezra had never answered, and now Adam was too late. She died almost immediately, Adam swearing to avenge her death on Ezra. At the time Ezra was away as a general in the Civil War, but a year or so later Adam met his wife at the home of her father in New York. The latter, a doctor with whom he had happened to come into contact, had taken a fancy to him. Adam didn't realize there was any connection, and when he was introduced to Christine he was surprised to hear her name. Out of hatred for his Mannon ancestry he himself had long before assumed the name of Brant, a shortened form of his mother's name. Despite his surprise at meeting Christine he resolved right then and there to take her away from Ezra. He soon became her lover. Yet being lovers only led to their falling in love, and Adam began to pay her indiscreet visits at the Mannon estate. To throw off suspicion Christine had him flirt with her daughter Lavinia. And it is then—on the day news is received of Lee's surrender—that the action of O'Neill's trilogy begins.

The inevitability of the events in the *Oresteia* stems from two things, the characters' own psychology and the participation of the gods in what they do. Orestes, for example, decides to kill his mother only after the deed has been sanctioned by Apollo through his divine oracle at Delphi. This sanction makes what Orestes does of divine or at least universally human significance. In other words, Clytemnestra's death at the hands of her son is inevitable by the very nature of things. For the nature of things, or natural law, is what the will of the gods expresses. All the other important happenings are inevitable by the same token. However, in *Mourning Becomes Electra* there are no gods as such participating in the action. The inevitability of the events derives entirely from the individual psychology of the characters. Here the workings of fate are the workings of the Oedipus complex. The fated victims are destroyed by their own incest wish, perpetuated in a cause-and-effect chain of childhood influences and the later acting out of these influences.

The first visible link in this chain is the marriage relationship of Ezra and Christine. While Christine's love for Ezra already began turning into disgust on their wedding night, Ezra has loved Christine unceasingly. The reason he has never stopped loving her is that his feeling springs from an unconscious source. For though Marie Brantôme lived in the Mannon house only a relatively short time, the young Ezra cared for her more than for his own mother and formed an unconscious attachment to her as if she were his mother. Her hair was even the same color as his mother's. And Christine's hair is just like hers. At one point, before Christine interrupts him, he says to her, "You're beautiful! You look more beautiful than ever—and strange to me. I don't know you. You're younger. I feel like an old man beside you. Only your hair is the same—your strange beautiful hair I always—"

Adam's love for Christine similarly springs from an unconscious source, as does Lavinia's repressed love for him. Christine is the image of Adam's real mother just as she is of Ezra's mother substitute. Moreover, her physical resemblance is only the outer appearance of an underlying psychic resemblance. Like Marie, she is of French descent and temperament, uninhibited rather than repressed in the Puritan way of the Mannons. This double device of physical and psychic resemblances, which was suggested to O'Neill by the Hamilton and Macgowan book or at least his own part in it, isn't very different from the single device of psychic resemblances in *Desire Under the Elms*. But it carries the fate idea one step further. Even the physical and circumstantial is now psychological and inevitable. This applies as much to the attachments to Adam as it does to the attachments to Christine. Adam resembles Ezra as well as every other male Mannon past and present, his resemblance signifying the psychic inevitability of both Christine's and Lavinia's love for him.

Ezra's fixation for Marie stems from realizing that she was his uncle's mistress, which happened when he was thirteen. Adam's fixation for her, along with his hatred of his father, goes back to a traumatic experience at the age of seven. And Lavinia's Oedipal fixations derive from her earliest childhood. In fact, when Christine tells her that she has felt disgust for Ezra ever since they were married, the reason for the complex of love, hatred, jealousy and revenge in which the whole family is caught comes out.

> LAVINIA. (*wincing again—stammers harshly*) So I was born of your disgust! I've always guessed that, Mother—ever since I was little—when I used to come to you—with love—but you would always push me away! I've felt it ever since I can remember—your disgust! (*Then with a flare-up of bitter hatred*) Oh, I hate you! It's only right I should hate you!
> CHRISTINE. (*shaken—defensively*) I tried to love you. I told myself it wasn't human not to love my own child, born of my body. But I never could make myself feel you were born of any body but his! You were always my wedding night to me—and my honeymoon!
> LAVINIA. Stop saying that! How can you be so—! (*Then suddenly—with a strange jealous bitterness*) You've loved Orin! Why didn't you hate him, too?
> CHRISTINE. Because by then I had forced myself to become resigned in order to live! And most of the time I was carrying

him, your father was with the army in Mexico. I had forgotten him. And when Orin was born he seemed my child, only mine, and I loved him for that! (*Bitterly*) I loved him until he let you and your father nag him into the war ...

LAVINIA. (*sternly*) It was his duty as a Mannon to go! ...

CHRISTINE. Well, I hope you realize I never would have fallen in love with Adam if I'd had Orin with me. When he had gone there was nothing left—but hate and a desire to be revenged—and a longing for love! And it was then I met Adam.

Just as Christine is to Adam the image of his mother, Adam is to Christine the image of her son. He is also the reincarnation of Ezra and of the love or at least attraction Christine once felt toward her husband, perhaps because Ezra answered an unconscious longing in her for her father. So the affair of Adam and Christine has a psychic necessity. And as all the events in the trilogy revolve around their affair, its necessity is crucial. The weakest link in the cause-and-effect chain may even be the way they met in the first place. For if Adam had come into contact with her father altogether unknowingly, their meeting would have been a mere accident. But there is a suggestion that on an unconscious level he sensed the man was her father and arranged to come into contact with him. In any event, motivated as he was, he would undoubtedly have found a way into the Mannon circle eventually.

Lavinia's fixated love for her father comes from his having turned to her for the love he failed to get from Christine. Correspondingly, Orin's attachment to his mother comes from Christine's having turned to him to express the love she couldn't give to Ezra. When Orin returns in the second play, "The Hunted," he is wholly on Christine's side in the family struggle. Lavinia succeeds in winning him over, but before she confronts him with what she knows she finds him paying his last respects to his father with mocking resentment. She berates him, saying that Ezra had been very proud of him and even boasted of Orin's having done one of the bravest things he had seen in the war. Orin defends himself by telling her what really happened, in the course of which the Oedipal source of his resentment is revealed.

He relates how, to cover up his fear, he volunteered for a mission infiltrating Confederate lines and had to kill two enemy soldiers by the time he got back. He killed them in the same way, which seemed like murdering the same man twice. And he had the feeling that war meant continuously murdering the same man, who would turn out in the end to be himself. He says, "Their faces keep coming back in dreams—and they change to Father's face—or to mine— What does that mean, Vinnie?" The nature of his dreams is soon made clear. After he has killed Adam aboard the clipper ship and ransacked the stateroom, he goes through Adam's pockets to finish making his death look like the work of thieves. Then he remains stooping over the body and staring into Adam's face.

> ORIN. By God, he does look like Father!
> LAVINIA. No! Come along!
> ORIN. (*as if talking to himself*) This is like my dream. I've killed him before—over and over.
> LAVINIA. Orin!
> ORIN. Do you remember me telling you how the faces of the men I killed came back and changed to Father's face and finally became my own? (*He smiles grimly*) He looks like me, too! Maybe I've committed suicide!
> LAVINIA. (*frightenedly–grabbing his arm*) Hurry! Someone may come!
> ORIN. (*not heeding her, still staring at* BRANT—*strangely*) If I had been he I would have done what he did! I would have loved her as he loved her—and killed Father too—for her sake! . . . It's queer! It's a rotten dirty joke on someone!

The joke is eventually seen to be on him. He has committed psychological suicide by killing Adam, who as his mother's lover was the projection of himself. Adam's complicity in the killing of his father had furthered Orin's identification with him, for unconsciously Orin also desired his father's death so he might take his place with his mother. Orin's likeness to Ezra and Adam signifies just this desire. In the same way Lavinia's resemblance to Christine signifies her unconscious desire to take her mother's place with her father. Orin begins to realize the joke is on him when Christine kills herself on learning of Adam's death. At that point there is no longer any possibility of his taking his father's place with her. There is also no possibility of Lavinia's taking her mother's place with her father or, more especially, with Adam, the image of her father. Yet by the very force of their desires they assume these roles. And in essentially the same way as the past had led Ezra and Christine to their fate, it leads Orin and Lavinia to theirs.

When they appear on the scene in "The Haunted," which is set about a year later, they are physical reincarnations of their father and mother. Lavinia has filled out and become much more feminine, wearing her hair and being dressed in green like Christine. Orin has become stiff and wooden in his movements, wearing a close-cropped beard and being dressed in black like Ezra. These physical reincarnations are basically psychic, however, and the events of the past soon begin to repeat themselves. The identifications with father and mother are unconscious, but Orin gradually becomes aware of his Oedipal desire to the point where he consciously surrenders to it. While Lavinia remains unknowingly in conflict with herself, he gives himself up to his need to repeat the experience of his guilt and be forgiven. And since Lavinia has taken her mother's place, it is with her that he must repeat the experience.

In the next-to-last act he gives Hazel a history he has written of the Mannon family crimes because he wants to keep Lavinia from marrying Peter, who has taken the place of Adam in the repetition of the past. And when Lavinia promises she will do anything he wants if only he makes Hazel give it back, he loses control of himself so far as to propose incest to her. At one point he says, "There are times now when you don't seem to be my sister, nor Mother, but some stranger with the same beautiful hair . . . Perhaps you're Marie Brantôme, eh? And you say there are no ghosts in this house?" Lavinia is the reincarnation of her mother and of Marie Brantôme both, Orin the reincarnation of Ezra Mannon and also of Abe Mannon. The pattern of events that began with the act of Abe Mannon's jealousy has now come full circle two generations later, coming necessarily by way of the Oedipus complex as it is a pattern formed wholly from within.

Genuinely horrified and repelled, Lavinia breaks down and in a hysterical outburst of hatred wishes Orin would kill himself. He realizes that, despite his reliving his guilt through Lavinia, she will always stand in the way of his forgiveness. And hypnotized by the thought of death as an atonement that will bring him forgiveness at last, he commits suicide in the same way his mother did. However, Orin's death doesn't free Lavinia from her own Oedipal desire. Instead the furies of his guilt attack her, and though she manages for the moment to repress them they take their revenge quickly enough. In the last act she is dressed again in the Mannon black of deep mourning. When Peter arrives, she is extremely anxious about losing him. Her fear begins to get the better of her, and she asks him to marry her that very evening. But since Orin's funeral has just taken place, this only makes him suspicious. Then in one last hysterical outburst she asks him to make love to her, revealing her unconscious desire to herself by a slip of the tongue.

LAVINIA. . . .Listen, Peter! Why must we wait for marriage? I want a moment of joy—of love—to make up for what's coming! I want it now! Can't you be strong, Peter? Can't you forget sin and see that all love is beautiful? (*She kisses him with desperate passion*) Kiss me! Hold me close! Want me! Want me so much you'd murder anyone to have me! I did that—for you! Take me in this house of the dead and love me! Our love will drive the dead away! It will shame them back into death! (*At the topmost pitch of desperate, frantic abandonment*) Want me! Take me, Adam! (*She is brought back to herself with a start by this name escaping her—bewilderedly, laughing idiotically*) Adam? Why did I call you Adam? I never even heard that name before—outside of the Bible! (*Then suddenly with a hopeless dead finality*) Always the dead between! It's no good trying any more!

Just as Christine and Orin had sensed earlier, all her actions have proceeded from a desire for Adam, a desire which at bottom is Oedipal. Lavinia doesn't understand it as such, though she is seemingly aware of it at this point to the extent Orin was. Realizing in any case her desire for Adam, she now accepts her guilt in all that has happened. Her jealousy has brought about the deaths of Adam, Christine and Orin, and, more indirectly, even of her father. There is no possibility of her being happily married to Peter. As with Orin, the only thing left her is the need for atonement. Besides, her love for Peter is little more than her desire for Adam. Deciding to make him leave her, she tells him she made love with one of the natives on the South Sea Island where she and Orin had stopped on their way back from the East. Peter immediately hurries off in Puritan shock and naiveté. And Lavinia, resolving to punish herself by living alone in the Mannon house for the rest of her days, orders Seth to nail up the shutters and have all the flowers in the rooms thrown out. Then as he begins she marches woodenly inside.

Lavinia's sealing herself up in the house as in a tomb is tantamount to her death. It is a psychological death, which fittingly brings the psychological cause-and-effect pattern of events to an end. But any tragic effect the Mannons' fate has issues from the spiritual significance of their struggle rather than from their inevitable defeat. On the cause-and-effect or Freudian level of the action their striving is nothing more than a repressed sexual instinct seeking gratification, a pagan desire for love that is really an Oedipal desire for physical incest and is in rebellion against the Puritan society that inhibits it. And a struggle deriving from the desire for physical incest, which in the civilized world must always be infantile and destructive, isn't a struggle for the highest. It isn't a struggle for life itself or life in its fullest sense and doesn't allow for an effect of heroic rebirth. On a second level of the action, however, the struggle of the Mannons is a struggle for such life and does allow for an effect of heroic rebirth. The gods who participated directly in the action in the *Oresteia* participate here symbolically, making what happens of ultimate importance. On this symbolic or Jungian level the attempt to escape from Puritan repression is a flight from spiritual death, and the Oedipal desire for physical incest is a longing to return to the womb of the soul either to die or be reborn.

The Puritanism in the trilogy represents the outside world, the world of the father. Just after Christine has killed herself Lavinia proclaims, "It is justice! It is your justice, Father!" She is referring here not only to Ezra's Puritan justice but to God the Father's as well. Accordingly, when she is struggling in the last play with her wish for Orin's death, her eyes are drawn to the Mannon portraits on the wall "as if they were the visible symbol of her God." The Mannons threaten her with an inexorable retribution. And they threaten it in reality from within. For the psychological world of the father exists in the unconscious along with that of the mother. The portraits of the Mannons, especially of

Abe Mannon, are like projections of guilt from out of the family unconscious.

Yet the incestuous longing for the mother lies deeper than the father's justice, belonging to the most primitive level of collective experience. It is repressed there by the morality of the father, which alone finds expression in the outside world. The Puritan morality of the Mannon fathers condemns sexual love generally rather than just incest. But at bottom it is aimed at incest, and for this reason those who violate it must pay the ultimate price of spiritual, if not physical, death. More significantly, though, the price to be paid even by those who observe it is spiritual death. This relationship of Puritanism and death is made clear enough by Ezra Mannon himself when he talks to Christine of the past.

> MANNON. . . .It was seeing death all the time in this war got me to thinking these things. Death was so common, it didn't mean anything. That freed me to think of life. Queer, isn't it? Death made me think of life. Before that life had only made me think of death!
> CHRISTINE. . . .Why are you talking of death?
> MANNON. That's always been the Mannons' way of thinking. They went to the white meeting-house on Sabbaths and meditated on death. Life was a dying. Being born was starting to die. Death was being born. (*Shaking his head with a dogged bewilderment*) How in hell people ever got such notions! That white meeting-house. It stuck in my mind—clean-scrubbed and whitewashed—a temple of death!

Then a few minutes later he says that he has been thinking of their going off on a voyage together, perhaps to some island where they could be alone and get back to each other, for he is sick of death and wants life. The reason he suggests going off on a voyage to some island is that the Islands are an unconscious image of the longing for the mother and rebirth. In his work diary O'Neill noted his intent to place "the one ship scene at the center of the second play (this, the center of the whole work) emphasizing sea background of family and symbolic motive of sea as means of escape and release." He continued,

> Develop South Sea Island motive—its appeal for them all (in various aspects)—release, peace, security, beauty, freedom of conscience, sinlessness, etc.—longing for the primitive—and mother symbol—yearning for pre-natal non-competitive freedom from fear—make this Island theme recurrent motive . . .

Later he alluded to the "death-in-life motive, return to death-with-peace yearning that runs through the plays" and then to the " 'Island' death fear and death wish." The Islands vary in significance with the individual characters, but they always act as a mother symbol representing the deepest part of the inner world. And the various aspects are really just two. One is the longing for psychological death, which characterizes Orin and also Adam and Christine following Ezra's murder. The other is the longing for psychological rebirth, which characterizes Lavinia and also Ezra right before his murder. Only Orin and Lavinia, however, are characterized by a longing for the mother in a motivating way. Taken together, their longings make up one ambivalent desire for death and rebirth.

The sea background of the family and the symbolic meaning of the sea were brought out by more than just the position of the ship scene at the center of the second play. Actually, the ship scene ended up as the fourth of five acts rather than the third, but it was still central to the trilogy as a whole.[77] The sea's influence on the Mannons is suggested almost immediately by the family business being shipbuilding. In addition, Adam is a clipper ship captain. And there is also the recurrent sea chanty "Shenandoah." O'Neill noted after the first draft the need to "use this more—as a sort of theme song—its simple sad rhythm of hopeless sea longing peculiarly significant—even the stupid words have striking meaning when considered in relation to tragic events in play." It is sung by Seth off-stage right after the curtain rises and repeated by him sometimes on and sometimes off the stage throughout. It is sung by sailors in the ship scene as well. With the exception of a refrain sung once by Seth, the words in each instance are the same.

> "Oh, Shenandoah, I long to hear you—
> A-way, my rolling river!
> Oh, Shenandoah, I can't get near you—
> Way—ay, I'm bound away
> Across the wide Missouri!
>
> "Oh, Shenandoah, I love your daughter
> A-way, my rolling river!"

The words express a longing for the river that corresponds to a longing for the sea. Once again the symbolism is of the ambivalent desire for psychological death and rebirth in the womb of the mother. In the image of the Islands this meaning is more manifest. Soon after his return Orin speaks of them to Christine. He identifies them not only with her, his individual mother, but with the mother-imago in the collective unconscious depths.

> ORIN. ...I used to have the most wonderful dreams about you. Have you ever read a book called "Typee"—about the South Sea Islands?
> CHRISTINE. (*with a start–strangely*) Islands! Where there is peace?
> ORIN. Then you did read it?
> CHRISTINE. No.
> ORIN. Someone loaned me the book. I read it and reread it until finally those Islands came to mean everything that wasn't

war, everything that was peace and warmth and security. I used to dream I was there. And later on all the time I was out of my head I seemed really to be there. There was no one there but you and me. And yet I never saw you, that's the funny part. I only felt you all around me. The breaking of the waves was your voice. The sky was the same color as your eyes. The warm sand was like your skin. The whole island was you. (*He smiles with a dreamy tenderness*) A strange notion, wasn't it? But you needn't be provoked at being an island because this was the most beautiful island in the world—as beautiful as you, Mother!

Orin's longing for the Islands is a longing to return to the peace and security of his childhood and always remain there. When he proposes incest to Lavinia and she wishes he were dead, he realizes that the peace of psychological death he desires is to be found only in physical death. And his thought of physical death as a return to the womb of the mother is what hypnotizes him into killing himself. As if in a trance he says, "Yes! It's the way to peace—to find her again—my lost island—Death is an Island of peace, too—Mother will be waiting for me there—"

While Orin's struggle is between the psychological death of the inner world and the physical death of the outer, Lavinia's is between life and death in each world. On her return from the Islands at the beginning of the third play Peter exclaims, "Gosh, you look so darned pretty—and healthy. Your trip certainly did you good! . . . I can't get over seeing you dressed in color. You always used to wear black." Lavinia replies, "I was dead then." For her the trip to the Islands was a psychological rebirth from out of herself. She goes on to tell Peter how the beauty and the spirit of love on the Islands set her free and made her forget death. There was only the here and now without consciousness of sin, only innocence and this world. Finally she says, "We'll make an island for ourselves on land, and we'll have children and love them and teach them to love life so that they can never be possessed by hate and death!... But I'm forgetting Orin!" Her struggle at this point is the one for life in the outside world, a struggle which she loses when Orin succumbs to his guilt and kills himself. For then her own guilt becomes too great and she psychologically dies again. Seth comes on the scene just as she fully realizes her guilt after her slip of the tongue. And to let her know he is there he sings to himself the chanty "Shenandoah."

> SETH. "Oh, Shenandoah, I can't get near you
> Way-ay, I'm bound away—"
> LAVINIA. (*without looking at him, picking up the words of the chanty—with a grim writhen smile*) I'm not bound away—not now, Seth. I'm bound here—to the Mannon dead! (*She gives a dry little cackle of laughter and turns as if to enter the house*).

The mother is now lost to her, as before to Orin. She accepts her defeat by the forces of the Mannon fate within her, and the life-and-death struggle comes to an end. Yet this final defeat has a tragic effect, an exultation. The tragic effect lies in the cyclic magnitude of the struggle, which leaves the audience with an impression of passionate will strong enough to make up for the final defeat. In the minds of the audience the Mannons, especially Lavinia, derive a symbolic or moral victory from the scope of their desires and suffering, from the intensity of their life-seeking.[78]

In its perfection of psychic cause and effect *Mourning Becomes Electra* is somewhat unreal. At the same time this unreality is precisely what O'Neill was after, which is why he chose to set the play after the Civil War. He noted with satisfaction after the third draft that the "Mannon drama takes place on a plane where outer reality is mask of true fated reality—unreal realism." What is real, then, is the underlying idea of individual fate, and what is unreal are

the individual characters embodying the idea. He noted
after the first draft exactly how he intended to treat the
characters:

> Exclude as far as possible and consistent with living people,
> the easy superficial characterization of individual
> mannerisms—unless these mannerisms are inevitable finger-
> print of inner nature—essential revelations. This applies to
> main people of trilogy. Townsfolk, on the other hand, should
> be confined to exterior characterization—main characters to
> interior—Peter and Hazel should be almost characterless,
> judged from either of these angles . . .

This plan of characterization, which he carried out exactly as intended, indicates his greater concern with the idea
than the individuals. The townsfolk, who make up a kind of
chorus commenting on the action, appear at the beginning
of each play. Together with Peter and Hazel, and also Seth,
who is more or less the leader of the chorus, they provide a
contrast that sets off the main characters. And the main
characters, each of whom is incomplete as an individual,
make up one whole tragic Self, or the idea of a tragic Self.
Such a scheme, however, has one serious disadvantage,
namely that abstract characters, whether exterior or interior, are too cold for evoking more than a limited pathos.

Even the cause-and-effect pattern loses some of its per-
suasive force from being abstract. While the portraits of the
Mannon ancestors imply that the fault lies ultimately with
the Puritanism far back in the family past, the events in the
trilogy are all traced to Abe Mannon's one act of jealousy.
The original cause resides in a single event, which is too
arbitrary a beginning and makes the whole pattern seem
contrived. In fact, the heavy weight laid on Puritanism by
this construction exposes its weakness as a substitute for the
Furies of natural law, especially in the light of recent
changes in sexual morality.

If these abstractions or overperfections are taken to be imperfections, only with the writing of *Long Day's Journey Into Night* a decade later was the fate idea fully realized. Here O'Neill made his characters complete in themselves and suggested that the cause-and-effect pattern had neither a beginning nor an end. There was a balance between the unreality of aesthetic distance and the reality of emotional intimacy. And the effect in the modern theater was more exulting, more like Greek tragedy, than ever before.

Another important reason for this was the more integral use he made of ritual elements in heightening the effect. *Mourning Becomes Electra* was filled with many devices toward this end—the masklike faces and portraits, the stark green and white and black color pattern, the chanty "Shenandoah," the repetition of the action in much the same words by different characters, and the rhythm of the scene sequence.[79] Yet most of these were on top of the drama rather than embedded in it. Actually, only the sea chanty and the repetition of the action were ritualistic in the sense of singing and dancing or movement. The scene sequence was more an architectural element, while the color pattern and the masklike faces and portraits were visual elements. O'Neill, of course, felt the architectural and visual elements to be part of the ritual. And they did contribute to the dramatic rhythm. This was conclusively—because negatively—shown to be true of the visual elements by two recent revivals. Both productions were flatter than they would have been if the masklike faces hadn't been omitted and, in one case, the portraits cut down.[80] But the contribution made by such elements was necessarily limited. In *Long Day's Journey Into Night* there was only ritual in the strict sense, and it intensified the action from within. Consequently, the fate of the individual characters was felt more fully, the pathos of the action being cumulative and without undue lapses into the prosaic or the merely pathetic.

Mourning Becomes Electra wasn't the first play among the tragedies with such ritualistic or rhythmic devices. *Beyond the Horizon* had been constructed so that the two scenes in each of the three acts alternated between the interior and exterior of the farmhouse or vice versa. O'Neill even complained once in a letter to Barrett Clark of the critics' failure to take account of this as a technical experiment. In the theater there had been long waits between the scenes, and the critics had accused him of bungling the construction through ignorance. In the letter he said, " . . .if I had wanted to, I could have have laid the whole play in the farm interior, and made it tight as a drum a la Pinero. Then, too, I should imagine the symbolism I intended to convey would be apparent even from a glance at the program." What he meant the alternation of settings to symbolize was the struggle between longing and frustration. Yet the cyclic rhythm of life as a whole was also suggested, particularly by the first and last scenes of the play being laid in the open. In the original production the long waits not only drew criticism but forced him to telescope the exterior scene of the last act into the interior. The symbolism and rhythm, however, were restored by an improved scene-shifting technique in a successful New York revival in 1926. In subsequent plays he tried other devices[81] such as the beating of the tom-tom in *The Emperor Jones*; the primitive tempo of Yank's speeches, along with the choral accompaniment and the coal shoveling of the stokers, in *The Hairy Ape*; the growing mask in *All God's Chillun Got Wings*; and the dance to celebrate the birth of the child in *Desire Under the Elms*. The interior monologues in *Strange Interlude* were also ritualistid since their function was to give the drama a rhythmic intensity as much as to reveal the thought process.

In *Mourning Becomes Electra* O'Neill used most of the devices from the earlier plays as well as the new ones of the color arrangements, the recurring sea chanty and the repetition of the action. As in *Beyond the Horizon* there was a "pattern of exterior and interior scenes, beginning and ending with exterior in each play," the one ship scene being in the center of the trilogy. Again, the effect of this was to suggest both the cyclic rhythm of life and the struggle between longing and frustration. The mask of *All God's Chillun Got Wings* and those of the ritual plays proper were present in the masklife faces and portraits. And equally present was the "tom-tom from 'Jones' in thought repetition." But pervading the trilogy was a more general ritual element that was to be the essential one in *Long Day's Journey*. The play O'Neill wrote and also had produced prior to starting on *Mourning Becomes Electra* was *Dynamo*, and the importance of sound effects in the production prompted a letter at the start of rehearsals to the Theater Guild Board of Managers.

> [Bobby Jones] once said that the difference between my plays and other contemporary work was that I always wrote primarily by ear for the ear, that most of my plays, even down to the rhythm of the dialogue, had the definite structural quality of a musical composition. This hits the nail on the head. It is not that I consciously strive after this but that, willy nilly, my stuff takes that form. (Whether this is a transgression or not is a matter of opinion. Certainly I believe it to be a great virtue, although it is the principal reason why I have been blamed for useless repetitions, which to me were significant recurrences of theme.) But the point here is that I have always used sound in plays as a structural part of them. Tried to use, I mean—for I've never got what the script called for . . .[82]

Actually, he strove for the musical quality more consciously than he said. *Lazarus Laughed*, for example, had been written a few years before this letter. And he was undoubtedly conscious of the musical factor in the plays he wrote after this letter. Following the third draft of *Mourning Becomes Electra* he noted his intent to "get more architectural fixed form into the outer structure—and more composition (in musical sense) into inner structure." The architectural shape of the trilogy was peculiarly suited to it because of the abstract character or formality of the cause-and-effect pattern. On the more individual level of action in *Long Day's Journey* there was no abstraction or formality, and O'Neill naturally didn't attempt an architectural shape. Yet it was through the latter element of musical composition that he was at last fully able, as he had once said hopefully of symbols, to "bring home to members of a modern audience their ennobling identity with the tragic figures on the stage."

Three of the Mannons after Ezra's homecoming in *Mourning Becomes Electra*, **original production in 1931, with (l-r) Alice Brady as Lavinia, Alla Nazimova as Christine, and Lee Baker as Ezra**

Photo by Gjon Mili

The four Tyrones at the climax of *Long Day's Journey into Night*, **original United States production in 1956, with Florence Eldridge as Mary, and (l–r) Bradford Dillman as Edmund, Jason Robards, Jr. as Jamie, and Fredric March as James**

168

o'neill himself

Long Day's Journey Into Night was written immediately after *The Iceman Cometh* and is characterized by very much the same mood and thought. Life is understood to be ultimately unlivable, bringing man sooner or later to a choice between psychological and physical death. As in *The Iceman*, however, O'Neill's main concern was aesthetic rather than philosophic. And just as he had been able by ritual means to celebrate life even while despairing of it, he was able to make it tragic. At the same time he wrote under a directly autobiographical compulsion, which, like his despair, tended not to be tragic. But by treating the autobiographical facts freely—eliminating, condensing and changing different ones—he was able to fit them into his aesthetic scheme.

For a long while there was a stipulation that the play was to be neither published nor produced until twenty-five

years after his death. The ostensible reason was the embar-
rassment the autobiographical revelations would have
caused Eugene O'Neill, Jr., his son by his first wife, Kathleen Jenkins. According to Carlotta, Eugene Jr. had asked
for the delay since O'Neill had first intended that the play
be released right after his death. Actually, this marriage was
one of the facts O'Neill had left out, though he had allowed
it a muted presence in the name of the servant girl, Cathleen. He had always wanted to spare both his son and his
ex-wife, who was also living. In other words, O'Neill might
have had other reasons for stipulating a delay. But whatever the case, Eugene Jr. committed suicide in 1950. And
on O'Neill's own death in 1953 the play was left to Carlotta
to dispose of as she saw fit. She eventually gave it to the
Royal Dramatic Theater in Stockholm for its world premiere in February 1956. Then after José Quintero's sensitive revival of *The Iceman* she gave it to him for its American
premiere in November of that year, following which it ran
for two full seasons. There have since been many productions both here and abroad.

As with *The Iceman*, O'Neill constructed the play according to the three old unities of time, place and action. Everything occurs from 8:30 in the morning to about midnight
on a day in August 1912 in the living room of the Tyrone
family's New London summer home. What occurs is the
final disintegration of the family and, in varying degrees, of
its individual members. The house is situated quite close to
the harbor, allowing for a symbolism of the sea, the fog and
the foghorn. This is the same symbolism first used many
years before in *Bound East for Cardiff*. But where in the early
play the meaning was intuitive and vague, here it is fairly
well defined.

As before, the sea generally signifies life itself. Yet the
fog, which had once simply suggested mystery, now specifi-

cally signifies the psychological death of illusion. And the foghorn, instead of being just a reminder of inevitable defeat, now represents the unbearable pain of reality. This precise meaning isn't wholly manifest until the last act. It becomes increasingly obvious, however, along with the family disintegration. When the disintegration is revealed in all its finality, life itself is revealed in its psychologically fated aspect at the same time.

The primary figure in the revelation of both the family disintegration and the fate of psychological death is Mary, the mother. The rest of the family is dependent on her, disintegrating as a result of her breakdown and seeing their own defeat in the life struggle in hers. It is Edmund rather than Mary who finally makes the symbolism entirely clear. But what he sees in the abstract, Mary embodies in the flesh, and through her his revelations have significance for the whole family. There is an especially close bond between Mary and Edmund, and she is dependent in turn on him. Jamie is described as looking more like his father with Edmund looking more like his mother. As in *Mourning Becomes Electra*, these resemblances are psychic as well as physical.

Actually, Mary's state of mind is dependent to a large extent on Jamie and Tyrone also. She tells Edmund in the first act, "It makes it so much harder, living in this atmosphere of constant suspicion, knowing everyone is spying on me, and none of you believe in me, or trust me." Yet allowing for this interdependency of Mary and the rest of the family, she is still the one on whom the family as a whole depends. When she relapses into her morphine addiction, Jamie, Tyrone and Edmund all suffer in their individual lives as a result. In the last act Jamie returns home drunk from the whorehouse uptown, and shortly afterwards he provokes Edmund into hitting him by referring to Mary as a hophead. Edmund apologizes for the blow, but Jamie admits he deserved it.

> JAMIE. (*huskily*) . . . My dirty tongue. Like to cut it out. (*He hides his face in his hands–dully*) I suppose it's because I feel so damned sunk. Because this time Mama had me fooled. I really believed she had it licked. She thinks I always believe the worst, but this time I believed the best. (*His voice flutters*) I suppose I can't forgive her yet. It meant so much. I'd begun to hope, if she'd beaten the game, I could, too. (*He begins to sob, and the horrible part of his weeping is that it appears sober, not the maudlin tears of drunkenness*).

Mary's failure to overcome her sickness has meant the loss of his hope that he would find the strength to struggle against his sickness of alcoholism. The disintegrating effect of her failure on Tyrone is no less profound, though it isn't the basis of his own failure in life. When the still hearty Tyrone realizes Mary has gone back to taking morphine, he immediately gives way to a sad and bitter weariness. From that point on his mood varies between dull anger, grief-stricken pleading and hopeless resignation. And by the end of the day it is apparent that the pain of Mary's failure is paralyzing. Her final defeat is his. As for Edmund, the disintegrating effect of Mary's defeat comes out in his bitter hurt and despair. It isn't altogether paralyzing, but at the very least he is left psychologically crippled by it.

So in a general way Mary's fate is the whole family's. She suffers a psychological death by finally withdrawing from the painful reality of life, and this withdrawal is symbolized by the fog. Her relapse begins the night prior to the disintegration when she takes some morphine because her anxiety over Edmund keeps her awake. As there is fog in the harbor, she is also kept awake by the foghorn. Then in the morning she tells Tyrone and Jamie she knows the fog will be coming back. And she explains self-consciously, "Or I should say, the rheumatism in my hands knows .... Ugh! How ugly they are! Who'd ever believe they were once beautiful?" To her the ugliness of her hands is the ugliness of what she has become over the last twenty-five years, which is why she uses the pain of the rheumatism in them as her reason for the morphine. When she takes morphine, she withdraws from the outer world of reality into the inner world of illusion, from the sight of her hands and the sound of the foghorn into the dense and muffling fog. In the third act she tells Cathleen, "It kills the pain. You go back until at last you are beyond its reach. Only the past when you were happy is real." More than a symbol of illusion in general, the fog is a symbol of the illusion of the past. The past is what displaces in her mind the reality of the present.

For Edmund the fog is even more of a retreat than for Mary. Around midnight he returns from a long walk he has taken to the beach and finds his father alone and half drunk. Tyrone begins to chasten him about not having more sense than to risk making his consumption worse, but he interrupts.

> EDMUND. To hell with sense! We're all crazy. What do we want with sense? ... (*Staring before him*) The fog was where I wanted to be. Halfway down the path you can't see this house. You'd never know it was here. Or any of the other places down the avenue. I couldn't see but a few feet ahead. I didn't meet a soul. Everything looked and sounded unreal. Nothing was what it is. That's what I wanted—to be alone with myself in another world where truth is untrue and life can hide from itself. Out beyond the harbor, where the road runs along the beach, I even lost the feeling of being on land. The fog and the sea seemed part of each other. It was like walking on the bottom of the sea. As if I had drowned long ago. As if I was a ghost belonging to the fog, and the fog was the ghost of the sea. It felt damned peaceful to be nothing more than a ghost within a ghost. (*He sees his father staring at him with mingled worry and irritated disapproval. He grins mockingly*) Don't look at me as if I'd

gone nutty. I'm talking sense. Who wants to see life as it is, if they can help it? It's the three Gorgons in one. You look in their faces and turn to stone. Or it's Pan. You see him and you die—that is, inside you—and you have to go on living as a ghost.

The reality of life is unbearable. And existence is possible only in a state of psychological death or illusion where the fog is indistinguishable from the sea, the illusion of life indistinguishable from life itself. The illusion of life is composed of the past. But while Mary's illusion is of the conscious past, Edmund's is of the unconscious past. He says that the fog made him feel as if he were walking on the bottom of the sea. For the sea is the maternal sea, and the bottom of the maternal sea is the source of life, the libidinal depths. He says that he felt as if he had drowned long ago, suggesting the very waters of the womb out of which he first came forth and to which in the fog he returns. Being psychically like his mother, he loves the fog and finds peace only by withdrawing from reality into it. The irony is that the pain of reality is unbearable to him primarily because of her withdrawal. After Tyrone is led by an argument over his miserliness to tell Edmund about some of the things in his past, Edmund responds in a like way. He describes the experiences of mystical union he has had, and the play's vision of life is made complete.

EDMUND. . . .Then the moment of ecstatic freedom came. The peace, the end of the quest, the last harbor, the joy of belonging to a fulfillment beyond men's lousy, pitiful, greedy fears and hopes and dreams! And several other times in my life, when I was swimming far out, or lying alone on a beach, I have had the same experience. Became the sun, the hot sand, green seaweed anchored to a rock, swaying in the tide. Like a saint's vision of beatitude. Like the veil of things as they seem drawn back by an unseen hand. For a second you see—and seeing the secret, are the secret. For a second there is meaning!

Then the hand lets the veil fall and you are alone, lost in the fog again, and you stumble on toward nowhere, for no good reason! (*He grins wryly*) It was a great mistake, my being born a man, I would have been much more successful as a sea gull or a fish. As it is, I will always be a stranger who never feels at home, who does not really want and is not really wanted, who can never belong, who must always be a little in love with death!

The veil of things drawn back is the individual appearance of things concealing the oneness of all life, the oneness of Nature. It is the same veil of Mâyâ which O'Neill first read of in Schopenhauer or in *The Birth of Tragedy*. The secret is of that oneness, or of what Nietzsche called "the mysterious Primordial Unity," here symbolized by the universal womb of the sea. But almost immediately the veil falls, and he who has seen the oneness is lost in confusion again, caught between his endless desires and frustrations, longing vainly to return where he was whole. Edmund says he would have been much more successful as a sea gull or a fish, by which he means if he had never come out of the womb of the maternal sea at all.

This despairing vision of life in *Long Day's Journey* is parallel to the hopeless outlook in *The Iceman*. Moreover, the parallel extends beneath the surface. The sickness of modern life underlying the sickness of the individual characters is the same in each play. It is the sickness caused by the death of the old God and the failure of the new. At one point Tyrone tells his two sons that their denial of Catholicism, the faith they were born and raised in, has brought them nothing but self-destruction. They retort that, for all his pretending, he is no better a Catholic than either of them, and Edmund asks him sarcastically if he has prayed for Mary. After replying that he has always prayed for her Tyrone says, "If your mother had prayed, too— She hasn't denied her faith, but she's forgotten it, until now there's no strength of the spirit left in her to fight against her curse." In part the family sickness Mary embodies is the loss of spiritual strength that comes from not having anything to believe in. At the end of the second act she is alone with Edmund and breaks down under his suspicion of her relapse.

> MARY. ...I've become such a liar. I never lied about anything once upon a time. Now I have to lie, especially to myself. But how can you understand, when I don't myself. I've never understood anything about it, except that one day long ago I found I could no longer call my soul my own. (*She pauses—then lowering her voice to a strange tone of whispered confidence*) But some day, dear, I will find it again—some day when you're all well, and I see you healthy and happy and successful, and I don't have to feel guilty any more—some day when the Blessed Virgin Mary forgives me and gives me back the faith in Her love and pity I used to have in my convent days, and I can pray to Her again—when She sees no one in the world can believe in me, and with Her help it will be so easy. I will hear myself scream with agony, and at the same time I will laugh because I will be so sure of myself.

Mary's loss of will, or loss of faith in herself, is really due to her loss of faith in the Blessed Virgin Mary. Her withdrawal into the past even takes the form of a search for her lost faith. And this relationship between her withdrawal and lost faith implies the sickness of the spirit generally. When God the Mother dies, all her children suffer. In the last act Tyrone tells Edmund, "When you deny God, you deny hope." His orthodoxy, not to mention his hypocrisy, qualifies what he says, but the remark emphasizes the underlying dilemma. As life in a godless world without faith or hope is unlivable, man is ultimately led to the point where he must psychologically die in illusion or physically destroy himself. Such is the total pessimism of the play.

Yet O'Neill manages to justify life by sounding the very

depths of its darkness. *Long Day's Journey* is even the most tragic—or triumphant—of his dramas. Perhaps the ways in which it differs from *Mourning Becomes Electra* make this clear. Most immediately, the pattern of fate here is more convincing. In the trilogy the unconscious motives of the characters take a direct expression, for which reason the events appear to happen schematically. But in *Long Day's Journey* the unconscious motives take only an indirect expression, for which reason the events appear to happen naturally.

Mary's relapse and the disintegration of the family occur because she can't face the prospect of Edmund's having consumption. What makes her so weak, however, is the nature of her own sickness. Her relapse really stems from having become addicted in the first place, and for this Tyrone's miserliness is to blame. She was first given morphine by a cheap doctor Tyrone called in when she was in pain after Edmund's birth. Then her will to be cured was weakened by his failure to give her a real home. But Edmund's sickness is still what makes reality so unbearable she must totally withdraw from it. And the dependence of her state of mind on Edmund's well-being is tied up in a strange way with her past dependence on her father. Tyrone remarks early to Jamie, "What makes it worse is her father died of consumption. She worshipped him and she's never forgotten." When she is completely back in the past at the end, she says she loves Mother Elizabeth in her convent school better than her own mother. Taken together with her adoration of her father, this means a much closer attachment to him than to her mother. By inference the tie between her attachments to her father and Edmund is Oedipal.

This Oedipal element in *Long Day's Journey* is different in degree, if not in kind, from the Oedipal element in

Mourning Becomes Electra. In the earlier work the attachments making up the fate pattern are pathologically Oedipal. They are all-motivating; there is nothing else. In the
later work the pattern has other elements, and the Oedipal
attachments are only what may be called normal or latent.
For example, Mary says to Edmund, "All you need is your
mother to nurse you. Big as you are, you're still the baby of
the family to me, you know." And the lasting nature of her
attachment to her father is suggested by the simple fact that
Tyrone was friendly with him and was introduced to her by
him. At one point Mary tells Tyrone that, while she couldn't
help loving him, she would never have married him had she
known he drank so much. This is curious in view of what
Tyrone subsequently tells Edmund, although he speaks
somewhat resentfully.

> TYRONE. . . .you must take her memories with a grain of
> salt. Her wonderful home was ordinary enough. Her father
> wasn't the great, generous, noble Irish gentleman she makes
> out. He was a nice enough man, good company and a good
> talker. I liked him and he liked me. He was prosperous
> enough, too, in his wholesale grocery business, an able man.
> But he had his weakness. She condemns my drinking but she
> forgets his. It's true he never touched a drop till he was forty,
> but after that he made up for lost time. He became a steady
> champagne drinker, the worst kind. That was his grand pose,
> to drink only champagne. Well, it finished him quick—that
> and the consumption— (*He stops with a guilty glance at his son*).

The intimation is that he and her father had more in
common than Mary admits, which, along with her naiveté
and romantic imagination, must have been a factor in her
falling in love with him. The Oedipal nature of Mary's
attachments as daughter to father and as mother to son is
only implied, but the implication is both forceful and essential. For it characterizes the loss of her father by consump-

tion as a traumatic shock from which she has never fully recovered. And it makes the threatened loss of her son by the same disease understandable as something too painful for her to face, combining as it does with the pain of her father's loss in the past. When Edmund tries to tell her he is seriously ill and likens himself to her father, she responds angrily, "Why do you mention him? There's no comparison at all with you. He had consumption . . . . I forbid you to remind me of my father's death, do you hear me?"

So the cause-and-effect pattern comes down to why Edmund has consumption, which is also explained in part by Oedipal forces. The basic reason, according to Mary, is that he was born with a nervous constitution which made him susceptible to physical breakdown. And the reason for this is the state of mind she was in when she was carrying him. She was afraid of what his not having a real home would do to him, afraid something terrible would happen as had happened three years before when her second baby, Eugene, died. She still felt guilty over the second baby's death and was fearful over having another one to take its place.

The death of Eugene, then, indirectly caused Edmund to be born nervous and overly sensitive. Further, it made the birth itself difficult enough for Mary to be in pain afterwards. In this way it was an originating factor in both Edmund's consumption and Mary's addiction. Eugene had died from measles contracted while Mary was on the road with Tyrone, who had written her to join him because he missed her and was lonely. But the real cause of Eugene's death was Oedipal jealousy on the part of Jamie, and to a lesser extent on the part of Tyrone. Jamie had gone into the baby's room when he had been sick with measles himself, which is how the baby had caught them. Mary says he did it on purpose, explaining, "He was jealous of the baby. He hated him . . . . Oh, I know Jamie was only seven, but he was never stupid. He'd been warned it might kill the baby. He knew. I've never been able to forgive him for that." Then when Edmund tells her he must go to a sanatorium, she accuses Tyrone of wanting to take him away from her out of a similar jealousy.

> MARY. (*dazedly, as if this was something that had never occurred to her*) Go away? (*Violently*) No! I won't have it! How dare Doctor Hardy advise such a thing without consulting me! How dare your father allow him! What right has he? You are my baby! Let him attend to Jamie! (*More and more excited and bitter*) I know why he wants you sent to a sanatorium. To take you from me! He's always tried to do that. He's been jealous of every one of my babies! He kept finding ways to make me leave them. That's what caused Eugene's death. He's been jealous of you most of all. He knew I loved you most because—

The other reason for Edmund's breakdown is that, on top of his susceptibility to it, he has led an unstable life. The main influence acting on him in this has been Jamie's. In the first act Jamie accuses his father of picking Doctor Hardy for Edmund only because Hardy is the cheapest doctor around, and Tyrone tries to defend himself by bringing up the ill effects of Jamie's influence. Jamie denies them, but before the argument is over his jealousy of Edmund comes out. And later, while drunk, he admits his jealousy to Edmund along with always having been aware of it deep down.

The question naturally arises why Jamie is the way he is. The reason for his failure to overcome his alcoholism lies with his dependency on his mother and her failure to overcome her addiction. But the reason he became an alcoholic rather than something less destructive lies with Tyrone. Mary recalls how Jamie always saw his father drinking, how there was always a bottle of whiskey around, how Tyrone's remedy for whenever Jamie had a nightmare or stomach ache was to give him a teaspoonful of whiskey to quiet him. Still she tells Edmund that his father didn't know any better since the Tyrones were such a poverty-stricken and ignorant family.

Actually, Jamie began to drink seriously when he found out about his mother's addiction. Yet his inclination to drink was developed in childhood by his father, who in the same unwitting way also encouraged Edmund to drink. Edmund's consumption has been brought about by a whole complex of things, including his own self-willed adventures as a beachcomer in Buenos Aires and a down-and-outer in a New York waterfront dive. But by one route or another they all lead back to Tyrone, to his jealousy, his ignorance and especially his miserliness. At the same time Tyrone is no less a victim of his own family past. He is a victim both in his personal life and in his career as a serious actor, which he sacrificed to a compulsive need for security. Consequently, in the last analysis it is impossible to know where the cause-and-effect pattern began or for that matter will end.

Like the Mannons, the Tyrones are defeated by a determining force beyond their control. But as the force is more complex and subtle here than in *Mourning Becomes Electra*, their defeat has a greater reality and evokes a deeper emotional response. Moreover, *Long Day's Journey* is set off from the trilogy by its compassion. Where the Mannon Puritanism was condemned, Tyrone's miserliness is forgiven. Edmund forgives him when, moved by his father's memories, he says with understanding, "I'm glad you've told me this, Papa. I know you a lot better now." Mary expresses her forgiveness several times, as when she says to Cathleen, "I've loved him dearly for thirty-six years. That proves I know he's lovable at heart and can't help being what he is, doesn't it?" Jamie fails to understand, but that is because he is so much the victim of his Oedipal feelings, being wholly dependent on his mother and hostile to his father. In addition, he is helplessly embittered by the failure of his own life. But though he can't redeem himself by forgiving, he is at least absolved by being forgiven. At one point Mary upbraids Edmund for turning on Jamie, telling him in her detached tone, "It's wrong to blame your brother. He can't help being what the past has made him. Any more than your father can. Or you. Or I." The past alone is unforgivable, there is no one to blame. The Tyrones, who are fuller characters than the Mannons, still hold to one another in their despair. The current of emotion in the play runs in all directions and on all levels.

In fact, what mainly separates *Long Day's Journey* from *Mourning Becomes Electra* is its pathos, which derives from its music acting on its pessimism. By the time O'Neill started writing the later play his darkened outlook had done away with every possibility of a triumph over defeat, whether personal on the part of the characters or symbolic on the part of the audience. Along with the Nietzschean process of Eternal Recurrence, the Jungian process of psychological rebirth had become just one more formula or pipe dream. To be sure, the figure of the Blessed Virgin in *Long Day's Journey* is another manifestation of God the Mother. Yet the loss of faith in the old God has destroyed her life-giving power, and Mary's return to her is a psychological withdrawal or death. The maternal sea is also a manifestation of the old life-giving Mother, a manifestation of life itself. Yet life itself is now understood to be unlivable for the individual, notwithstanding its cycle of birth, death and rebirth for the race. And Edmund's ecstatic sensations of union with it have no value beyond what he experiences while they last—they are too fleeting and fragile to redeem his own life in any significant way. So there is no personal triumph over defeat by means of a transforming inner conquest. Nor is there a symbolic triumph by means of the very size or grandeur of the defeat. The tragic effect of *Long Day's Journey* comes rather from another aspect of the defeat, the aesthetic quality as against the quantity of it.

Despite the final disintegration of the family the Tyrones love one another as before. Edmund even has a greater understanding of his family and love for them than previously. The hostility between Jamie and his father is perhaps more rancorous, but underlying the rancor is the frustration of their love for Mary. This is emphasized at the climax by the appeal each one makes to her to come back to them, though they all know it is hopeless. Similarly, Mary is a victim of the frustration of her love for them. More than anything else it is the pain of being unable to prevent herself from hurting them, especially Edmund whom she loves most, which makes her withdraw from them entirely. The sum of this unrequited love on all sides is suffering. And suffering generates pathos, the aesthetic equivalent that O'Neill had long been striving for but always missing to an extent.* In *The Birth of Tragedy* Nietzsche had stated the following.

> The effect of tragedy never depended on epic suspense, on a fascinating uncertainty as to what is to happen now and afterwards: but rather on the great rhetorical-lyric scenes in which the passion and dialectic of the chief hero swelled to a broad and mighty stream. Everything was directed toward pathos, not action; and whatever was not directed toward pathos was considered objectionable.*

O'Neill didn't pretend to any great rhetorical-lyric

---

*To say that Nietzsche's pathos is really equivalent to Aristotle's pity and terror would turn Nietzsche over in his grave. But with a certain reservation this is true. They are at least analagous. And with a certain reservation Nietzsche's Dionysian communion really corresponds to Aristotle's catharsis. The reservation is essential, however. Aristotle's catharsis is brought about by the moral significance of the action. Nietzsche's communion is brought about by the aesthetic manner of the action. The catharsis is effected morally, the communion aesthetically, which is scenes, at least not in his later plays. But considering its naturalistic idiom, the last act of *Long Day's Journey* comes closer to being one than anything else he ever wrote. This is because of the poetry that Edmund and Jamie quote. O'Neill used the poetry to achieve a lyrical effect such as he himself as a writer of prose, or for that matter the modern prose theater, was incapable of.[83] The poetry was a ritual device designed to get "more composition'(in musical sense) into inner structure," as he had noted his intention somewhat vainly for *Mourning Becomes Electra*. Many of the poems are lamentations for a lost love, corresponding in their elegiac mood to the emotions of the characters in the dramatic situation. And the lyrical intensity of the poems serves the purpose of gradually swelling these feelings to the point where the audience is submerged in a pathos that is general.

The lyrical climax coincides with the dramatic climax. It is achieved by Jamie's bitter quoting from Swinburne's "A Leave-taking," following Mary's dreaded entrance when completely lost in the fog of the past. Jamie recites three verses, the first after Tyrone's desperate appeal to her to come back to them, the second after his own, and the third after Edmund's. The Swinburne poem is made to express the unrequited love of the whole family. The tragic image is of all four Tyrones, and a pathos of tragic proportions is released at the very moment the final disintegration of the family is revealed. The disintegration isn't overcome by the feeling of unrequited love on stage, but it is by the audience's experience of the pathos called up by that feeling.

why O'Neill's dramaturgy has as much importance as his philosophical outlook. Further, Aristotle's pity and terror are first created by the moral significance of the action and then released. Nietzsche's pathos is there to begin with as the emotion of all life's suffering and has to be elicited from the depths. Aristotle is a moralist and speaks a practical truth. Nietzsche is a mystic and speaks *the* truth.

As in *The Iceman*, both the Apollonian and Dionysian artistic principles are embodied in the play. The dramatic image is Apollonian, a conscious view of individual experience, but the aesthetic effect is Dionysian, an emotional upsurge which is communal. And this Dionysian aesthetic effect is achieved by means of ritual intensifying the action from within. The ritual used in *The Iceman* consists of singing and dancing, the ritual in *Long Day's Journey* of singing only. The singing in the latter, however, is present in more than just the lyricism of the quoted poetry. It is embedded in what amounts to an operalike structure of the whole drama. Throughout the first three acts there is only a suggestion of this, though it becomes stronger as the action deepens. In the first act there are no really long speeches, but in the succeeding ones Mary's become longer and longer as she recedes more and more into the past. They become like arias, as it were, set off by interludes of recitative. Then in the last act, in which there are long speeches by Edmund, Tyrone and Jamie as well, the operatic structure becomes manifest.[84]

The beginning of the last act is much like a long duet between Edmund and his father. The middle part is like a duet between Edmund and Jamie, this second duet giving way to a trio on Tyrone's return. The two duets and the trio all contain outbursts of poetry. Edmund and Jamie recite Dowson, Baudelaire, Wilde, Rosetti and even Kipling. Tyrone quotes Shakespeare, as does Jamie a couple of times rather mockingly. As for the probability of the poetry, it is always in character. Tyrone's being an actor allows for his quotes, and the reading Edmund and Jamie have done allows for theirs. The setting helps in this regard with two bookcases containing among other works those quoted. In addition, the conversation either prepares for the poetry in advance or justifies it as it comes. Shortly before quoting from "A Leave-taking" Jamie says to Edmund, "And who steered you on to reading poetry first? Swinburne, for example? I did!" The last part of the act begins with Mary's entrance. The pathos is heightened just before she comes in by her awkward playing of a Chopin waltz that she remembers from her convent days. She enters immediately after, and in the ensuing quartet, the tragic ensemble of all four Tyrones, the pathos reaches its climax.

So just as the utter despair of life in *The Iceman* is celebrated aesthetically, the inevitability of defeat in *Long Day's Journey* is made tragic aesthetically. "How can the ugly and the unharmonious, the substance of tragic myth, excite aesthetic pleasure?" Nietzsche asked. If the ugly and unharmonious are taken in this case for hopelessness and pain, the answer of Nietzsche's quoted by O'Neill in the program to *The Great God Brown* again applies:

> Here it becomes necessary to raise ourselves with one daring bound into a metaphysics of Art. Therefore I repeat my former proposition that only as an aesthetic phenomenon may existence and the world appear justified: and in this sense it is precisely the function of tragic myth to convince us that even the ugly and unharmonious is an artistic game which the will plays with itself in the eternal fullness of its joy.

With *Long Day's Journey* O'Neill finally succeeded in creating a modern tragedy equivalent to the ancient Greek. The Freudian and Jungian experiment had led him to the abstract perfection of *Mourning Becomes Electra* and then to a drama of psychological inevitability on the individual level. And through the inspiration he had first found in Nietzsche—together with the impetus given this inspiration by his pessimism—everything was finally directed toward pathos, not action. His concept of fate became moving to the point of exultation as well as intellectually acceptable.

Like *The Iceman*, the play brought both emphases of his idea of the theater together. In its naturalistic form the ritual of *The Iceman* was a celebration of the individual life struggle, and in its musical composition the life struggle of *Long Day's Journey* was a ritual of celebration.

The ritual elements in O'Neill were what constituted his power. His rhythms of word and action, his singing and dancing reinforced by his visual and architectural devices, were the means by which he communicated his personal tension. If he and the theater were both incapable of poetry in the strict sense, he was led to find another way of eliciting the tragic feelings. His tension was carried directly from the actors performing on stage to the spectators sitting out front, holding them to the drama and making them take part in it on its various levels. This tension, however, could pass only in the live theater as against the movie theater or the theater of a reader's mind. There had to be actors to do the carrying, using their voices and bodies so the rhythms could be heard and seen. There had to be actors speaking and gesturing right there, creating the impression of spontaneity but also the impression of formality, as if what they said or did had as much value in its character as a performance as in its meaning, as if there were equal importance in the acting out as in what was acted out. Life had to be imitated, or celebrated, before an audience's eyes. Otherwise the audience was left outside, observing rather than participating, and the drama appeared flat and overdrawn.[85]

One reason the movies made from O'Neill's plays have generally misfired is that the film medium is by its nature indirect. The screen acts as a third party between the actors and the spectators, cutting down, if not interrupting altogether, the flow of tension. Moreover, there is no risk in the performance, which lessens the possible reward. When

Long Day's Journey was made into a film, the director, Sidney
Lumet, elected to cut the voiced climax of the Swinburne
poetry in favor of a visual climax of rotating lights and
shadows. This was a perfect use of the medium and also a
good dramatic device since the quoted poetry was unlikely
to come off on the screen. But as a movie the play failed to
have an exulting or tragic effect despite a heightening of its
starkness. The recent color film of *The Iceman*, directed by
John Frankenheimer, had little effect of any kind, and not
only because Lee Marvin was miscast as Hickey. The same
can be said of the film of *Mourning Becomes Electra*, made in
the 1940s by Dudley Nichols, one of the few serious movie
people around at the time as well as a close friend of
O'Neill's. And the Hollywood versions of *The Emperor Jones,
The Hairy Ape, Strange Interlude* and *Desire Under the Elms*
among others[86] were of no distinction at all. The movie
screen has never been able to do what the stage image does
since ritual tension has to be transmitted from one flesh and
blood human being to another. There is a great difference
between a film of people dancing and the physical presence
of people dancing. This lack of presence or immediacy is
even more in evidence with television, where there is a
miniature screen and a scattered audience, though well-
acted, filmed TV versions of *The Iceman* and *Long Day's
Journey* still had power. The point is that a Dionysian communion, at least for the average personality, can occur only
in a group made up of both live actors and spectators.

O'Neill himself came to consider the film, even at its best,
an entirely different medium. One of the better movies
made from his plays was *The Long Voyage Home*, based on the
four Glencairn one-acters. When O'Neill saw it, he liked the
silent parts better then the talking parts. In other words, he
ended up liking what was visual about the movies rather
than what was dramatic.[87] Hollywood interested him

primarily as a source of money. Occasionally he wrote screen treatments of his plays, or tried to help with the adaptations by making some suggestions, but the film that was turned out had little to do with his art. And though he had his guilt feelings at times, the alimony he had to pay Agnes for the support of his two children made him accept almost every substantial offer. Early in 1941 he was even open to the possibility of a weekly family radio series based on *Ah, Wilderness!* and filled with patriotic and moralistic platitudes. Fortunately for his conscience, if not his finances, the deal fell through. Where there was a question concerning his own medium, however, he never compromised. Broadway was like Hollywood, "the Amusement Racket which New York vaingloriously calls The Theater," as he once described it.[88] But the particular theater where a play of his was being done was always different.

O'Neill's idea of the theater was what shaped his plays, and any evaluation of those plays must start from it. Once again, there are really only two kinds of theater, religious theater and political theater. The theater is religious when its primary intention is to evoke emotions, whether tragic or comic or in some combination. The theater is political when its primary intention is to be instructive, usually in the ways of a higher morality. Just plain commercial theater is only the religious corrupted by lack of faith. It flourishes in a culture grown cynical. In his soul O'Neill was naive. He was a man of the religious theater uncorrupted. Aesthetics took the place of formal religion with him, art made life livable. He tried to convert the theater back into a church because he had a deep psychological need to do so.

Clearly, to criticize his work for its basic indifference to moral or social questions is irrelevant, if not dull. His plays weren't meant to change people's lives through ideas, and so they weren't aimed at the intellect or geared for the intelligentsia. O'Neill wanted them to be popular in the same way the plays of Aeschylus and Shakespeare were popular. Besides, their intellectual content has far more scope and subtlety than his intellectual critics are aware of. The accusations that his work is middlebrow or simply melodramatic point up the rigidity and stuffiness of his accusers.

The question that does arise with O'Neill, though, is whether his religious aesthetic itself is valid. Taking up this question, of course, assumes that the plays cannot simply be dismissed for failing to bring off the aesthetic. It even assumes that to dismiss them on such a basis is to dismiss the tragedies of Aeschylus and Shakespeare as well. For O'Neill's plays have gone to the heart of the religious experience as much as theirs. In fact, in the middle decades of the twentieth century O'Neill has been more moving in the theater than any Greek or Elizabethan could possibly be. What one feels watching the great tragedies of the past is less an emotional than an intellectual excitement, though academicians often find it hard to tell the difference. O'Neill did what he wanted to do, however many men of cerebral temperament were left outside the pale.

Now, the question of the religious aesthetic boils down to whether it is a self-indulgence or a discipline. Socrates was anti-tragic because he thought tragedy was a self-indulgence and as such dangerous. Its music weakened the intellect and carried one back to the irrationality of childhood. But the young Nietzsche, in opposing Socrates, wasn't simply indulging himself. If Dionysian emotion was a self-indulgence, it was a necessary one. Apollonian discipline was meaningless without it. Indeed, tragedy was the discipline of giving form to that emotion, of recognizing and dealing with it. And the older Nietzsche, who had come rather grudgingly to admire Socrates, still held that view. In other words, what has guided the evoking of the tragic emotions hasn't been a pleasure or escape principle but a pain or reality principle. It has been the need to discover and come to terms with one's innermost self. If the pleasure principle had been the guide, tragedy would be decadent.

Yet then one asks how O'Neill's aesthetic can be a discipline when he tried to make the individuals in his audience submerge themselves in an unthinking whole, when he tried to evoke the longing to return to the womb. The answer is simply that he tried to make them return and be spiritually reborn. He tried to make them feel "an urge toward life and ever more life." He never left his audience in the womb, not in his best plays at any rate. In one manner or another he made the individuals in his audience emerge cleansed of their retrogressive longings. Political theater, or political art in general, tends to ignore this unconscious aspect of reality, dealing with reality mostly on a horizontal plane of social relationships. But religious theater, or religious art in general, concerns itself with just this aspect, dealing with reality mostly on a vertical plane. Its principle or discipline is to bring the basic longings and fears—the psychic forces of love and violence, union and death—into consciousness and release them. So without carefully weighing O'Neill's plays one by one, let it be said that about ten of them do this to varying degrees and the two masterpieces of his maturity go all the way. Nobody could ask more from any artist in living up to his own highminded idea of his art.

While *The Iceman* and *Long Day's Journey* were O'Neill's greatest plays, they weren't his last. Following the completion of *Days Without End* he had begun working on an elaborate cycle first conceived in 1928, if not earlier. That year he had written De Casseres of a scheme he expected to be working on for a long time to come. "It will have scope enough to contain all of life I have the guts to grasp and make my own. And it will not be like anything ever written before in its form and intensity . . . . It will have ten or more 'Interludes' in it, each deeper and more powerful than 'S.I.' and yet it will all be a unity." The scheme was perhaps tied up in his mind then with the autobiographical "Sea-Mother's Son" idea. Only by the time he started on the cycle he had given up the thought of an autobiographical sea play for the sake of more objectivity. The autobiographical emotions were to be projected back into American history, and in a very selective way. An idea for the unwritten last play in the *Dynamo* trilogy may have been the starting point for the cycle narrative.[89] But O'Neill wrote to Barrett Clark in September 1937, "There will be nothing of *Ah, Wilderness!* or *Days Without End* in the cycle. They were an interlude. The Cycle goes back to my old vein of ironic tragedy—with, I hope, added psychological depth and insight."

Taking time out for other plays, he worked on the cycle for over a decade. As a whole it came to be called "A Tale of Possessors Self-Dispossessed." His final intent was to follow an Irish-American family from the French and Indian War down through the Depression years in a cause-and-effect pattern of events and influences. The characters were to be in their youth in one play and be parents or grandparents in another. And the early experiences of the first generation of characters were to determine its later experiences, which in turn were to determine the early experiences of the next generation of characters. Many people have the impression that O'Neill's main concern here was to dramatize the failure of American materialism. But in a letter to Lawrence Langner in August 1936 he made clear that his emphasis was to be less on American materialism than on the process of inevitability itself.

I hope you yourself don't believe the Cycle is "an American life" in any usual sense of the word, or you're going to be disappointed. I mean, I'm not giving a damn whether the dramatic event of each play has any significance in the growth of the country or not, as long as it is significant in the spiritual and psychological history of the American family in the plays. The Cycle is primarily just that, the history of a family. What larger significance I can give my people as extraordinary examples and symbols in the drama of American possessivess and materialism is something else again. But I don't want anyone to get the idea that this Cycle is much concerned with what is is usually understood by American history, for it isn't. As for economic history—which so many seem to mistake for the *only* history just now—I am not much interested in economic determinism, but only in the self-determinism of which the economic is one phase, and by no means the most revealing—at least, to me.

The cycle was to be a family history like *Mourning Becomes Electra* and later *Long Day's Journey*. Along with the Mannon and Tyrone fates there was to be a Harford fate. At its furthest stage the cycle consisted of nine plays, including two double-length ones that were to be reworked into two plays each, making eleven in all. O'Neill had apparently completed more than half of these at one point, at least in rough draft. But a hereditary nerve tremor that had handicapped him in his work since 1943 finally incapacitated him altogether, and the cycle ended up by being abandoned. He destroyed everything he had done with the exception of the completed version of *A Touch of the Poet*, which was the projected fifth play, a typescript rough draft of *More Stately Mansions*, the sixth, and one scene from *The Calms of Capricorn*, the seventh.

A Touch of the Poet, which was premiered in Stockholm before running through the 1958-59 season in New York, has to do with the conflict of illusion and reality. In this— as well as in its compassionate and complex sense of character—it is like *The Iceman* and *Long Day's Journey*. Yet alone it is neither a ritual celebration nor a tragedy, and the aesthetic difference is telling. In addition, it differs philosophically by ending on a note of hope, though O'Neill put the note in a minor key by breaking his hero's will along with his pride. Major Melody is finally compelled to give up his Byronic pose, but his ensuing humility is little more than a sign of humiliation. It is the humility of lifelessness and utter defeat. His return to the arms of his maternally loving and selfless wife covers this up, and so the play appears rather optimistic or at least ambiguous. But if the cycle were complete and *A Touch of the Poet* were seen as part of the whole, the underlying idea of an inevitable fate would likely make itself felt. O'Neill even wanted to withhold the plays until they were all finished and then have them presented on successive evenings to get the full aesthetic effect of the inevitability. For this he had in mind a no-star repertory company created especially for the purpose. The idea of an O'Neill repertory group had occurred to him long before as the only way he could ever build his own kind of theater.[90]

The other cycle play, *More Stately Mansions*, was introduced in Stockholm in an edited version, cut down from about ten hours to three, in the fall of 1962. It drew mixed reactions. Then a few years later, with José Quintero directing and Ingrid Bergman in the leading role, it had its American premiere. Here again the response was less than enthusiastic. The main trouble was that the characters, left by O'Neill in extremely rough form, were still rough— their motives were abstract and their actions stilted, faults the editing couldn't remedy without adding or changing words, which on principle hadn't been done. The play might have succeeded, however, if more had been cut, enough to give the motives and actions a surrealistic quality. Perhaps in Stockholm *More Stately Mansions* will eventually receive a new and better production. The Swedes have always been sympathetic to O'Neill and kept his plays in repertory. O'Neill wanted all the last plays presented there first for that reason. Temperamentally, he was much closer to the Swedes than to his own countrymen or the English. The Swedes had given birth to Strindberg, who had taught O'Neill to sing of the horrors and beauties of the human abyss, and they had adopted O'Neill himself as a sort of orphan.

Simultaneously with "A Tale of Possessors Self-Dispossessed" O'Neill had been working on a cycle of six or eight one-act plays, essentially monologues of character revelation. This was to be entitled "By Way of Obit" (each monologue being about a person who has recently died) and something of a technical departure. He similarly left only one of these, written in 1941-42 and called *Hughie*. Like *A Touch of the Poet*, which was also put in its final form in 1942, it primarily deals with the illusion and reality conflict. A night clerk in a cheap midtown hotel is forced to respond to the pose of a Broadway "sport" because just as much as the Broadway sport himself he needs to pretend his life is something more than it is.

Seen in the context of the planned cycle, this play, too, would likely have a suggestion of inevitability or at least of deeper forces being at work. The technical departure is really a return to the mood creation of such early pieces as *Bound East for Cardiff* and *The Moon of the Caribbees*. Much of the mood is trapped in the stage directions, which are more like psychological descriptions. But these descriptions might be interpreted with lights or projections on a screen or even in more concrete ways. Actually, O'Neill wasn't that interested in the play, being content to let whoever put it on figure out his own technique. He himself would have preferred a filmed background with a sound track, which was the technique he had first thought of as an inexpensive way to stage *Lazarus*. Nothing experimental has been done with *Hughie* either in Stockholm or New York. Yet the original New York production, with Quintero directing and Jason Robards, Jr.,[91] as the Broadway sport, was strong and convincing.

In 1943 O'Neill wrote his last play, *A Moon for the Misbegotten*. It was a follow-through on *Long Day's Journey*, dramatizing an interlude in the final days of Jamie when he is beyond hope of anything but release from the pain of life in physical death. The interlude is a night of peace, the peace of psychological death in the womb. Josie Hogan, the would-be Earth Mother, is forced by Jamie's bitter suffering to give up her last hope of fulfillment as a woman. And resigning herself to being the unmarriageable virgin she really is, she becomes the Virgin Mother he needs to hear his confession and ease his last days with forgiveness. The play has its own compelling tone, its own pathos mixed of innocence and despair. But for all its evocativeness, its quality as a ritual of confession, it lacks the force of inevitability. After the passion of *Long Day's Journey* it is simply, as others have called it, O'Neill's Pietà.

Other things were left incomplete besides the cycles. Along with ideas for plays about Robespierre, Malatesta and Aeschylus, there was one about the ancient Chinese emperor Shih Huang Ti, and another about the Spanish Philip II and his brother Don Juan of Austria. The eruption of World War II had caused O'Neill to project a symbolical fantasy to be called "The Last Conquest," dealing with the attempt of Evil embodied in a World-Dictator "to stamp out even the unconscious memory of Good in Man's spirit." He had made some notes for a Negro play to be called "Gag's End." And he had also thought at one point of writing a sequel to *Ah, Wilderness!*, perhaps to prick that old bubble of fulfillment blown in a dream of make-believe.

But with all the work of the last years, finished and unfinished, O'Neill's being as an artist had already fully expressed itself in his autobiographical tragedy. Prior to the opening of *The Iceman* in 1946, he remarked that the play was part of an interlocking series, the other parts of which were *A Moon for the Misbegotten, A Touch of the Poet* and *Long Day's Journey*. The connection he had in mind was presumably the idea of psychological inevitability. Further, all four expressed, though *A Touch of the Poet* less so, the deep pessimism he felt.

Long Day's Journey and *A Moon for the Misbegotten* were pessimistic because of the family suffering he had known. *The Iceman* and *A Touch of the Poet* were pessimistic because of the dilemma he saw in human nature generally. On the one hand, there was illusion or self-deceit with all the cruelty and waste of life needed to support it. On the other, there was reality or self-acceptance with all the hopelessness and humiliation that comes from not having anything left to live for. At bottom the problem seems to have been a matter of individual egoism. For the individual had nothing larger than himself to which he could belong and to which he could surrender his egoism. There was nothing to believe in. This, of course, was the existential condition, O'Neill simply defining it psychologically rather than philosophically. In these last plays he tried to overcome his pessimism by aesthetic means. In *A Moon for the Misbegotten* and *A Touch of the Poet*, which were never really intended to stand alone and where his attempt was anti-climactic, he didn't wholly succeed. But in *The Iceman* and *Long Day's Journey* he succeeded to the extent of making the American theater equivalent to what the Theater of Dionysus had been some 2,400 years ago.

O'Neill once explained, "I do not write for critics. They are too steeped in the theater and they react from that standpoint and not from the insights of one living in life.

They see the play first and life second—whereas I write first about life and then try to cram it into a play form." Yet for the most part the life he wrote about was the one within him. The existence he justified as an aesthetic phenomenon was his own. It was an existence tortured by childhood longings, alienated and withdrawn, irreconcilably lonely. It was a constant struggle against depression and loss of will. But writing could make him feel intensely alive. And when, shortly before *The Iceman* opened, a reporter saw fit to ask him if he was happy, he could allow the artist in him to respond, "I'm happier now than I've ever been—I couldn't ever be negative about life. On that score you've got to decide YES or NO. And I'll always say YES. Yes, I'm happy."[92]

CHRONOLOGY OF FIRST PRODUCTIONS

Play	Written*	Producer	Premiered
Bound East for Cardiff	spring 1914	Provincetown Players	Provincetown, Mass.—July 28, 1916 (New York, in Greenwich Village—Nov. 3, 1916)
Thirst	early 1914	Provincetown Players	Provincetown—August 1916
Before Breakfast	summer 1916	Provincetown Players	New York, in Village—Dec. 1, 1916
Fog	early 1914	Provincetown Players	N.Y., in Village—Jan. 5, 1917
The Sniper	1915	Provincetown Players	N.Y., in Village—Feb. 16, 1917
In the Zone	early 1917	Washington Square Players	N.Y., in Village—Oct. 31, 1917
The Long Voyage Home	early 1917	Provincetown Players	N.Y., in Village—Nov. 2, 1917
Ile	early 1917	Provincetown Players	N.Y., in Village—Nov. 30, 1917
The Rope	early 1918	Provincetown Players	N.Y., in Village—April 26, 1918
Where the Cross Is Made	summer 1918	Provincetown Players	N.Y., in Village—Nov. 22, 1918
The Moon of the Caribbees	early 1917	Provincetown Players	N.Y., in Village—Dec. 20, 1918
The Dreamy Kid	summer 1918	Provincetown Players	N.Y., in Village—Oct. 31, 1919
Beyond the Horizon	early 1918	John D. Williams	N.Y., on Broadway,—Feb. 2, 1920
Chris Christopherson	1919	George C. Tyler	Atlantic City—March 9, 1920
Exorcism	1919	Provincetown Players	N.Y., in Village—March 26, 1920
The Emperor Jones	1920	Provincetown Players	N.Y., in Village—Nov. 3, 1920
Diff'rent	fall 1920	Provincetown Players	N.Y., in Village—Dec. 27, 1920
Gold	1920	John D. Williams	N.Y., on Broadway—June 1, 1921
Anna Christie	summer 1920	Arthur Hopkins	N.Y., on Broadway—Nov. 2, 1921
The Straw	1918-1919	George C. Tyler	N.Y., in Village—Nov. 10, 1921
The First Man	early 1921	Augustin Duncan	N.Y., in Village—March 4, 1922
The Hairy Ape	Dec. 1921	Provincetown Players	N.Y., in Village—March 9, 1922
Welded	1923	Experimental Theater, Inc., with Edgar Selwyn	N.Y., on Broadway—March 17, 1924

Play	Written*	Producer	Premiered
The Ancient Mariner	1924	Experimental Theater, Inc.	N.Y., in Village—April 6, 1924
All God's Chillun Got Wings	1923	Experimental Theater, Inc.	N.Y., in Village—May 15, 1924
Desire Under the Elms	1924	Experimental Theater, Inc.	N.Y., in Village—Nov. 11, 1924
The Fountain	1921-22	Experimental Theater, Inc.	N.Y., in Village—Dec. 10, 1925
The Great God Brown	early 1925	Experimental Theater, Inc.	N.Y., in Village—Jan. 23, 1926
Marco Millions	1923-25	Theater Guild	N.Y., on Broadway—Jan. 9, 1928
Strange Interlude	1926-27	Theater Guild	N.Y., on Broadway—Jan. 30, 1928
Lazarus Laughed	1925-26	Pasadena Community Players	Pasadena, Cal.—April 9, 1928
Dynamo	1928	Theater Guild	N.Y., on Broadway—Feb. 11, 1929
Mourning Becomes Electra	1929-31	Theater Guild	N.Y., on Broadway—Oct. 26, 1931
Ah, Wilderness!	fall 1932	Theater Guild	N.Y., on Broadway—Oct. 2, 1933
Days Without End	1932-33	Theater Guild	N.Y., on Broadway—Jan. 8, 1934
The Iceman Cometh	1939	Theater Guild with Armina Marshall	N.Y., on Broadway—Oct. 9, 1946
			(Circle in the Square revival in Village — May 8, 1956)
A Moon for the Misbegotten	1943	Theater Guild	Columbus, Ohio—Feb. 20, 1947
			(Carmine Capalbo & Stanley Chase production, N.Y., on Broadway—May 2, 1957)

Play	Written*	Producer	Premiered
Long Day's Journey into Night	1940-41	Dramaten (José Quintero, Leigh Connell & Theodore Mann	Stockholm, Sweden—Feb. 10, 1956 production, N.Y., on Broadway—Nov. 7, 1956)
A Touch of the Poet	1935-43	Dramaten (Robert Whitehead production, N.Y., on Broadway—	Stockholm—March 29, 1957 Oct. 2, 1958)
Hughie	1941-42	Dramaten (Theodore Mann & Joseph Levine with Katzka-Berne	Stockholm—Sept. 18, 1958 production, N.Y., on Broadway—Dec. 22, 1964)
More Stately Mansions	1935-43	Dramaten (Elliot Martin production, N.Y., on Broadway—	Stockholm—Sept. 11, 1962 Oct. 31, 1967)

*Based on O'Neill's own dates in Yale Collection.

notes

In tracing the development of O'Neill's aesthetics I have naturally followed in the footsteps of those scholars and critics who have gone down the same path. To my knowledge nobody has made the same critical turnings I have, or arrived at the same final understanding, but I had the benefit of various signposts along the way. And the more significant of these I have pointed out at the appropriate places in the notes, if not the text. Let me add, however, that my views have been accessible to others since 1960, especially in my article, "Dionysus in *The Iceman Cometh*," *Modern Drama*, Spring 1962.

For the sake of readability I have refrained from listing obvious sources or giving precise references for every phrase and fact. Quotes from the plays can be found in any edition of the plays. Information about the productions can be found in the Theater Collection of the New York Public Library located at Lincoln Center. Letters and remarks to Barrett Clark can be found in his book *Eugene O'Neill, the Man and His Plays*, letters and remarks to Lawrence Langner in his book *The Magic Curtain*. Material drawn from O'Neill's unpublished notes and manuscripts can be found in the Eugene O'Neill Collection of Yale University Library. Biographical material can be found either in *O'Neill* by Arthur & Barbara Gelb or the two-part life by Louis Sheaffer—*O'Neill, Son and Playwright* and *O'Neill, Son and Artist*. All exceptions to these rules are, of course, treated in the notes.

202

1. If one sees in religion—with its incantatory rituals and prayers—a form of musical therapy or healing, the persistent appeal of religion in the face of science and materialistic philosophy is more easily understood. At the same time religion has lost much of its force among the educated. So the need for art and drama to take the place of religion, to fill the psychological vacuum, has grown. A recurring theme in Louis Sheaffer's two-volume *O'Neill* (Boston, 1969 and 1973) is that O'Neill was an emotional hemophiliac whose wounds never healed—except temporarily as he treated them in his plays. The description is apt. And the connection between O'Neill's hemophilia, his being a lapsed Catholic, and his devotion to religious theater is obvious. An important thing to remember, however, is that emotional hemophilia, peculiar as it may seem, is a common disease.

2. Susan Glaspell, *The Road to the Temple* (New York, 1927), p. 254.

3. *Ibid.*, pp. 309-10.

4. Arthur Hobson Quinn, *A History of The American Drama from the Civil War to the Present Day*, 3rd ed. (New York, 1945), II, 199.

5. Barrett Clark, *Eugene O'Neill, the Man and His Plays*, rev. version (New York, 1947), p. 25, described O'Neill as being "familiar with Nietzsche in translation before he went to Harvard" to take George Pierce Baker's playwriting workshop in 1914. In his own letter to Baker seeking admission O'Neill wrote that he had read "many books on the subject of the Drama," q.v. in Wisner Payne Kinne, *George Pierce Baker and the American Theater* (Cambridge, Mass., 1954), p. 13.

6. George Bernard Shaw, *The Quintessence of Ibsenism* (New York, 1949, Dramabooks reprint), p. 49.

7. Kenneth Macgowan, *The Theater of Tomorrow* (New York, 1921), pp. 176-77. At the time he published this book Macgowan was an associate editor of *Theater Arts* magazine, which had been edited by Sheldon Cheney since its founding in 1916. In 1914 Cheney had published a book called *The New Movement in the Theater*, in which he assessed the developments in the European theater, especially the New Stagecraft and what he called "psychologic" drama. Macgowan's book, while focusing on the same developments, went a step further, emphasizing the religious experience as being at the core of the new theater. Moreover, his book was less an assessment than an invocation, i.e., a manifesto.

8. O'Neill, "Memoranda on Masks," *The American Spectator Year Book*, ed. George Jean Nathan et al. (New York, 1934), pp. 166-67. For the first and only use of the subtitle see the original edition of *Lazarus Laughed* (New York, 1927.)

9. Doris Alexander deserves the credit for exploring this first and most fully. See her analysis, "*Strange Interlude* and Schopenhauer," *American Literature*, May 1953, and her biographical study, *The Tempering of Eugene O'Neill* (New York, 1962).

10. Young Boswell (Harold Stark), *People You Know* (New York, 1924), p. 246.

11. Glaspell, p. 301.

12. George Jean Nathan, *The Intimate Notebooks of George Jean Nathan* (New York, 1932), p. 10.

13. Edwin Engel, *The Haunted Heroes of Eugene O'Neill* (Cambridge, Mass., 1953), first traced the influence on O'Neill of *The Birth of Tragedy* and related Dionysian currents. Yet for all his scholarship and insights he treated the phenomenon with such distaste, not to say hostility, that the spirit of O'Neill's devotion to Nietzsche was badly distorted and its full significance missed.

14. Friedrich Nietzsche, *The Birth of Tragedy*, trans. Clifton Fadiman, in *The Philosophy of Nietzsche* (New York, 1927), pp. 954 ff. for this and subsequent quotes. Actually, O'Neill used the 1909 William Haussmann translation, but for Nietzsche's sake I quote throughout from the more idiomatic one by Fadiman.

15. Nietzsche said, "The tradition is undisputed that Greek tragedy in its earliest form had for its sole theme the sufferings of Dionysus, and that for a long time the only stage-hero was simply Dionysus himself. With equal confidence, however, we can assert that, until Euripides, Dionysus never once ceased to be the tragic hero; that in fact all the celebrated figures of the Greek Stage—Prometheus, Oedipus, etc.—are but masks of this original hero, Dionysus. There is godhead behind all these masks; and that is the one essential cause of the typical 'ideality', so often wondered at, of these celebrated characters." *Ibid.*, p. 1000.

16. Macgowan wrote me in a letter dated Dec. 28, 1960, "I don't remember that I read *The Birth of Tragedy* before I wrote the *Theater of Tomorrow*, or *Themis*. While I was on the *Boston Transcript* I covered four lectures by Gilbert Murray on Greek tragedy and interviewed him also." Regarding O'Neill, Hamilton Basso wrote in "The Tragic Sense—III," *The New Yorker*, March 13, 1948, pp. 46-47, "To his right were several bookshelves. Among the books were . . . big volumes of reproductions of paintings, books on explorations, books on the habits and customs of primitive peoples."

17. Jane Harrison, *Themis*, 2nd ed. (London, 1927), pp. 443 ff. for this and subsequent quotes.

18. Francis Fergusson, *The Idea of a Theater* (Garden City, N.Y., 1954). The view has its limitations. In analyzing the ritual experience in the theater Fergusson intellectualized it, placing too much emphasis on moral perception and too little on pure emotional, i.e., musical or rhythmic, elements. Accordingly, he paid no heed to O'Neill in the book and had nothing but scorn for *Lazarus Laughed* in an earlier article, "Eugene O'Neill," *The Hound and Horn*, Winter 1930. He made what I have come to think of as the Aristotelian error, which, despite *The Birth of*

Tragedy and O'Neill, is still commonplace, even among contemporary dramatists such as Arthur Miller who have sought to write tragedy.

19. Mary B. Mullett, "The Extraordinary Story of Eugene O'Neill," *The American Magazine*, Nov. 1922, p. 34.

20. Helen Deutsch and Stella Hanau, *The Provincetown: A Story of the Theater* (New York, 1931) recorded all the ins and outs of the group's history.

21. Macgowan, pp. 248 ff. for this and subsequent quotes. The Theater of Cruelty, conceived by the French writer Antonin Artaud and described in a series of essays and letters about ten years later, was even more Dionysian than the Theater of Tomorrow. Artaud not only asked for ritualistic effects, especially dancelike movements, but for action with violence as a means of catharsis, action that celebrated life as a cruel force. Recently there has been much interest in Artaud because of the ceremonial violence in the plays of Jean Genêt and the more or less abandoned improvisations involving the audience by the Living Theater group. But it should be noted that the same intellectual and theatrical forces were already at work in Europe and America half a century ago.

22. *The American Spectator*, Nov. 1932, p. 3, then expanded for *The American Spectator Year Book*, 1934.

23. See Mardi Valgemae, "O'Neill and German Expressionism," *Modern Drama*, Sept. 1967, for the details.

24. "Eugene O'Neill Writes About His Latest Play," New York *Evening Post*, Feb. 13, 1926, p. 6. Reprinted in Clark, pp. 104-6.

25. Clark, p. 5, related that O'Neill went off to a rehearsal of *The Great God Brown* in 1926 with "a worn copy" of *The Birth of Tragedy* in his pocket. And Macgowan recalled in his letter to me of Dec. 28, 1960, that "if there were excerpts from it in the program . . . I think he supplied them."

26. "A Mystical Month on Broadway," *Theater Arts*, March 1924, p. 148.

27. For an account of the community theater movement see Macgowan, *Theater of Tomorrow*, pp. 201-8.

28. Deutsch and Hanau, pp. 60-62, stated only that the dome was the first in New York. But Travis Bogard, *Contour in Time* (New York, 1927), p. 71, has asserted it was the first in America, which seems reasonable.

29. Macgowan, in Dec. 28, 1960, letter to me: "I tried hard to get *Lazarus Laughed* produced professionally, having some correspondence with Max Reinhardt and others about it." And in April 10, 1961, letter to me: "Otto Kahn provided the money for Morris Gest to bring Reinhardt Productions—not to mention the Moscow Art Theatre—to America. Accordingly, either O'Neill or his agent, or perhaps I myself, sent *Lazarus* to Kahn, who apparently couldn't get excited about it." As for actual finances, O'Neill wrote Nathan he thought a production would cost

about $40,000—Isaac Goldberg, *The Theater of George Jean Nathan* (New York, 1926), p. 165—while the Provincetown Players later estimated $75,000. Ward Morehouse, *Matinee Tomorrow* (New York, 1949), pp. 202-3, reported that *The Miracle* cost $500,000 and made a profit of $300,000. This profit figure, though, is contradicted in "Morris Gest, Colorful Showman, Dies Suddenly in N.Y. Hospital at 61," *Variety*, May 20, 1942, p. 50, where the story is that Gest went into bankruptcy owing $600,000 from the loss he suffered in producing *The Miracle*, the show supposedly ending up on the road without money enough to pay off the actors. I assume that, where the fate of actors is concerned, *Variety* tends to imagine the worst. But either way, and allowing for the difference between *The Miracle* and *Lazarus*, O'Neill's play foundered professionally because it had to make its way in big-time show business.

30. O'Neill might also have read Jung's *Psychological Types*, published in translation in 1923, and made use of it in the mask scheme for *Lazarus*. Oscar Cargill has emphasized this, *Intellectual America* (New York, 1941), p. 699. But O'Neill's familiarity with *Psychological Types* or any other Jung work apart from *Psychology of the Unconscious* is far from certain and not especially significant. See discussion of his psychoanalytical reading in OEDIPUS section.

31. Benjamin De Casseres, "The Triumphant Genius of Eugene O'Neill," *Theatre Magazine*, Feb. 1928, p. 62.

32. Clark, p. 25; Croswell Bowen with the assistance of Shane O'Neill, *The Curse of the Misbegotten* (New York, 1959), pp. 168-69; Agnes Boulton, *Part of a Long Story* (Garden City, N.Y., 1958), p. 61. The misquoted passage among the *Lazarus* notes, which are in the Yale Collection, runs, "A God wilt thou create for thyself out of thy seven devils! Thou luminous one, thou goest the way of the creating one." Cf. the lines in "The Way of the Creating One," First Part of *Zarathustra* as translated by Thomas Common.

33. *Thus Spoke Zarathustra*, in *The Portable Nietzsche*, ed. and trans. Walter Kaufmann (New York, 1954), pp. 124-27 *et passim* for this and subsequent quotes. O'Neill first read the 1896 Alexander Tille translation, then the Thomas Common, published in 1909 and for a long time the standard one. But here again, for Nietzsche's sake, I quote from a more idiomatic version. In eliminating the bogus biblical style imposed on Nietzsche by the first two translators, as well as in adhering more closely to the German, Kaufmann is the first to render *Zarathustra* faithfully into English.

34. *Ibid.*, p. 428. Zarathustra says, "To be sure: except ye become as little children, ye shall not enter into *that* kingdom of heaven. (And Zarathustra pointed upward with his hands.) But we have no wish whatever to enter into the kingdom of heaven: we have become men—*so we want the earth*."

35. Arthur and Barbara Gelb, *O'Neill* (New York, 1962), p. 600, for reading of Bergson and Freud. In a letter about *Lazarus* to Quinn, II, 253, O'Neill said, "His laughter is the direct expression of joy in the Dionysian sense, the joy of a celebrant who is at the same time a sacrifice in the eternal process of change and growth and transmutation which is life . . . And life itself is the self-affirmative joyous laughter of God."

36. Harrison, *Themis*, pp. 208-9, and Carl Gustav Jung, *Psychology of the Unconscious*, trans. Beatrice Hinkle (New York, 1953 reprint), pp. 468 ff. The corresponding totem animal for Dionysus was most often the bull. O'Neill was also familiar with totem animal rituals through Freud's *Totem and Taboo*.

37. Gelb, pp. 602-3.

38. *American Spectator Year Book*, p. 165.

39. Bogard, p. 209n. The play was given another scaled-down student production at the University of California in Los Angeles in 1964. In the program for this latter production a reference is made to all the previous ones—Pasadena, Fordham, Berkeley and . . . Sweden! There is no mention, however, of Mexico, which, together with the lack of information about a Swedish production, suggests an error. For a thorough account of O'Neill's fortunes in Sweden through 1963 see Lennart A. Björk, "The Critical Reception of Eugene O'Neill in Sweden," Princeton University Ph.D. dissertation, 1966.

40. See Bella A. Landauer, "The International O'Neill," *American Book Collector*, July 1932, for relatively complete listing as of that year; and Jordan Yale Miller, "A Critical Bibliography of Eugene O'Neill," Columbia University dissertation, 1957, II, 448, for Bantu performance in 1936. In a letter to me dated Dec. 10, 1958, A. Chakovsky, editor at the time of a foreign literature periodical in Moscow called *Redakcija zhurnala*, verified the fate of the projected *Lazarus* production by the Moscow Art Theater: "My inquiries proved that this play was not staged in the Soviet Union."

41. O'Neill's letter to Nathan about *Dynamo* (see n. 12) was also printed in the program for the Theater Guild production.

42. The published version of *Dynamo*, which I quote from here, differs considerably from what was produced by the Theater Guild. A good many of the plays differ in print from on stage, O'Neill leaving things in for the reader that a live audience was better off without. The variations are generally slight, but after the failure of *Dynamo* he partly rewrote the play to make the theme less explicit. While this particular speech remained as before, it was originally said to Ada, Mrs. Fife's daughter and Reuben's mistress. The rehearsal script is in the Yale Collection.

43. Doris Falk, *Eugene O'Neill and the Tragic Tension* (New Brunswick, N.J., 1958) applied the psychoanalytical system of Karen Horney to O'Neill's plays, seeing them as a sequence of unstable resolutions of a

conflict between two false self-images, one characterized by pride and the other by humility. Philip Weissman, "Conscious and Unconscious Autobiographical Dramas of Eugene O'Neill," *American Psychoanalytical Association Journal*, July 1957, took a more Freudian view, seeing in the plays unintended projections of Oedipal feelings. Weissman's view has since been echoed in Bogard's study of the plays. My own view is too limited in scope to bear comparison with theirs. It is, however, not inconsistent with them. At best all such views are only partially true; they can never be exclusive. For one thing, a patient, or an author, can hardly be analyzed without his active participation. For another, the whole psychic truth might well be unknowable. The most comprehensive and, consequently, balanced idea of O'Neill's psychology is Louis Sheaffer's, developed in his two-part biography. His view of O'Neill as an emotional hemophiliac is eclectic, containing all other views, including mine. But the question in any case has little bearing on the effect of O'Neill's plays in the theater, which is all that counts. A knowledge of O'Neill's life and psyche doesn't really change one's response to his work or help in assessing that response.

44. *The Plays of Eugene O'Neill*, Wilderness ed. (New York, 1934), XI, ix.

45. Hamilton Basso, "The Tragic Sense—II," *The New Yorker*, March 6, 1948, p. 48.

46. Lionel Trilling, "Eugene O'Neill," *After the Genteel Tradition*, ed. Malcolm Cowley (New York, 1936), p. 138. Trilling is unusual among O'Neill critics because, while highly rational in temperament and very socially aware, he has sympathized with O'Neill's emotional struggles and religious concerns. See also his "Introduction" to O'Neill, *The Emperor Jones*, Modern Library (New York, 1937).

47. Parritt's mother actually takes as much from a real-life model as she does from Tiberius' mother, at least in her relationship with Larry. Her promiscuity comes from the anarchist mistress of O'Neill's companion and mentor in the early days, Terry Carlin. In fact, it is in Terry Carlin's image that Larry is drawn, though in his dramatic role Larry is directly parallel to Caligula. Similarly, Hickey has much in common not only with Lazarus but with Charles Chapin, who in 1918 murdered his wife, claimed at his widely publicized trial that he did it out of love for her, and then stuck to his claim in an autobiography published while he was in prison two years later. For an account of the Chapin case see Sheaffer, *O'Neill, Son and Artist*, p. 494.

48. Mullett, p. 118.

49. José Quintero, "Postcript to a Journey," *Theater Arts*, April 1957, p. 28. See Quintero's memoir, *If You Don't Dance They Beat You* (Boston, 1974), for his intuitive, musical approach generally. Not surprisingly, Eric Bentley's experience in co-directing *The Iceman* in Zurich in 1950

was quite the opposite. Focusing on O'Neill's line of argument, the author of *The Playwright as Thinker* found it boringly repetitious, if not also confused, and ended up cutting the play by almost an hour. The production made no special impression. Bentley tells the story as part of "Trying to Like O'Neill," *In Search of Theater* (New York, 1953). Bentley's antipathy to O'Neill, moderated of late but lasting in print some 20 years, had seemingly less to do with O'Neill's shortcomings than Bentley's own temperament. Levels of sophistication being equal, value judgments are inevitably matters of temperament, however brilliantly they may be rationalized. In this regard Bentley was strictly a man of what I have called political theater. As a devotee of Shaw and disciple of Brecht, that is the only kind he was searching for, or was then equipped to find.

50. Quoting from Jung and also Gilbert Murray's *The Classical Tradition in Poetry*, in which Murray compared the Hamlet and Orestes stories, Maud Bodkin, *Archetypal Patterns in Poetry* (London, 1934), made a strong case for the existence of the archetypal in both poetry and drama. The argument, however, needn't be based on Jung and the collective unconscious. Freudian theory, which assumes the individual to pass through stages paralleling the development of the race, allows for it equally.

51. Mullett, p. 118.

52. *The Birth of Tragedy*, pp. 961-62, where Nietzsche told the following anecdote. "There is an ancient story that King Midas hunted in the forest for the wise *Silenus*, the companion of Dionysus, without capturing him. When Silenus at last fell into his hands, the king asked what was the best and most desirable of all things for man. Fixed and immovable, the demigod said not a word; till at last, urged by the king, he gave a shrill laugh and broke out into these words: 'Oh, wretched ephemeral race, children of chance and misery, why do ye compel me to tell you what it were most expedient for you not to hear? What is best of all is beyond your reach forever: not to be born, not to *be*, to be *nothing*. But the second best for you—is quickly to die.' " This anecdote was the second quote from *The Birth of Tragedy* in the program to *The Great God Brown*.

53. Stark, p. 246.

54. Mullett, p. 118.

55. "Introduction" to O'Neill, *Nine Plays* (New York, 1932), p. xvii.

56. Martha Carolyn Sparrow, "The Influence of Psychoanalytical Material on the Plays of Eugene O'Neill," Northwestern University thesis, 1931, pp. 76-77. Much of O'Neill's letter was published by Sparrow's thesis adviser, Arthur B. Nethercot, "O'Neill on Freudianism," *Saturday Review of Literature*, May 28, 1932.

57. O'Neill's copy of *Group Analysis and Its Relation to the Ego*, signed by him and inscribed "Bermuda '25," is among the O'Neilliana at Yale. If he read it for the psychology of the crowds in *Lazarus*, he made little use of it. See n. 30.

58. W. David Sievers, *Freud on Broadway* (New York, 1955), p. 132, came to a similar conclusion about O'Neill: "Some of his most important plays owe more to Jung than to Freud, to the mystic rather than the clinical approach to human behavior. If there is one persistent theme in O'Neill, it is the search for Godhead—male or female."

59. O'Neill read the original C.J.M. Hubback translation of *Beyond the Pleasure Principle*, but I quote from the more rounded one by James Strachey (New York, 1950), p. 23.

60. Beatrice Hinkle's 1916 translation of *Psychology of the Unconscious* is the only one of the book in its original form. Jung made extensive revisions in 1952 for a new German edition, and the latter has been translated by R.F.C. Hull under the title *Symbols of Transformation*.

61. *Totem and Taboo*, trans. A.A. Brill, in *The Basic Writings of Sigmund Freud* (New York, 1930), p. 927.

62. O'Neill might have been familiar with Freud's earlier writings indirectly. *An Interpretation of Dreams* appeared in English in 1913, *A General Introduction to Psychoanalysis* in 1920. See n. 56.

63. In all fairness to Freud it should be pointed out that in his later writings, where the ego and its motives received greater emphasis as a primary force, man's psyche had more possibilities and the workings of the system were less mechanical.

64. Jung developed his libido theory in chapters V-VII, especially pp. 330 ff.

65. O'Neill's sense of the hero (see n. 53) bears the unmistakable mark of Schopenhauer. Yet it also runs parallel to Jung's sense: "The hero is a hero because he sees in every difficulty of life resistance to the forbidden treasure, and fights that resistance with the complete yearning which strives towards the treasure, attainable with difficulty, or unattainable, the yearning which paralyzes and kills the ordinary man."

66. Yale Collection, Author's Foreword to *The Great God Brown*. Published, with commentary, by Mardi Valgemae in *Yale University Library Gazette*, July 1968.

67. *Children of the Sea*, 1914, original typescript in the Library of Congress or film reproduction in New York Public Library. Conrad's *Nigger of the Narcissus* was first published in America in 1897 under the same title. For "Sea-Mother's Son" see Gelb, p. 146.

68. While *Gold* was overwritten even as a drama of circumstance and suspense, it could be played with theatrical effect if the first act were simply left out. The first act succeeds only in telegraphing the remaining four. And there is so much exposition in the remaining four that leaving out the first would hardly require a word to be added or changed. An interesting sidelight on the play, as Sheaffer suggests in *O'Neill, Son and Artist*, p. 12, is that it was a comment by O'Neill, conscious or otherwise, on his actor-father. James O'Neill's perennial stage vehicle, *The Count of*

Monte Cristo, was—spiritually if not physcially—a treasure chest filled with worthless trinkets. Again, however, such biographical insight has nothing to do with the play on stage.

69. "The Mail Bag," *The New York Times*, Dec. 18, 1921, VI, 1. In an earlier version of the play, which failed in a production try-out in Atlantic City under the title *Chris Christopherson*, the lighter element was even stronger. While the emphasis was more on the father, Anna was merely an unhappy ex-typist, not an unhappy ex-prostitute. So in rewriting the play O'Neill had tried to darken it, and to some extent he succeeded. For all the ambiguity of the ending, the final version allowed a 1923 Berlin production in which Anna, perhaps expressing the mood of Germany at the time, committed suicide.

70. Wilderness ed., III, xi. O'Neill was presumably intrigued by the figure of the deposed black ruler because of Jung's assumption that "the mode of adaptation which today is unconscious for us is carried on by the savage Negro of the present day," *Psychology of the Unconscious*, p. 433. An apparent dramaturgical influence was Gordon Craig's book *The Theater Advancing*. Sheaffer, *O'Neill, Son and Artist*, p. 28, tells that O'Neill read this in 1920 before writing *The Emperor*.

71. "Eugene O'Neill Talks of His Own and the Plays of Others," New York *Herald Tribune*, Nov. 16, 1924, VIII, 14. Quoted in Clark, p. 84.

72. Oliver M. Sayler, "The Real Eugene O'Neill," *Century Magazine*, Jan. 1922, pp. 358-59.

73. "The Ordeal of Eugene O'Neill," *Time*, Oct. 21, 1946, p. 76. The anonymous writer of this cover story was James Agee.

74. "Working Notes and Extracts from a Fragmentary Work Diary," *European Theories of the Drama*, ed. Barrett Clark, rev. ed. (New York, 1947), pp. 530 ff. for this and subsequent quotes.

75. Doris Alexander, "Psychological Fate in *Mourning Becomes Electra*," *PMLA*, Dec. 1953, first made the case for the book being reflected in the play. As for O'Neill actually getting a copy, Macgowan wrote me in his Dec. 28, 1960, letter, "I rather suspect that Dr. Hamilton or I may have sent it."

76. Quinn, II, 255, quotes a letter from O'Neill about it: "The Trilogy of Aeschylus was what I had in mind. As for individual characters, I did not consciously follow any one of the Greek dramatists. On the contrary, I tried my best to forget all about their differing Electras, etc. All I wanted to borrow was the theme-pattern of Aeschylus (and the old legends) and to reinterpret it in modern psychological terms with Fate and the Furies working from within the individual soul."

77. In the original production a five-minute intermission preceding the scene served to point up its thematic and dramatic import. The only other intermissions in the entire performance were the dinner hour after "Homecoming" and fifteen minutes after "The Hunted."

78. Joseph Wood Krutch is the critic who most appreciated O'Neill's tragic outlook, especially this form of it. As late as 1929, when he discussed tragedy in *The Modern Temper*, Krutch was convinced the genre had died with the Elizabethans, who appeared as if they would be the last to have both the religious belief in man's significance and the art essential to it. A few years later, however, thinking of *Mourning Becomes Electra*, he wrote of O'Neill that "he has created his characters upon so large a scale that their downfall is made once more to seem not merely pathetic, but terrible." (*Nine Plays*, p. xxii.) Yet Krutch's idea of tragedy—much like Francis Fergusson's, which shares its acute awareness of the religious element—is too Aristotelian. All Krutch could do to explain the effect of the religious was invoke the standard formula of pity and terror, and without any understanding of inevitability. He had little sense of the musical nature of tragedy, of pathos as a communal emotion released by ritual.

79. O'Neill also tried real masks, half-size à la *Lazarus*, and interior monologues à la *Interlude* in the course of the four drafts he wrote. As he explains in his notes, he eliminated these devices as such because they slowed down or confused the action rather than intensified it.

80. Michael Kahn directed one revival for the American Shakespeare Festival in Stratford, Conn., summer 1971, and Theodore Mann the other for the Circle in the Square in New York, winter 1973. Both productions were hopelessly earthbound because they attempted to make the trilogy realistic, which is why the masklike faces were omitted. Such an attempt betrays a basic lack of understanding of what O'Neill was about. He didn't want realism here but stylization, and the masks were part of that. For the final draft he noted, "Keep mask conception—but as Mannon *background*, not foreground:—what I want from this mask concept is a dramatic arresting visual symbol of the separateness, the fated isolation of this family, the mark of their fate which makes them dramatically distinct from the rest of the world—I see now how to retain this effect without the use of built masks—by make-up—in *repose* (that is, *background*) the Mannon faces are like life-like death masks... I can visualize the death-mask-like expression of characters' faces in repose suddenly being torn open by passion as extraordinarily effective—moreover, it's exact visual representation of what I want expressed..." In addition, when revising his "Memoranda on Masks" in 1934, he said, "I should like to see 'Mourning Becomes Electra' done entirely with masks, now that I can view it solely as a psychological play, quite removed from the confusing preoccupations the Classical derivation of its plot once caused me." If anything, the masklike faces should have been abandoned for real masks, not real faces, particularly when the workings of extreme Puritanism have come to seem comical on a realistic plane. Unfortunately, the ordinary Ameri-

can director, like the ordinary American playwright, has only a social imagination.

81. For O'Neill on the rhythm in *Beyond the Horizon* and *The Hairy Ape*, see Mullett, p. 118. Every movement in the plays from singing and dancing to dining and smoking has been traced by Egil Törnqvist, *A Drama of Souls* (New Haven, Conn., 1969). Yet what finally emerges is an indiscriminate catalogue. A much more reasoned and sensitive study of O'Neill's dramaturgy is the one by Timo Tiusanen, *O'Neill's Scenic Images* (Princeton, N.J., 1968). Even the latter, however, fails to fathom O'Neill's aesthetic purposes. To do that it is necessary to consider not only what is happening on stage but in the audience.

82. Theresa Helburn, *A Wayward Quest* (Boston, 1960), pp. 260-61. Actually, Phillip Moeller, who directed five O'Neill plays for the Theater Guild, was also aware of their musical structure. See Sheaffer, *O'Neill, Son and Artist*, pp. 428 & 489; and *Boston Herald*, Dec. 31, 1933, p. 28.

83. Lionel Abel, "O'Neill and His Critics," *The New Leader*, Jan. 6, 1958, pp. 25-26, made clear that O'Neill, while never managing to rise above prose, still had a superior command of language. Examining Krutch's assumption, stated apologetically more than once, that O'Neill was an eminent dramatist despite being a faulty writer, he argued: "What matters on the stage is not that a speech should be elegant—unless the character is—but that the words spoken should be discovered by the character himself in the act of saying them. O'Neill was certainly able to make characters speak authentically at the critical points of their life experience . . ." This holds true of the characters, even when quoting poetry, at the climax of *Long Day's Journey*.

84. Actually, there are aria-like speeches in many of the plays. For one thing, they came naturally to O'Neill's musical instinct. For another, he found them the best means of expressing the inner reality of his characters. Partly for this reason the plays are very adaptable into opera. So far *The Emperor Jones* and *Mourning Becomes Electra* have made their way to the stage of the Metropolitan, the latter with considerable force. *The Emperor* had music and a libretto by Louis Gruenberg and was premiered in 1933; *Electra* had music by Marvin David Levy with a libretto by Henry Butler and was premiered in 1964. In addition, *Ile* was set to music by Beatrice Laufer and performed in 1958 at the Blanche Theatern in Stockholm. The operatic possibilities for *Long Day's Journey* are obvious.

85. In the last analysis ritual, or pathos evoked by ritual means, might be all that is needed for a tragic theater. A personal or symbolic triumph of the characters over inevitable defeat could be foregone if the audience experienced an aesthetic triumph. Even the inevitability of the characters' defeat could be foregone if the defeat then suffered still had a universal significance. Such is the case, for example, in Chekhov's *The Three Sisters*, where the defeat of the characters stems simply from human

vulnerability, from the vanity of human designs and desires, and where a pathos of communal proportions is evoked, at least when the play is produced with feeling for its rhythmic structure.

86. *Anna Christie* was made into a film twice, first into a silent film and then into a talkie with Garbo. *Ah, Wilderness!* was turned into a musical called *Summer Holiday*. And a melodrama under the title of *The Constant Woman* was loosely drawn from O'Neill's apprentice play *Recklessness*. None of these amounted to anything either.

87. Helbrun, pp. 276-77.

88. Yale Collection, note to Lawrence Langner, dated Jan. 27, 1934, on special set of uncorrected page proofs of *Days Without End*.

89. See Sheaffer, *O'Neill, Son and Artist*, pp. 440-41.

90. Helburn, p. 269.

91. Much of the credit for the impact made by O'Neill's last plays in New York must go to Robards, evidently something of an O'Neill character personally. With great perception and sense of theater he also created an astonishing Hickey in the first revival of *The Iceman*, a poignant while bitter Jamie in the premiere of *Long Day's Journey*, and a very human ghost of Jamie in the highly successful 1973 revival of *Moon for the Misbegotten*.

92. *Time*, Oct. 21. 1946, p. 76.

select bibliography

Abel, Lionel. "O'Neill and His Critics." *The New Leader* 41 (Jan. 6, 1958), 25-26.

Alexander, Doris. "Psychological Fate in Mourning Becomes Electra." *PMLA*, 68 (Dec. 1953), 923-34.

———. "*Strange Interlude* and Schopenhauer." *American Literature*, 25 (May 1953), 213-28.

———. *The Tempering of Eugene O'Neill.* New York: Harcourt, Brace and World, 1962.

Basso, Hamilton. "The Tragic Sense." *The New Yorker* 24 (Feb. 28, 1948), 34-38; (Mar. 6), 34-38; (Mar. 13), 37-40.

Bentley, Eric. *In Search of Theater.* New York: Knopf, 1953.

Bodkin, Maud. *Archetypal Patterns in Poetry.* London: Oxford University Press, 1934.

Bogard, Travis. *Contour in Time: the Plays of Eugene O'Neill.* New York: Oxford University Press, 1972.

Boulton, Agnes. *Part of a Long Story.* Garden City, N.Y.: Doubleday, 1958.

215

Bowen, Croswell, with the assistance of Shane O'Neill. *The Curse of the Misbegotten*. New York: McGraw-Hill, 1959.

Brustein, Robert. *The Theater of Revolt*. Boston: Little, Brown, 1964.

Cargill, Oscar. *Intellectual America*. New York: Macmillan, 1941.

Chabrowe, Leonard. "The Classical Idea in Eugene O'Neill." Columbia University Master's thesis, 1960.

———. "Dionysus in *The Iceman Cometh*." *Modern Drama* 4 (Spring 1962), 377-88.

Clark, Barrett H. *Eugene O'Neill, the Man and His Plays*. Rev. version. New York: Dover, 1947.

Deutsch, Helen, and Stella Hanau. *The Provincetown: A Story of the Theater*. New York: Farrar and Rinehart, 1931.

Engel, Edwin A. *The Haunted Heroes of Eugene O'Neill*. Cambridge, Mass.: Harvard University Press, 1953.

Falk, Doris. *Eugene O'Neill and the Tragic Tension*. New Brunswick, N.J.: Rutgers University Press, 1958.

Fergusson, Francis. "Eugene O'Neill." *The Hound and Horn* 3 (Winter 1930), 145-60.

———. *The Idea of a Theater*. Garden City, N.Y.: Doubleday Anchor, 1954.

Freud, Sigmund. *Beyond the Pleasure Principle*. Trans. James Strachey. New York: Liveright, 1950.

———. *Totem and Taboo*. Trans. A.A. Brill. Rpt. in *The Basic Writings of Sigmund Freud*. New York: Modern Library. 1938.

Gelb, Arthur and Barbara. *O'Neill*. New York: Harper and Row, 1962.

Glaspell, Susan. *The Road to the Temple*. New York: Stokes, 1927.

Hamilton, G.V., and Kenneth Macgowan. *What Is Wrong with Marriage*. New York: Albert and Charles Boni, 1929.

Harrison, Jane. *Themis*. 2nd ed. London: Cambridge University Press, 1927.

Helburn, Theresa. *A Wayward Quest*. Boston: Little, Brown, 1960.

Jones, Robert Edmond, and Kenneth Macgowan. *Continental Stagecraft*. New York: Harcourt, Brace, 1922.

Jung, Carl Gustav. *Psychology of the Unconscious*. Trans. Beatrice Hinkle. Rpt. New York: Dodd, Mead, 1953.

Kinne, Wisner Payne. *George Pierce Baker and the American Theater*. Cambridge, Mass.: Harvard University Press, 1954.

Krutch, Joseph Wood. "Introduction," in Eugene O'Neill, *Nine Plays*. New York: Modern Library, 1932.

———. *The Modern Temper*. New York: Harcourt, Brace, 1929.

———. "O'Neill Again." *The Nation* 134 (Feb. 17, 1932), 210-11.

Langner, Lawrence. *The Magic Curtain*. New York: Dutton, 1951.

Macgowan, Kenneth. *The Theater of Tomorrow*. New York: Boni and Liveright, 1921.

——— and Herman Rosse. *Masks and Demons*. New York: Harcourt, Brace, 1921.

Mullett, Mary B. "The Extraordinary Story of Eugene O'Neill." *The American Magazine* 94, (Nov. 1922), 34.

Nathan, George Jean. *The Intimate Notebooks of George Jean Nathan*. New York: Knopf, 1932.

Nethercot, Arthur H. "O'Neill on Freudianism." *Saturday Review of Literature* 8 (May 28, 1932), 759.

Nietzsche, Friedrich. *The Birth of Tragedy*. Trans. Clifton Fadiman, in *The Philosophy of Nietzsche*. New York: Modern Library, 1927.

———. *Thus Spoke Zarathustra*, in *The Portable Nietzsche*. Ed. and trans. Walter Kaufmann. New York: Viking, 1954.

O'Neill, Eugene. Author's Foreword to *The Great God Brown*. Eugene O'Neill Collection at Yale University Library. See also Valgemae.

———. "Working Notes and Extracts from a Fragmentary Work Diary." *European Theories of the Drama*, ed. Barrett H. Clark. Rev. ed. New York: Crown, 1947.

O'Neill and His Plays: Four Decades of Criticism. Ed. Oscar Cargill, N. Bryllion Fagin and William J. Fisher. New York: New York University Press, 1961.

"The Ordeal of Eugene O'Neill." *Time* 48 (Oct. 21, 1946), 71-72.

Quinn, Arthur Hobson. *A History of the American Drama from the Civil War to the Present Day*. 3rd ed. New York: Appleton-Century-Crofts, 1945.

Quintero, José. "Postscript to a Journey." *Theater Arts* 41 (April 1957), 27-29.

―――. *If You Don't Dance They Beat You*. Boston: Little, Brown, 1974.

Raleigh, John Henry. *The Plays of Eugene O'Neill*. Carbondale: Southern Illinois University Press, 1965.

Sayler, Oliver M. "The Real Eugene O'Neill." *The Century Magazine* 103 (Jan. 1922), 351-59.

Sheaffer, Louis. *O'Neill, Son and Playwright*. Boston: Little, Brown, 1968.

―――. *O'Neill, Son and Artist*. Boston: Little, Brown, 1973.

Sievers, W. David. *Freud on Broadway*. New York: Hermitage House, 1955.

Sparrow, Martha Carolyn. "The Influence of Psychoanalytical Material on the Plays of Eugene O'Neill." Northwestern University Master's thesis, 1931.

Törnquist, Egil. *A Drama of Souls: Studies in O'Neill's Super-Naturalistic Technique*. New Haven, Conn.: Yale University Press, 1969.

Tuisanen, Timo. *O'Neill's Scenic Images*. Princeton, N.J.: Princeton University Press, 1968.

Trilling, Lionel. "Eugene O'Neill," in *After the Genteel Tradition*, ed. Malcom Cowley. New York: Norton, 1936.

―――. "Introduction," in Eugene O'Neill, *The Emperor Jones*. New York: Modern Library, 1937.

Valgemae, Mardi. "Eugene O'Neill's Preface to *The Great God Brown*." *Yale University Library Gazette* 43 (July 1968), 24-29.

―――. "O'Neill and German Expressionism." *Modern Drama* 10 (Sept. 1967), 111-23.

Weissman, Philip, M.D. "Conscious and Unconscious Autobiographical Dramas of Eugene O'Neill." *American Psychoanalytical Association Journal* 5 (July 1957), 432-60.

Young Boswell (Harold Stark). *People You Know.* New York: Boni and Liveright, 1924.

index

Abbey Theater, 60
Abel, Lionel, 213 n83
Adams, Henry, 61
Aeschylus, 12, 15, 146, 190, 196, 211 n76
Agee, James, 211 n73
Ah, Wilderness!, 66-67, 129, 142, 192, 196; as film, 2R4 n86; or radio, 189
Alexander, Doris, 203 n9, 211 n75
Alienation, xxii, 121-25
All God's Chillun Got Wings, 22, 25-26, 48, 126-28, 164-65; in Russia, 125
American Mercury, 126
American Shakespeare Festival, 212 n80
Anarchism, 79, 90, 125-26, 208nn47
Ancient Mariner, The (O'Neill adaptation), 22, 25-26
Anderson, Maxwell, 128
Anna Christie, 16, 117, 119-20, 134, 211 n69; in Berlin, 211 n69; in Russia, 125; as film, 214 n86
Apollo: as Year-God, 11-12; as individualizing principle, 3-5, 8, 14, 45, 98, 185, 190; as natural law, 148

Appia, Adolphe, xvii, 20
Archetypes: in characterization, 17-18, 113, 129, 134; in plot, 75, 96-97, 209 n50. *See also* Collective unconscious; Oedipus complex; *Totem and Taboo*
Aristotle. *See* Tragedy
Artaud, Antonin, 205 n21

Baker, George Pierce, 37, 203 n5
Baker, Lee, 167 (fig.)
Barton, James, 71 (fig.)
Basso, Hamilton, 204 n16
Baudelaire, Charles, 185
Belasco, David, 32
Bentley, Eric, 208 n49
Bergman, Ingrid, 194
Bergson, Henry, 49
Beyond the Horizon, xxi, 16, 117-18, 120, 164-65
Beyond the Pleasure Principle (Freud), 107-9
Bible, 19, 25, 42, 46, 49
Birth of Tragedy, The (Nietzsche): basic concepts of, 2-8, 204 n15; affirmed

220

by Cambridge School, 12-14; influence on O'Neill, xvii, 8, 14, 28-29, 41, 53-58, 94, 98-99, 175, 183, 186, 204 nn13 & 16, 205 n25, 209 n52 (*see also* Imaginative Theater; Pathos; Ritual)
Bodkin, Maud, 209 n50
Bogard, Travis, 57, 205 n28, 208 n43
Boris Godunov (Moussorgsky), 56
Boulton, Agnes, 24, 46, 64, 140-41, 143, 145, 189
Bound East for Cardiff, xiii, 102, 115-16, 124, 170, 195
Brady, Alice, 167 (fig.)
Brecht, Bertold, 209 n43
Brown, Gilmor, 40
Buddhism, 31-32, 44, 104
Butler, Henry, 213 n84
"By Way of Obit," 195

Caliban (P. MacKaye), 36-37
Calms of Capricorn, The, 193
Cambridge School of Classical Anthropologists, 8-14, 204 n16
Cargill, Oscar, 206 n30
Carlin, Terry, 208 n46
Catholicism, 60, 63-65, 175-76, 182, 203 n1. *See also* Christianity
Chaliapin, Fyodor, 56
Chapin, Charles, 208 n46
Chekhov, Anton, 213 n85
Cheney, Sheldon, 203 n7
"Children of the Sea," 116
Chorus: in Nietzsche, 6-8; in Harrison & Murray, 13; in Reinhardt, 20-21; in O'Neill, 16-18, 30-33, 54, 57, 74-77, 89, 91-96, 162, 164. *See also* Music
Chris Christopherson, 134, 211 n69
Christianity, 25, 28, 43-45, 48, 51-53, 104, 128. *See also* Catholicism
Circle in the Square, 96, 212 n80
Clark, Barrett, xxiii, 56, 58-59, 73-74, 104-5, 164, 192, 203 n5, 205 n25
Cohan, George M., 69
Coleridge, Samuel Taylor, 25
Collective unconscious, 16, 113-14, 209 n50; in plays, xxii, 105, 121-24, 127-28, 130-33, 137-38, 156-59, 211 n70. *See also* Archetypes; Jung

Common, Thomas, 206 n32-33
Community Drama, 36-37
Conrad, Joseph, 116, 210 n67
Continental Stagecraft (Jones & Macgowan), 21-22
Cook, George Cram, xiv, xvii, 1, 8, 16, 38, 102
Count of Monte Cristo, The (stage adaptation), 210 n68
Craig, Gordon, xvii, 20, 211 n70
Criticism & Critics. *See* O'Neill
Cycle, 191-95
Cyclorama, 37-38

Dancing. *See* Ritual
Dante, 38
Darwinism, 19
Days Without End, 60-61, 63-67, 105, 142, 191-92
De Casseres, Benjamin, 44-45, 61, 191
Desire Under the Elms, xvi, 106, 114, 120, 122, 128-134, 150, 164; in Russia, 125; as film, 188
Diff'rent, 122
Dillman, Bradford, 168 (fig.)
Dionysus: as Year-God, 11-13, 51, 207 n36; as communion principle, in Nietzsche, 3, 6-8, 14, 44, 183, 190, 204 n15, 209 n52, and in O'Neill et al., xvi, xviii, 21, 27-30, 42, 44-45, 49, 68, 98-99, 142, 185, 188, 204 n13, 205 n21 (*see also Birth of Tragedy*)
Dithyramb, 13, 29-30, 53, 96. *See also* Chorus; Interior monologues; Repetition, in dialogue
Divine Comedy, The (Geddes adaptation), 38
Dome. *See* Cyclorama
Don Juan of Austria, 196
Dowson, Ernest, 185
Dvorak, Antonin, 36
Dynamo, 1-2, 59-63, 66-67, 105, 165, 192, 207 nn41 & 42

Ecce Homo (Nietzsche), 44
Education of Henry Adams, The (Adams), 61
Eldridge, Florence, 168 (fig.)
Electra (Hofmannsthal), 142

Emperor Jones, The, xxii, 16, 38, 105, 113, 120-23, 164, 211 n70; as film, 188; as opera, 213 n84
Engel, Edwin, 204 n13
Eternal Recurrence, xviii, 26-27, 44, 48, 50-53, 59, 66-67, 77, 86-87, 89, 182. *See also Thus Spoke Zarathustra*
Euripides, 8, 204 n15
Everyman (Hofmannsthal), 21
Experimental Theater, Inc., xvii-xviii, 19-28 passim, 32, 39, 126-28
Expressionists, German, 23

Falk, Doris, 207 n43
Fadiman, Clifton, 204 n14
Fate, xv-xvi, xx-xxii, 101-2, 106-15; as circumstance, 116-20; as internal, primitive forces, 120-24, 127-28; as Oedipal forces, 129-34, 143-46, 149-56, 161-62, 211 n76; as psychological forces generally, 171-72, 177-81, 192-97
Faust (Goethe), 22-23, 65
Fergusson, Francis, 14, 204 n18, 212 n78
Festspiel (Hauptmann), 21
Films: for the plays, 55, 195; of the plays, 187-89, 214 n86
First Man, The, 16, 18-19, 24, 26-27, 122
Fog, xviii, 2, 16, 28
Fountain, The, xviii, 16, 26-27, 123
Frankenheimer, John, 188
Freud, Sigmund, xx-xxi, 20, 49, 102-17 passim, 129, 135-36, 139, 156, 186, 207 n36, 208 n43, 209 n50, 210 nn58, 62 & 63. *See also* Oedipus complex; Repetition, of past

"Gag's End," 196
Garbo, Greta, 214 n86
Geddes, Norman-Bel, 35, 38-39; ii (fig.)
General Introduction to Psychoanalysis, A (Freud), 210 n62
Genêt, Jean, 205 n21
Gest, Morris 32-33, 35, 206 n29
Ghost Sonata, The. See Spook Sonata
Glaspell, Susan, 1, 102
"Glencairn." *See* "S.S. Glencairn"

Gold, 117-18, 210 n68
Gorki, Maxim, 98-99
Götterdämmerung, Die (Wagner), 57
Great God Brown, The, xvi, xviii, 22, 26-30, 39, 43-44, 52; *Birth of Tragedy* quoted in program, 99, 186, 205 n25, 209 n52
Green, Paul, 54-55
Group Psychology and the Analysis of the Ego (Freud), 105, 209 n57
Gruenberg, Louis, 213 n84

Hairy Ape, The, 16-18, 26, 113, 123-25, 164; in Russia, 125; in S. Africa, 58; as film, 188
Hamilton, Gilbert van Tassle, 140-43, 150, 211 n75
Hamlet, 15, 209 n50
Harrison, Jane, 9-14, 204 n16
Hauptmann, Gerhart, 21
Haussmann, William, 204 n14
Hell Hole, 73-74
Herbert, Victor, 36
Higher man, 46-47, 50-51, 64, 66, 86, 109, 125. *See also Thus Spoke Zarathustra*
Hinkle, Beatrice, 210 n60
Hofmannsthal, Hugo von, 142. *See also Everyman*
Horney, Karen, 207 n43
Howells, William Dean, xiv
Hubback, C. J. M., 210 n59
Hughie, 195-96
Humperdinck, Engelbert, 35
Huston, Walter, 129
Hyde, James, 40

Ibsen, Henrik, xiii, xvii, 98-99
Iceman Cometh, The, xvi-xvii, xix-xx, 58-60, 67-68, 73-99, 105, 169-70, 185-87, 191, 194, 197, 208 n47; 214 n91; O'Neill interview for premiere, 126, 198; in Zurich, 208 n49; as film, 188; on TV, 188; 71-72 (figs.)
Ile, 117; as opera, 213 n84
Imaginative Theater, xviii, 33, 41, 53, 74, 93, 203 n8. *See also* Dionysus; Ritual

In the Zone, 116-17
Inevitability. *See* Fate
Interior monologues, 134, 139, 212
    n79. *See also* Chorus; Dithyramb;
    Repetition, in dialogue
Interpretation of Dreams, An (Freud),
    102, 210 n62

Jenkins, Kathleen, 170
Jimmy the Priest's, 73
John, Saint, 25, 42, 49
Jones, Robert Edmond, xvii-xviii, 19,
    21, 36, 39, 165
Joyce, James, 134
Jung, Carl Gustav, xx-xxi, 16, 20, 42,
    48, 52, 97, 102-17 passim, 129-30,
    133, 137, 156, 182, 186, 206 n30,
    209 n50, 210 nn58, 60 & 65, 211
    n70. *See also* Collective unconscious,
    Oedipus complex

Kahn, Michael, 212 n80
Kahn, Otto, 39, 205 n29
Kaiser, Georg, 23
Kaufmann, Walter, 206 n33
King Lear, 15
Kinsey, Alfred, 143
Kipling, Rudyard, 185
Krutch, Joseph Wood, 101, 212 n78,
    213 n83

Langner, Lawrence, 59, 66, 95, 192
"Last Conquest, The," 196
Laufer, Beatrice, 213 n84
Lawson, John Howard, 128
Lazarus Laughed, xvi, xviii-xix, 21-22,
    25, 38-58, 63, 66, 104-5, 165, 196,
    203 n8, 204 n18, 205 n29, 206 nn30
    & 32, 207 n35, 209 n57, 212 n79; as
    basis for *Iceman*, xix-xx, 59-60, 68,
    73-78, 86-99 passim; productions,
    in Pasadena, 40-41, 54, 56-58, in
    Mexico, 58, at Fordham, 57, in
    Berkeley, 57, and at UCLA, 207
    n39; ii, 69-70 (figs.)
Levy, Marvin David, 213 n84
Lincoln Center Repertory Company,
    32

Little Theater movement. *See*
    individual companies
Living Theater, 205 n21
Long Day's Journey Into Night, xvi,
    xxii-xxiii, 133, 163-66, 169-87,
    191-97 passim, 213 nn83 & 84, 214
    n91; as film, 188; on TV, 188; 168
    (fig.)
Long Voyage Home, The, 117; as film,
    188
Lower Depths, The (Gorki), 98-99
Lumet, Sidney, 188

Macbeth, 15
Macgowan, Kenneth, xvii-xviii, 8,
    19-22, 26, 33, 35, 39-41, 128, 140,
    142-45, 203 n7, 204 n16, 205 nn25
    & 29, 211 n75
MacKaye, Percy, 36-37
MacKaye, Steele, 36-38
Maeterlinck, Maurice, 34
Malatesta, Errico, 126, 146, 196
Mann, Theodore, 212 n80
March, Fredric, 168 (fig.)
Marco Millions, xvi, xviii, 22, 30-32, 39,
    54, 61-62
Marvin, Lee, 188
Masks, xviii, 21-23, 25-32, 42, 54-57,
    65-66, 127-28, 163-65, 204 n15, 206
    n30, 212 nn79 & 80
Masks and Demons (Macgowan & Rosse),
    21-22, 38
Mâyâ, veil of, 5, 6, 175
"Memoranda on Masks," 22-23, 27,
    65-66, 212 n80
Mencken, H. L., xvii
Metropolitan Opera, 213 n84
Miller, Arthur, 205 n18
Miracle, The (Vollmoeller), 21, 34-41,
    53, 57, 206 n29
Moeller, Philip, 62, 213 n82
Monterey, Carlotta, 40, 59, 63-65,
    141-42, 145, 170
Moon of the Caribbees, The, 17, 116-17,
    195
Moon for the Misbegotten, A, 196-97, 214
    n91
More Stately Mansions, 193-94
Morehouse, Ward, 206 n29

Moscow Art Theater, 58, 205 n29, 207 n40
Mourning Becomes Electra, xvi, xx, xxii, 59, 67, 104-8, 122, 139, 142-66, 171, 193, 211 n77, 212 nn78, 79 & 80; in relation to *Long Day's Journey*, 163-66, 177-86 passim; as film, 188; as opera, 213 n84; 167 (fig.)
Murray, Gilbert, 8, 9, 13, 204 n16, 209 n50
Music: in theater generally, 3, 5-7, 20, 35-36, 40-41, 203 n1, 204 n18, 205 n21, 212 n78; in O'Neill, 40-41, 56-57, 74-75, 94-96, 158-59, 163-66, 183-87, 213 nn81, 82 & 84. *See also* Chorus
Myth, 7-8, 13-14, 19, 98-99, 101, 106, 111-13, 129, 139, 142, 186. *See also* Dionysus; Jung; Oedipus complex; *Oresteia*

Nathan, George Jean, xvii, 1, 19, 61, 95, 126, 205 n29
Nazimova, Alla, 167 (fig.)
Neighborhood Playhouse, xiii, 18, 36
Nemirovitch-Dantchenko, 58, 125
New Stagecraft, xvii, 20-23, 35, 37, 203 n7
Nichols, Dudley, 188
Nietzsche, Friedrich, xvii, xx, xxiii, 1-8 passim, 12, 14, 23-24, 26, 28, 40-50 passim, 64, 66, 98-99, 104, 109, 113, 125, 175, 182-83, 186, 190, 203 n5, 204 nn13 & 15, 209 n52. *See also* Eternal Recurrence
Nigger of the Narcissus (Conrad), 210 n67
Nobel Prize, 24, 66

Oedipus complex, 106-15 passim, 119-20, 122, 129-34, 136, 144-45, 149-56, 177-80, 182, 208 n43. *See also* Freud; Jung
Oedipus Rex, xx, xxii, 21, 101
O'Neill, Agnes. *See* Boulton
O'Neill, Carlotta. *See* Monterey
O'Neill, Eugene: criticism of, 191, 204 nn13 & 18, 208 nn46 & 49, 212 n78, 213 n83 (*see also individual plays*);

psychoanalysis of, 64-65, 140-42, 203 n1, 207 n43; on critics and analysts, 103-4, 197; on theater and emotions, xv-xvi, xviii, xxi, 16, 28, 54-55, 95, 113; on politics and society, 125-26; on God and life, 2, 61, 101, 103, 198, 207 n35
O'Neill, Eugene Jr., 170
O'Neill, James, 210 n68
O'Neill, Kathleen. *See* Jenkins
Opera, xvii, 3, 40-41, 56-57, 185-86, 213 n84
Oresteia, xx, xxii, 12, 101, 146-49, 156, 211 n76
Orestes, 21
Overman. *See* Higher man

Paganism, 28, 44. *See also* Dionysus; Nietzsche
Parsifal (Wagner), 3, 57
Pasadena Community Playhouse, xix, 40-41, 54, 56, 58; 69 (fig.)
Pathos, xx, 7, 101-2, 115, 212 n78, 213 n85; in the plays, xxii-xxiii, 127, 133-34, 139, 162-64, 182-84, 186, 196. *See also* Tragedy
Philip II, 196
Pichel, Irving, 40-41, 56; 70 (fig.)
Pinero, Arthur, 164
President Sam of Haiti, 120, 211 n70
Primitivism. *See* Archetypes; Cambridge School; Collective unconscious; *Theater of Tomorrow*; *Totem and Taboo*
Processional (Lawson), 128
Productions. *See individual plays*
Provincetown Players, xiii-xiv, xxii, 1-2, 16, 19, 38-40, 102, 119, 122, 206 n29
Psychoanalysis. *See* Collective unconscious; Freud; Hamilton; Jung; Oedipus complex; O'Neill
Psychological Types (Jung), 206 n30
Psychology of the Unconscious (Jung), 42, 52, 97, 102-12 passim, 210 nn60 & 65, 211 n70
Pulitzer Prize, 120
Puritanism, 122, 130, 149, 155-57, 162, 181, 212 n80

Quinn, Arthur Hobson, xv, 100-101, 211 n76
Quintero, José, 96, 170, 194, 196, 208 n49

Rebirth: in earlier societies, 10-15 passim; in Jung, 48, 111-14; in O'Neill, 28-29, 42, 48, 52, 66, 75, 87, 96-97, 133, 156-59, 182 (*see also* Eternal Recurrence)
Recklessness: as film, 214 n86
Reinhardt, Max, xvii, 20-21, 32-36, 38-41, 58, 205 n29
Religion. *See* Bible; Buddhism; Catholicism; Christianity; Dionysus; O'Neill, on God; Rebirth; Theater, religious; Tragedy, O'Neill's sense of
Repetition: in dialogue, 75, 95-96, 165 (*see also* Chorus; Dithyramb; Interior Monologues); of past, 107-8, 135-36, 153-54, 163 (*see also* Freud; Oedipus complex)
Research in Marriage, A (Hamilton), 143
Revelation, Book of (O'Neill adaptation), 25
Ritual: in earlier societies, 8-15 passim, 51, 109, 207 n36; in theater generally, 20-22, 34-37, 40-41, 204 n18, 205 n21, 212 n78, 213 n85; in O'Neill, xii, xvi-xix, xxiii, 15-16, 28-33, 53-58, 67, 74-75, 93-98, 100, 104, 113, 163-66, 184-85, 187-88, 196. *See also* Theater, religious
Robards, Jason Jr., 196, 214 n91; 72, 168 (figs.)
Robespierre, Maximilien de 126, 146, 196
Rosetti, Dante Gabriel, 185
Rosse, Herman, 21, 38
Rubáiyát of Omar Khayyám, The (Fitzgerald), 67
Russia, 58, 125-26

Saint Louis (P. MacKaye), 36
Sanctuary (P. MacKaye), 36
Scarecrow, The (P. MacKaye), 36
Schopenhauer, Arthur, xx-xxi, 5, 62, 117, 175, 203 n9, 210 n65

"Sea-Mother's Son," 116, 192
Shakespeare, William, 15, 20, 36-37, 185
Shaw, Bernard, xiii, xvii, 209 n43
Sheaffer, Louis, 19n, 203 n1, 208 n43, 210 n68
Shih Huang Ti, 196
Siegfried (Wagner), 40, 57
Sievers, W. David, 210 n58
Silenus, 99, 209 n52. *See also Birth of Tragedy*
Singing. *See* Ritual
Sisk, Robert, 146
Sister Beatrice (Maeterlinck), 34
Socrates, 8, 190
Sophocles, 15
Sparrow, Martha Carolyn, 209 n56
Spook Sonata, The (Strindberg), 23
"S.S. Glencairn" cycle, 17, 115-17, 188
Stallings, Lawrence, 128
Stanislavski, Konstantin, 58
Stockholm. *See* Sweden
Strachey, James, 210 n59
Strange Interlude, xvi, 60, 62, 107, 134-41, 145, 165, 188, 192, 203 n9, 212 n79
Straw, The, 117-18
Strindberg, August, xvii, 19, 23, 195
Superman. *See* Higher man
Suppressed Desires (Cook & Glaspell), 102
Sweden, 170, 193-95, 207 n39, 213 n84
Swinburne, Algernon, 184, 186, 188
Symbolism. *See individual plays*

"Tale of Possessors Self-Dispossessed, A," 192-95
Tempest, The, 37
Theater: ancient Greek, xii, xvi, xviii, 9, 12-15, 20, 38, 98, 197 (*see also Birth of Tragedy, Oedipus Rex, Oresteia*); Elizabethan, xii, xviii, 14-15, 20, 38, 212 n78; medieval, 14; physical innovations in, 37-38, 205 n28; political, xi, xxiii, 23, 124-25, 189, 191, 209 n49; religious, xi-xviii passim, xxiii, 1-2, 14-15, 19-25, 28-30, 33, 37, 58, 60-61, 65-66, 74, 93-94, 100,

189-91, 203 nn1 & 7 (*see also* Ritual; Tragedy)

Theater Advancing, The (Craig), 211 n70

Theater Arts, 203 n7

Theater of Cruelty, 205 n21

Theater of Dionysus, xvi, 98, 197

Theater of the Five Thousand, xvii, 20-21, 40

Theater Guild, 32, 39, 54, 56, 59, 95, 146, 165, 207 nn41 & 42, 213 n82

Theater of Tomorrow, The (Macgowan), xviii, 19-21, 26, 33, 40, 203 n7, 204 n16, 205 n21

Themis (Harrison), 9-14, 204 n16

Thomas, Augustus, xiii

Three Sisters, The (Chekhov), 213 n85

Thus Spoke Zarathustra (Nietzsche), xviii, 41-50 passim, 206 nn32 & 34. *See also* Eternal Recurrence; Higher man

Tille, Alexander, 206 n33

Tiusanen, Timo, 213 n81

Törnquist, Egil, 213 n81

Totem and Taboo (Freud), 102, 105, 109-10, 207 n36. *See also* Archetypes, in characterization

Touch of the Poet, A, 193-95, 197

Tragedy: Aristotelian vs. Nietzschean, xxiii, 7-8, 183n, 204 n18, 212 n78, 213 n85; O'Neill's sense of, xv-xvii,

xx-xxiii, 3, 8, 14, 100-115 passim, 118, 127-29, 133-34, 136-39, 156, 161-66, 182-86, 190-91, 196, 210 n65. *See also Birth of Tragedy*; Fate; Ritual

Trilling, Lionel, 67, 208 n46

Tristan and Isolde (Wagner), 3, 40

Ulysses (Joyce), 134

Vollmoeller, Karl, 34-35

Wagner, Richard, ii, 3, 40-41

Washington Square Players, xiii, 32, 36

Weissman, Philip, 208 n43

Welded, 19, 24-27

What Is Wrong with Marriage (Hamilton & Macgowan), 143-45, 150, 211 n75

What Price Glory? (Anderson & Stallings), 128

Where the Cross Is Made, 117-19

Wild Duck, The (Ibsen), 98

Wilde, Oscar, 185

Wit and Its Relation to the Unconscious (Freud), 104

Woolcott, Alexander, 35

World as Will and Idea, The (Schopenhauer), xx-xxi, 5

World Finder, The (S. MacKaye), 36-37

Wright, Frank Lloyd, 38